contemporary moral issues

joe jenkins

Heinemann

Heinemann Educational Publishers
Halley Court, Jordan Hill, Oxford, OX2 8EJ
Part of Harcourt Education

Heinemann is the registered trademark of Harcourt
Education Limited.

Copyright notice

British Library Cataloguing in Publication Data
A catalogue record for this book is available from the
British Library

ISBN 0 435 30309 0

Designed and typeset by Artistix
Picture research by Jennifer Johnson
Printed and bound in UK by Bath Colourbooks

Acknowledgements

The author would like to thank the following individuals
and organizations: Albert Bowkett for his contributions to
Units 30–34; Francis Beswick, author of *Christian
Medical Ethics* (First and Best in Education Ltd., 1996);
Dr Patrick Dixon; Karen K Giuliano RN, CCRN, MSN,
University of Virginia; Nathaniel Handy for his work on
Adressess/Websites; Thony Handy for his contribution to
Unit 74; David Jeffery for his contributions to Units 48,
88, 92; Andy Jones, VSO; Robert Fisk of *The
Independent*; Matthew Fox; David Kostinchuk for his
research on televangelists; Newsletter of the Muslim
Parliament of Great Britain: *Islamophobia: The Oldest
Hatred*; Majlis al-Shura (Vol. 1, Issue 5, Dec 1997);
Nicola Haisley for her editorial precision and for writing
the Index; Professor George Joffe, Director of Studies at
The Royal Institute for International Affairs; Nigel Kelly
for the publishing pragmatics and vision; Jayne Lennard
for keeping me on the straight but not so narrow; Jack
Williams-Mathevosian for the initial technological
advice; Jennifer Johnson for picture research; Bruce
Kent; Louise Matthews for her proofreading and office
skills; W Owen Cole for his consultancy and his
editorship of the seminal *Spirituality in Focus*; Sarah
Mitchell for her unstinting enthusiasm, clarity and
professionalism; His Holiness, the Dalai Lama; Aki
Nawaz; John Pilger; Arundhati Roy; Nitin Sawnhey; D.J
Timmi; Yusuf Mahmoud of ZIFF for their continued
inspiration; *Roots World* for the Baaba Maal and Youssou
N'Dour interviews; Anup Shah for his website 'Global
Issues that Affect Everyone'; Kevin Elliott RN for his
advice on Units 24–25; Simon Tomlin for his assiduous
work on the manuscript and The World Congress of
Faiths, for *Testing the Global Ethic* (1998).

Photograph acknowledgements appear on p. 205.

Websites

Links to appropriate websites are given throughout the
book. Although these were up to date at the time of
writing, it is essential for teachers to preview these sites
before using them with pupils. This will ensure that the
web address (URL) is still accurate and the content is
suitable for your needs.

We suggest that you bookmark useful sites and consider
enabling pupils to access them through the school
intranet. We are bringing this to your attention, as we are
aware of legitimate sites being appropriated illegally by
people wanting to distribute unsuitable or offensive
material. We strongly advise you to purchase suitable
screening software so that pupils are protected from
unsuitable sites and their material.

If you do find that the links given no longer work, or the
content is unsuitable, please let us know. Details of
changes will be posted on our website.

Tel: 01865 888058 www.heinemann.co.uk

Contents

SOCIAL HARMONY 70

RIGHTS 106

WAR AND PEACE 132

1 Introduction

Trying to make sense of the modern world makes for an exciting yet challenging experience. This book aims to:

- give you relevant facts and improve your understanding about a range of contemporary moral issues

- explore the beliefs of people from around the world and help you recognize the thoughts and feelings of others

- increase your awareness of the rights and responsibilities of global citizenship

- encourage you to engage in discussion with others and learn what is involved in reasoned argument. These include:

  - giving reasons to support your opinions

  - being prepared to change your opinions

  - listening to and analysing the views of others

  - defending a viewpoint in the face of criticism

  - respecting differences.

Good reasons

We have all, at some time or another, made moral judgements about other people. Other people too make moral judgements about us. Have we a right to judge others? Have others a right to judge us? How do we know what is right?

Throughout our lives we are faced with choices about a whole range of issues. It would be impossible to live secure and stable lives if some of our principles did not match other people's ideas about right and wrong. Society would be a complete nightmare if it did not maintain some values upon which people are able to rely on.

However, how do we know that other people's views, or our own views for that matter, are the right ones? Thinking for ourselves is not always easy, particularly when we are faced with the 'this is right and that is wrong' message from friends, families, the media, politicians and religions. One of the best ways of discovering whether your views or other peoples' views make any sense is to look at the reasons people give for their views. If I do not give any reasons for my opinions then people are less likely to take me seriously. If I do give reasons and they are **clear**, **relevant**, and **factual**, then my views are more likely to be respected.

Launching your learning

A Can you think of some of the reasons people might give to support the following statements:

'People should be told if convicted sex offenders live in their neighbourhood.'

'Police have no right to read citizens' text messages and emails.'

'Cloning human beings will, in time, lead to psychologically damaged cloned teenagers.'

B Not all reasons however are necessarily *good* reasons. Look at the following statements and for each one decide whether it is: a) good reason; b) a reason but not a good one; or c) not a reason at all.

'Cigarette adverts are evil because my dad says so.'

'I believe that cigarette adverts should be banned.'

'Cigarette adverts lie and deceive people into believing that it is cool to smoke.'

'If advertisers say cigarettes make you cool then you are cool.'

C Think of examples of:

   a) a moral act, for example an act you consider to be right

   b) an immoral act, for example an act you consider to be wrong

   c) an amoral act, for example an act that shows no understanding of right or wrong.

FOR DISCUSSION

Popular thinking sees morality (the study of right and wrong) as simply being about old-fashioned rules designed to stop people enjoying themselves, usually in relation to sex. This is a very narrow view, for morality in its fullest sense is about seeking the 'good life', not being a 'goody-goody', but living a life that is real. It is about *the art of living successfully* – what the Ancients called 'wisdom'. But what is success? Discuss the following statements by Dr Martin Luther King (see Unit 58). Think of some reasons Dr Martin Luther King might have given to support these statements:

'We are prone to judge success by the size of our salaries or the size of our cars rather than by the quality of our service and relationship to humanity.'

'As long as there is poverty in the world I can never be rich. I can never be what I ought to be until you are what you ought to be.'

CITIZENSHIP CHALLENGE

Look at the photograph below. How can you square what you see with what the Danish poet Piep Hein says: *'We are global citizens with tribal souls.'*

Although it might seem easy to decide what is right and wrong in some situations, in others it is not so simple. Every situation is different and the way we approach a situation may be different every time. Many of the problems we face as individuals are very complicated and it is not always easy to know the right way to react to them. However, because we are capable of thinking reasonably we are able to choose what we think is the right or wrong way to behave. Can you think of some reasons that the men in the photograph might give for justifying their actions? Do you think these reasons are good reasons?

▲ Global citizens with tribal souls?

2 Relationships: LOVE

Top of the Pops

'Tender loving, sweet devotion,
Every second, minute, hour,
I'll be waiting for you
Come put your loving on the line.'

Artful Dodger, *Twenty Four Seven Love*

Ever since people have written songs and poems one of the most popular themes has been love. If we look at the top thirty singles chart we can be sure that many of the songs will be about love.

Research in 2001 by sociologists found that teenage crushes and the emotional turmoil of early relationships can lead to depression. Young women in Britain are twice as likely to suffer from depression as young men – especially vulnerable are girls who fall in love before the age of seventeen. So what is this thing called 'love'?

The Greeks

The Ancient Greeks thought that the word 'love' meant many different things. Consequently, they had definitions for different types of love:

- **storge** – warm affection or liking something, for example, 'I love Manchester United'; 'I love playing the guitar'

- **eros** – sexual affection, passion, desire to fall in love. The word 'erotic' comes from the Greek word 'eros'

- **philos** – love, of friends

- **agape** – selfless love for others, including charity, tolerance and respect towards all people. Agape is a type of love that expects nothing in return – called **unconditional love**.

Falling in love

Love is a two-way process. We both receive love and give love. People who find it difficult to love may not always have received love in the first place. Love can bring out some very strong emotions. Sometimes relationships can cause confusion. We can 'fall head over heels in love' with somebody we 'fancy' because we are attracted to them. The 'fickle' nature of 'falling in love' can make every experience different for every individual.

FOR DISCUSSION

- Sometimes we can fall in love with somebody and find out later that we do not even like them.

- Sometimes we can 'fall out of love' as quickly as we 'fall in love'.

- We may even find ourselves falling in love with somebody we did not fancy or find attractive when we first met them. We can grow into love.

- Sometimes we fancy someone but are too shy to tell them. Sometimes we can tell someone we are in love with them but they just do not want to know. These sorts of experiences can be very painful. They are called '**unrequited love**'.

- Sometimes we can fall in love with somebody who is not even very nice to us; even someone that all our friends dislike as a person – sometimes '**love is blind**'.

True love

'Love is patient, love is kind and envies no one. Love is never boastful, nor conceited, nor rude; never selfish, not quick to take offence. Love keeps no score of wrongs; does not gloat over other men's sins, but delights in the truth. There is nothing love cannot face; there is no limit to its faith, its hope and endurance. Love will never come to an end.'

I Corinthians 13

In the Tenakh, the Jewish Bible, love is compared to fire:

'Love is strong as death … Its flashes are flashes of fire … many waters cannot quench love, neither can floods drown it.'

The Song of Songs 8: 6–7

Love of God

Religions have expressed the ultimate aim of love as union with God – '**mystical love**'.

Ramakrishna (1836–86) the Hindu Saint said: 'Sex life with a woman! What happiness is there in that? The realization of God gives ten million times more happiness. When a man or woman attains ecstatic love of God all the pores of the skin, even the roots of the hair, become like so many sexual organs, and in every pore they enjoy the happiness of communion with the **Atman** (soul).'

TALKING POINTS

- 'Greater love hath no man than this, that a man lay down his life for his friends.' (Jesus in John 15: 13)

- 'All you need is love.' (Lennon/McCartney)

- 'Experience shows us that love does not consist in gazing at each other but in looking together in the same direction'. (Antoine de Saint Exupery – twentieth-century French writer)

- 'Love means not ever having to say you're sorry.' (From the 1970 film *Love Story*)

- 'Those who have courage to love should have courage to suffer.' (Anthony Trollope – nineteenth century English novelist)

Launching your learning

Using some of the words and phrases below, either:

A write an essay entitled 'What is love?'; or

B make up a text message about love. **Storge, eros, erotic, philos, agape, lust, unconditional love, unrequited love, 'love is blind', love of God, mystical love, Atman.**

3 Relationships: SEX 1

Introduction

There is a lot of misinformation about sex in modern society. Television, videos, billboards, films, pop songs and magazines can make it difficult to sort out truth from fiction. Sex is sellable. It has become a commodity, easily commercialized and sold without regard for the damage it may do. Sex is so powerful that if approached without responsibility it can ruin people's lives.

The sexual act is a giving of oneself in a very deep way. Sexual relationships can create new life and enrich human relationships and self-discovery.

The sex drive

Sexuality is a creative act of the universe. Every flower and blossom on this planet is a reproductive organ. The sexual drive is one of the strongest drives. At its biological level it is the desire to reproduce. At an emotional and psychological level our sex drive is linked to our overall well-being. Sexual intercourse is more often than not **non-procreative**. People have sex for reasons other than for producing new life. To experience happy relationships we must respect others not as objects but as people with the same feelings and hopes as us.

Exchange versus relationship

There is a world of difference between a client and a prostitute having sexual intercourse and a couple, in love, making love. The client and prostitute are merely *engaging* whereas the lovers are in *relationship* where body and mind meet.

Moods

During puberty, moods go up and down like a yoyo – wildly happy one minute, so miserable the next … you may fall in love for the first time!

When you fall in love it takes a while to learn how to handle the powerful new emotions that accompany the experience.

▶ The sexual act is a giving of oneself in a deep way

For many people in our western society the first time they fall in love is not the only time. Many people fall in and out of love quite frequently. The person who is just right for you when you are fifteen or sixteen may not necessarily be the person you want to spend the rest of your life with. Falling in love can help you learn a lot about yourself and other people. Any permanent relationship when you are older will be based more on knowing about people, than on knowing about sex.

Marriage made in Heaven?

In some cultures, for example Hinduism, young people are guided by their elders who search for the right partner to make the 'marriage made in Heaven'. A marriage perfectly matched. These are sometimes called **arranged marriages** (see Unit 9).

FOR DISCUSSION

A Is pleasure the deepest reason for sex?

B Should people have sex as and when they wish, either outside or inside marriage?

C Why do you think that Britain has the highest rate of teenage pregnancies in Europe?

D Why do you think research shows that teenagers who can talk with their parents about sex are less likely to engage in high-risk behaviour than those who do not feel they can talk to their parents about sex?

E Why do you think teenage boys are sometimes under pressure to talk about 'sexual conquests', yet girls are called names if it is believed that they have had more than one sexual relationships?

F Sex is often thought of as being something 'naughty', 'rude' or 'dirty'. Why do you think this is so? (See Unit 5.)

G If sex is not just for procreation, if its purpose is also to unite people in love, then can you see the day when permanent, loving relationships between homosexuals will be legally approved?

H The thinker Gabriel Marcel believed that European society had reduced the *mystery of sex* to a *problem about sex*.

TALKING POINTS

It has been said that in earlier generations teenage sex was less common than it is today because of three fears: fear of *detection*, fear of *infection* and fear of *conception*. What will future generations be saying? Discuss the statements below as possibilities:

A 'Virginity is not valued as it once was.'

B 'Contraceptive devices may have improved but education about the reasons for using them has not.'

C 'Sex is so powerful and meaningful that justice can only be done to it in a life-long relationship.'

D 'The media titillates.'

E 'Teenagers naturally want to experiment.'

4 Relationships: SEX 2

Masturbation – a definition

Masturbation is defined as: 'sexual activity involving only one person', 'self-stimulation', 'auto-eroticism' and 'self-pleasuring'. Two negative terms which are not often used today are 'self-abuse' and 'onanism'.

Scientists have completely reversed their beliefs about masturbation since the nineteenth and early twentieth century when it was incorrectly linked to 'deterioration of eyesight', 'insanity' or 'hair growth on the palms'. Today there is wide-ranging agreement among health professionals that masturbation is not psychologically or physically unhealthy.

Masturbation and religion

Traditionally, religions have taught that sex is meant for two people and so activities like lone masturbation go against the true purpose of sexuality.

What about mutual masturbation? Religions tend to agree that in a loving relationship within marriage, mutual masturbation is acceptable.

In, the New Testament, Jesus says of sexual fantasies:

> '... whosoever looketh on a woman to lust after her hath committed adultery with her already in his heart.'
>
> Matthew 5: 28

That is, a person who fantasizes about making love to another person has committed adultery – fantasies are often present when a person masturbates.

Christian opposition to masturbation has softened greatly in recent years. Liberal Christians do not base their moral code solely on the Bible. They include the findings of science, medicine and research into human sexuality. Most mental health professionals have concluded that sexual fantasies are normal and healthy. Sexual attraction to other people is natural and, to a degree, an automatic and unavoidable response. A religious liberal would probably conclude that manual stimulation of the genitals is in no way sinful and fantasizing about a person whom one is in love with, or would like to be in love with, is harmless.

Some may go even further: enjoying the feelings arising from manual stimulation is a gift like listening to your favourite music on a paradise beach and feeling the sun's rays beating down on you with a cool drink at hand. In each case, some external agent stimulates nerve endings giving us pleasant feelings. The only difference with masturbation is the intensity of those feelings.

CITIZENSHIP CHALLENGE

In groups of two to three, imagine that you had to plan a **Sex Education Programme** for people of your own age. There are three sessions of 45 minutes to organize. Discuss what topics you would like to cover. Write down on a piece of paper your suggestions and fold the paper before handing it to the teacher who will arrange a class discussion.

Thanking and hoping

For Christians, the Bible teaches fundamental truths about human behaviour. The problem today is that the Church's teachings often seem 'old-fashioned'. Jack Dominian, a Roman Catholic theologian and psychiatrist, challenges this view:

> 'Sexual intercourse is first of all a body language, through which couples talk to and do things for one another. When couples make love they rejoice in each other's presence and the pleasure they exchange. For this they want to give thanks. Thus sex is a recurrent act of **thanksgiving**.
>
> Because people want to make love repeatedly, they trust that their partners will respond to them again. So sex is also a recurrent act of **hope**: the hope of being desired again.
>
> In the course of the day couples hurt one another. Most of these hurts are forgiven and forgotten on the spot. But some are too painful to be forgiven so easily. Such hurts need a deeper level of love and communication to erase them. So sexual intercourse can also be an act of **reconciliation**.
>
> Every time a couple makes love, they are saying to each other: 'I recognize you, I want you, I appreciate you.' In this way it is a recurrent act of personal **affirmation**.
>
> This is the case for Christian morality: not that sex is dangerous and needs marriage and procreation to protect it; but rather that sex is so powerful and meaningful that justice can only be done to it in a **continuous and enduring relationship**.'

From *The Capacity to Love*, 1985

Launching your learning

Using some, or all, of the words and phrases below, explain what Christian attitudes to sex are.

Thanksgiving, hope, reconciliation, affirmation, continuous enduring relationship.

What is safe sex?

If two people have sexual intercourse and one of them has HIV or another sexually transmitted disease, they could give it to their partner(s). By 2001 there were one and a quarter million cases of sexually transmitted diseases reported in Britain (see Unit 6).

Doctors believe that if the man wears a latex condom whenever he has intercourse it helps to protect him and his partner from giving each other HIV. That is why people call sexual intercourse with a latex condom 'safe sex'.

Is it true that you cannot get pregnant the first time that you have sex?

NO. You can get pregnant any time you have sexual intercourse. Wearing a latex condom is an effective way of preventing pregnancy.

5 Relationships: SEX 3

Taboo – a definition

A **taboo** is defined as 'a strong social custom forbidding certain things'.

In 2001 the British film censors allowed a film called *Intimacy*, featuring scenes of oral sex and erect penises, to be shown uncut. But why have oral sex and erect penises been taboo up until now – only visible in illegal pornographic films?

Religions

The removal from public view of erections and various sexual activities is very recent. It is almost exclusively restricted in cultural traditions stemming from **The Religions of The Book** (Judaism, Christianity and Islam). Jewish sexual morality, as outlined in the Tenakh, is the morality of herdsmen anxious to increase the number of children. A man must not do anything that misdirects his 'seed' from reproductive uses. Oral sex, homosexuality and masturbation were considered **'abominations'** because they misdirect the 'seed' from reproductive uses.

The early Christians, expecting Christ to return at anytime, thought they should remain **celibate**. The 'spirit' was 'good' whereas the body was thought to be 'bad' and must be disciplined.

This led to extremes like the early Christian, Origen, (185–255CE) castrating himself to escape his sexual longings. Christianity became **puritanical**. Sexual pleasure was regarded as evil. This attitude reached ridiculous proportions in nineteenth century Britain when all penises on Greek statues in the British Museum were chipped off to save the blushes of Victorian visitors. They remain, to this day, locked in a drawer in the museum.

Other cultures have a widespread celebration of sexuality in art and religion and an absence of pornography. The painted pottery of the classical world, and the beautiful art of India, China and Japan depicts all forms of heterosexual and homosexual activity, and erect penises are celebrated as a positive symbol.

▲ Indian temple art celebrates sex as a divine gift

Celibacy – a definition

Celibacy is defined as 'the state of being unmarried, especially as the result of a religious promise'.

Over the last 40 years, the idea of celibacy among priests has become a controversial issue in the Roman Catholic Church. In 1966 the National Association for Pastoral Renewal (NAPR) was formed. Their aim is to work for, among other things, optional celibacy.

Controversy over celibacy has been highlighted in the press over recent years with stories of priests having relationships and even fathering children. This has caused the Roman Catholic Church much distress and many people within the Church are calling for more understanding and for counselling services to be readily available to priests who are torn by their love for a woman and their love for the Church. However, successive popes have ruled that celibacy among priests must remain. They argue that celibacy enables a priest to dedicate himself entirely to his ministry.

Islamic view

Muslims believe that humans should appreciate the good things of life, including our sexual side, as a **blessing** of God. Islam is, therefore, totally opposed to monasticism and celibacy. Islam aims at teaching people not to deny their sexual urges, but rather to fulfil them in a responsible way. It recognizes the sexual needs of human beings and believes that the natural instincts should not be suppressed. Islam says that all the biological parts of our body have a purpose. In Islamic texts the idea of marriage is not restricted to a **platonic relationship** between husband and wife, nor is it confined to sex for the purpose of procreation. The legal term for marriage is *nikah*, which literally means 'sexual intercourse'. Sex within marriage is openly recommended in the Qur'an and the sexual urge is counted as a creative command of God and cannot be associated in any way with sin and evil. Marriage and sex are among the signs of God's power and blessings.

Chastity – a definition

Chastity is defined as 'the state of being sexually pure'.

Some people decide that they will not have sexual relations. This is called 'chastity' and those people who decide not to have sex are called **chaste**. This is sometimes also known as **sexual abstinence**. People decide to be chaste for a number of reasons:

- to practise self-control
- to concentrate all their energies in other directions
- as an experiment within a relationship
- to practise birth control
- to dedicate themselves to some religious ideal; in monasteries (communities of monks) and convents (communities of nuns), men and women make three vows – poverty, chastity and obedience.

FOR DISCUSSION

A To what extent, if any, do you think the media makes sex a taboo subject?

B Is there enough serious discussion about sex in modern society?

Launching your learning

Using some, or all, of the words and phrases below, write an essay entitled 'Sex and religion', making reference to any differences in opinion you can find.

Taboo, The Religions of The Book, abominations, Original Sin, puritanical, celibacy, monasticism, blessing, platonic relationship, chastity, sexual abstinence.

6 Relationships: *VIRGINITY*

Thinking about virginity

Making the decision about whether it is right for you to have sex is not the same as going to the dentist or starting a part-time job. Instead, every individual must use his or her own judgment and decide for himself or herself if it is the right time – and the right person. This decision is not always easy; pressures, emotions and other people's attitudes can confuse even the most clear-headed teenager when it comes to sex.

Friends

Nobody wants to feel left out. Teenagers everywhere want to be liked. They want to belong, to feel as if they are part of a crowd. Unfortunately, some teenagers feel that they have to lose their virginity to keep up with their friends or to be accepted. It is not uncommon to feel pressure from one another to do certain things.

Maybe some of your friends have already had sex with their boyfriends or girlfriends. Maybe they act like it is not a big deal. But sex is not something that is only physical; it is emotional, too. And since everyone's emotions are different, it is hard to rely on your friends' opinions to decide if it is the right time for *you* to have sex. What matters to *you* is the most important thing, and your values may not match theirs. That is fine – it is what makes us all different and unique. But having sex to make your friends happy, or to prevent yourself from feeling left out, will not make you feel very good about yourself in the long run. And most importantly, true friends do not really care whether a person is a virgin or not – they will respect your decisions, no matter what.

Messages

Even if your friends are cool with your decision to remain a virgin for the time being, it is easy to be misled by the media. Television programmes and films often give out the message that makes it seem as if every teenager in Britain is having sex. Writers and producers sometimes make a programme or film plot exciting by showing teenagers being sexually active. However these teenagers are actors – they are not *real* people with *real* concerns. They do not have to worry about what might happen as a result of having sex or about how they will feel later on. In other words, these TV or film plots are stories, not real life. In real life, every teenager can, and should, make his or her own decision.

Pressures

Some teenagers who are going out do not pressure each other about sex. However, in many relationships, one person wants to have sex although the other one does not. Maybe one person is more curious and has stronger sexual feelings than the other. Or one has religious reasons why he or she does not want to have sex and the other one does not feel the same way. Whatever the situation, it can place stress on a relationship – you want to keep your boyfriend or girlfriend happy, but you do not want to do what you think is wrong, or you are not yet ready to have sex.

As with almost every other big decision in life, you need to do what is right *for you* and not anyone else. Anyone who tries to pressure you into having sex by saying, 'if you truly cared you would not say no', or 'if you loved me you would show it by having sex', is not really looking out for you. If you feel that you should have sex because you are afraid of losing that person, then maybe you should dump that person. Sex is an expression of love – not something a person feels that he or she *ought* to do. If a boyfriend or girlfriend truly loves you, he or she will not pressure you into doing something you are not ready for yet, or do not believe in.

Saying 'No'

Some teenagers may wait longer before having sex. They may have thought carefully about what it means to lose their virginity and begin a sexual relationship. For these teenagers, there are many reasons for abstinence (not having sex). Some do not want to worry about unplanned pregnancy, or sexually transmitted diseases (STDs). Some STDs, like AIDS, can literally make sex a life-or-death situation, and some teenagers take this very seriously. It is a frightening fact that in 1990 624,000 people in Britain suffered from STDs, but by 2000 the number had soared to 1,250,000. There are around 90,000 teenage pregancies in England every year (*Social Exclusion Unit Report, 1999*).

Some teenagers do not have sex before marriage because they follow the teachings of their religion. For instance, sex before marriage is absolutely forbidden in Islam and most Christians agree with the Roman Catholic Church's teaching: 'Every sexual act must be within the framework of marriage'. This is a commonly-held teaching of most of the major religions.

Others may abstain – not have sex – because they have a very strong belief system of their own. Other teenagers may feel like they are not ready emotionally and they want to wait until they are absolutely sure they can handle a sexual relationship.

Hypocrisy

More people today accept that sex before marriage is not wrong. It is common for people to have sex with different partners before they get married. Although attitudes may have changed, there is as much hypocrisy as ever. Sexually active males may be called 'Casanova', or 'a bit of a lad' if they have a lot of different sexual partners. But if females are sexually active they may be called horrible names. There is no history of men being punished for losing their virginity. Women on the other hand have sometimes been brutally treated.

In some countries in the past, a father could kill his daughter if she lost her virginity before marriage. The attitude that it is more acceptable for men to be sexually active is still common. In reality, both men and women are capable of feeling jealous if their partner has already 'slept around'.

Summing up

When it comes to sex, there are two very important things to remember. Firstly, you are the person in charge of your own happiness, and secondly, you have a lot of time to wait until you are totally sure about it. If you decide to put off sex, it is fine – no matter what anyone says. Being a virgin is one of the things that proves *you* are in charge, and it shows that you are powerful enough to make your own decisions about your life. People should respect you for your decision. If you find yourself feeling confused about sex you may be able to talk to an adult for advice. Keep in mind, though, that everyone's opinion about sex is different. Even though another person may be able to share useful advice, in the end, the decision is up to you.

FOR DISCUSSION

- In small groups read this unit aloud and then talk about it.

- What do you think about the following two statements? Compare and discuss them.

  A 'It is a good idea to have sex before marriage so that you will be experienced when you meet your marriage partner.'

  B 'If you sleep around you soon lose the wonder and mystery of sex, which should only be shared with your loved one.'

7 Relationships: THE FAMILY

Social animals

Human beings are essentially social animals. We all depend upon other people. Once we would have been totally dependent on people close to us – our family or tribe – for food, shelter, protection, help with raising children, and for company. Human society today is more complicated: supermarkets provide us with food; contractors build our houses; the state protects us; schools share the upbringing of our children; we can join chat rooms and make friends across the world. But many of our closest relationships are still found within the family.

The family – a definition

The family is our basic social unit. It is the smallest and most common group in our society. It is found in every culture and in every period throughout history. Every family is different. The picture of the 'ideal' family in advertising (sometimes referred to as 'the cereal packet family') – mum, dad and two kids living happily together – can be very different from many people's experiences in the real world.

Different kinds of family

- **A nuclear family** is where two parents live with one or more children in the same house. About half the people of Britain belong to this kind of family.

- **An extended family** can include several generations living possibly in the same house or closely together in the same neighbourhood. It can include parents, grandparents, uncles, aunts and cousins. This is the most common family unit in countries like India and parts of Africa.

- **A reconstituted family** is where divorced or bereaved people have remarried or live together to bring their children into their new relationship. Two families are brought up together. This can also be called a **blended** family and involves step-parents and often step-brothers and/or step-sisters. Reconstituted families have become much more common over recent years.

- **A one-parent family**, (also known as a **single parent family**, or **lone family**) is where one parent brings up a child, or children, on their own. Parents can be on their own for many different reasons. They may have chosen to bring a child up on their own, they may be divorced, or their partner may have died. An estimated 22% of families in the UK with children are headed by one parent.

- **A community family** involves several people choosing to live together and share work, property and bringing the children up. These are sometimes called communes. Some people, like monks, live together in a religious community.

- **An expanded family** is where a group of similar people, for instance the aged or disabled people, live together and, with the help of outside professional agencies, support each other.

- **Same sex families** occur where, for example, a woman brings up her children with her partner, another woman.

- **A childless family** is where there are no children living in the home. Maybe the couple are not able to have children, or they choose not to have children, or the couple's children have grown up and left home.

Happy families?

Although family life can be very creative it can also be very destructive. Although many families are happy, many are not. Many of the problems experienced by adults can be traced back to their childhood. There can be many tensions within the family. Overcrowding and poor housing, unemployment, money worries, divorce, alcohol and drug abuse and sickness, can all have a devastating effect on family life. Children are sometimes neglected, physically, emotionally or sexually abused. A family that suffers from these sorts of pressures is sometimes called a **dysfunctional** family. Those who were not loved as children can have huge problems in later life. People who have been abused as children are more likely than others to become abusers themselves.

Why are families important?

- Families exist for mutual support, companionship and the welfare of children.

- We all need close and loving relationships. Stable relationships are important for the long process of bringing up children.

- Families prepare us for adult life and teach us, from an early age, how to live together.

- Families are important because they form the group in which most humans spend most of their time.

- Our early experiences within the family environment have a huge effect on the sorts of people we become.

- The family provides us with an identity, a history, a name, as well as many values and opinions.

- Through families, we can learn about the customs and traditions of our cultures.

Religious views

- All the world religions teach that the family is very important and each family member has responsibility for the others.

- Harmony in family life is based on love, freely given and received.

- Family life should be respected and all family members are to be cared for and treasured.

- Children are expected to respect their parents' authority. Parents must be aware that they have to earn respect by being kind, understanding, tolerant and supportive of their children.

- Each individual in the family has a duty to work hard to keep the family happy and stable. If people within the family perform their duties then other members of the family will benefit.

- Marriage is seen as the basis for family life and all religions mark this by special ceremonies (see Units 8 and 9). Children are seen as a gift from God. The ceremonies of Baptism and Confirmation in Christian traditions for instance, welcome the young person into the family of the Church.

- Jewish, Muslim, Sikh and Hindu families are very close-knit and often live as extended families with elderly relatives, usually living in the home, looked after and treated with respect. This situation is very different from much of modern living in Europe where, especially in towns and cities, the old are often neglected and put into homes.

FOR DISCUSSION

A In the Tenakh, it says: 'Honour your mother and father' (Exodus 20: 12 – the fifth Commandment). What do you think this means? Can you think of situations where this is not possible?

B Islam teaches that the condition of a society can be traced directly back to the strength or weakness of the family. Why do you think family background and type is important in making us the way we are?

8 Relationships: MARRIAGE 1

Christian marriage

Purpose

A summary of the teachings of the Christian marriage ceremony can be found in the acronym '**purpose**':

Procreation – marriage is the most stable relationship in which to have children

Union – marriage enables two people to live together in an atmosphere of love and support

Rearing children – marriage is the most loving relationship in which to bring up children

Pattern for society – marriage provides society with family units of mutual support

One flesh – marriage lets people express their sexuality honestly, passionately and lovingly

Sacred – marriage is a 'holy institution', which is blessed by God

Eternal – marriages are everlasting faithful relationships.

Preparation

A couple wanting to get married in a Christian place of worship usually have some form of **preparation** in the weeks leading up to the service. A clergyman will emphasize that marriage is a life-long **commitment** and will talk to the couple about any questions or worries they might have. To help couples prepare for their marriage some churches ask couples to attend a number of 'engaged couples' courses. These will cover subjects such as:

Cohabitation

Commitment

Compromise

Communication and quite often cash!

The Bible and marriage

The teachings in the Bible on marriage are important for Christians. In the New Testament, Jesus teaches that marriage was created by God:

> 'But from the beginning of creation, God made them male and female. For this reason a man shall leave his father and mother and be joined to his wife, and the two shall become one flesh. So they are no longer two, but one flesh. Therefore what God has joined together, let no one separate.'

Mark 10: 6–9

The first recorded miracle performed by Jesus was at a wedding at Cana in Galilee (John 2: 1–11). St Paul compared the love of a husband and wife to the love Christ has for his people, the church (Ephesians 5: 21–33).

The service

Almost all Christians get married in a church. The main difference between a church service and getting married in a Registry Office is that Christians believe that during a church service they make their promises before God. The service is performed by a clergyman who will remind the couple of the purposes of marriage. The couple **vow** to love, honour, comfort and protect the other, and to be faithful as long as they live. Each then **promises**:

> '... to have and to hold, from this day forward; for better or worse, for richer or poorer, in sickness and in health, to love and to cherish, till death us do part, according to God's holy law; and this is my solemn vow.'

After exchanging wedding rings the clergyman pronounces that the couple are 'husband and wife.' He then repeats the words of Jesus: 'Therefore what God has joined together, let no one separate.'

Orthodox marriage ceremony

An Orthodox marriage ceremony takes place in two parts. The first part is the **betrothal**. This takes place at the entrance to the church where the couple promise to love and care for each other. The second part of the ceremony is called the **crowning**. This usually takes place at a table in the centre of the church. The priest chants the **three great prayers** of marriage. These are that the couple should try and have children and that they should care for all God's creation and that the marriage is a sign of the unity between Christ and his church, with the family becoming a small church of its own. Then comes the coronation when a **stefana** – made of flowers, leaves, silver or gold – is held above the couple and then placed on their heads. The priest joins their hands and blesses them and their life together. At the end, after the Lord's Prayer, the couple drink wine three times from the same cup, to symbolize that they now share a common life.

Sex and marriage

Christians believe that sex within marriage is a gift from God. It is potentially a beautiful and creative act of love – views reflected in this statement from the Roman Catholic Church:

> 'The sexual act should reflect the total self-giving of two couples in love, through marriage. Likewise it should express the quality and the potential of the relationship as open, loving and life-giving.'

Christian teaching is that sexual intercourse is wrong unless it happens within a marriage. God intended men and women to live together as married couples but not to **cohabit** (to live together before marriage). The Roman Catholic and Orthodox Churches are totally opposed to people cohabiting, while some Protestant Churches accept cohabitation although they always encourage people to marry in church.

Rings

A ring is traditionally worn on the third finger of the left hand, a place where a vein runs directly to the heart. The symbolism of the ring is taken from the Jewish tradition:

- **Round** – symbolizing the eternity of marriage
- **Gold** – symbolizing the purity of marriage
- **Plain** – symbolizing the simplicity of marriage.

Marriage as a sacrament

Marriage is a **public sign** of a couple's commitment to each other. Roman Catholics, Orthodox Christians and some Anglicans believe that marriage is a **sacrament**. A sacrament is a public sign of an inward invisible blessing. During a marriage the love of God is gracefully and mysteriously present.

FOR YOUR FOLDERS

- What vows do the bride and bridegroom make before the ring is placed on the bride's finger?
- What is the meaning of the ring in marriage?
- 'Only Christians who go to church regularly should be allowed to marry in church.' Do you agree? Give reasons for your answer showing you have thought about both sides of the question.
- What, in your opinion, is the importance, if any, of marriage? Could many of the purposes of marriage (as outlined in the acronym in this unit) be fulfilled outside of marriage?

Launching your learning

Find out the meaning of the following words and phrases:
Preparation, commitment, companionship, vows, promises, betrothal, crowning, stefana, cohabit, public sign.

9 Relationships: MARRIAGE 2

Hindu marriage

Hindu marriage is a life-long commitment. It is the strongest bond that takes place between a man and a woman. Hindus believe that men and women are soul-mates who, through the institution of marriage, can direct their instincts and passions into the progress of their souls.

During the wedding the bride and groom walk three times around a fire. They touch each others' heart and pray for harmony then step on a stone and pray for their love to be firm and steadfast like the stone. They make the following **seven promises**:

> '... to nourish each other ... to grow together in strength ... to preserve our wealth ... to share our joys and sorrows ... to care for our children ... to be together forever ... to remain lifelong friends ... the perfect halves to make a perfect whole.'

Arranged marriages

Most, but not all, Hindu marriages are **arranged** by the elder members of the family. Marriage is a union not only of the couple, but of their families, too. The success of arranged marriages and the low divorce rates in Hindu culture lies in the families' judgement to base the union on practical matters which will outlast 'falling in love' and last through the years. An ancient scripture called Atharva Veda says that a couple should 'never stop loving'.

In seeking a bride for a son or a groom for a daughter the aim is to find a partner **compatible** in age, education, social status, religion and character. Elders may first seek a partner among families they know and respect. **Mutual attraction** and the full **consent** of the couple are important too. **Astrology** is always consulted for compatibility. Once a potential spouse is selected inquiries are made. The families then gather at the girl's home to get acquainted and to allow the young couple to meet and discuss their expectations. If all agree to the match, gifts are exchanged between families.

It used to be common for a bride's parents to give a **dowry** to the bridegroom's parents. This was the daughter's natural inheritance from her father's property. The size of the dowry affected the bride's status in her new home and sometimes caused problems. A law abolishing dowry came into force in India in 1985.

Love marriages

Sometimes, particularly in countries like Britain, young Hindus who fall in love may want to marry before any arrangements between elders have been made. These are sometimes called **love marriages**. If young people choose their own partners, the choice is usually only approved by parents if the families are of equal social standing. In her new home a bride has to look after her parents-in-law and other senior relatives. If there are differences between the family traditions she will experience difficulties with regard to religious rituals and food.

The ideal age for women to marry is from 18–25, men from 21–30. The couple should be prepared to work with their marriage, not expecting it to take care of itself. They should approach the marriage as holy. It is important to marry a spouse who is dependable and serious about raising children in the Hindu way. When problems arise in marriage, Hindus study the Scriptures and seek advice of family, elders and spiritual leaders.

Muslim marriage

Islam regards marriage as the natural human status for adults. The only proper way for a Muslim to take part in sexual activity is within marriage. Finding a good life partner and building up a relationship is regarded as 'half the faith'. The Hadith teaches that:

> 'Whoever gets married has completed half of his faith; therefore let him be conscious of Allah in the other half of his faith.'

Marriage is a social contract and a partnership which brings **rights** and **duties** to both husband and wife. One aim of marriage is that the partners should become best friends. A husband and wife will share any worries and responsibilities together in an atmosphere of love and trust. Islam supports the basic equality of the sexes.

In the Muslim world, because **modesty** is emphasized so strongly, there is often little contact between young men and women. The selection of a marriage partner is often arranged by the parents. It is acceptable to arrange marriages by recommendation as long as the couple agree. If parents choose the future spouse and the couple concerned have no say in the matter this could be a recipe for disaster. One of the conditions of a valid marriage is the **consent** of the couple. Marriage by definition is a **voluntary union** between two people. There is no dating, living together or physical relationship before marriage. For Muslim couples, love comes after the marriage and not before.

The Prophet Muhammad (pbuh) permitted marriages between people of vastly different social status, knowing it was not these factors which made for **compatibility** but what sort of people they are in their hearts. The most important ingredients in a Muslim marriage are shared values and beliefs so that even if the couple come from different backgrounds they have the same basic attitudes and habits which will bind them together.

Polygamy

'Marry women of your choice, two, three or four; but if you fear that you shall not be able to deal justly with them, then marry only one.'

Qur'an, Surah 4: 3

The ideal Muslim family is **monogamous** – one husband and one wife. However it is not forbidden or unlawful for a man to have more than one wife. Although the practice of men having more than one wife is referred to as **polygamy**, in fact it should properly be called **polygyny**. True polygamy – either sex having more than one spouse – is not allowed.

Polygynous marriages can create problems like jealousy, inequality, disharmony and conflicts between the children of different wives and in these marriages the man must take care of, and treat, his wives equally well.

TALKING POINT

'Do not marry only for a person's looks; their beauty might become the cause of moral decline. Do not marry for wealth, since this may become the cause of disobedience. Marry rather on the grounds of religious devotion' – The Hadith (Muslim text).

FOR DISCUSSION

Why are the caste and family traditions of a bride and groom important in Hindu marriage?

'Love comes after the marriage and not before.' Do you think this is true? Give reasons.

Romance can die out quickly. Does the media give young people unrealistic expectations about love and relationships?

Statistically, arranged marriages prove to be more successful and lasting than romantic types of courtship. Why do you think this is so?

Launching your learning

Write one sentence down for each of the following words and phrases:
The seven promises, arranged marriages, compatible, astrology, mutual attraction, consent, dowry, love marriages, rights and duties within marriage, modesty, voluntary union, monogamous, polygamy, polygyny.

10 Relationships: DIVORCE

Not all marriages are successful and an estimated one in three marriages in Britain end in divorce. A combination of factors has led to this increase over the last 30 years.

British law

These changes have been reflected in British law, which can be summarized as follows:

It is only possible to divorce after twelve months of marriage and only if the marriage has *irretrievably broken down* – this means that there is no way that the marriage can be retrieved. There are five different ways to prove the '**irretrievable breakdown**':

1 one **spouse** has '**committed adultery**' (had sex with another person)

2 one spouse has behaved in such a way that the other cannot reasonably be expected to go on living with him/her

3 the couple have lived apart for two years, and one spouse agrees to a divorce

4 one spouse has lived apart for five years or more

5 one spouse has **deserted** for two years or more.

Christian view

In the New Testament, Jesus condemns divorce:

> 'What therefore God hath joined together, let no man put asunder.'
>
> Mark 10: 9

Today, however, many Christian churches accept that some marriages *do* break down and a divorce is the only way forward. The **Anglican Church** and most other Protestant denominations allow divorce, although only as a last resort.

If the marriage has become destructive then it is in the best interests of those involved for the marriage to end. Anglicans can re-marry in church. Other churches will allow couples to re-marry though they may be reluctant to carry out the re-marriage.

The Roman Catholic Church teaches that marriage is a **sacrament** and no one has the right to unmake something created by God. Catholic couples whose marriage has broken down will live separately but cannot re-marry. The Church does not accept that the religious marriage can end though they accept that the couple may go through a legal divorce. In very rare cases what is known as an **annulment** may be granted:

1 if the marriage has not been **consummated** (no sex)

2 if one partner had been forced to marry against their wishes

3 if one partner cannot meet the requirements of marriage

4 if one partner was not baptized as a Catholic.

The Orthodox Church

The Orthodox Church (see Addresses/ websites) allows divorce if a marriage cannot be repaired. In theory, it allows divorce only in the case of adultery, but in practice the Orthodox Church often allows divorce for other reasons. An Orthodox Christian might be **excommunicated** for a time after a divorce if he or she was the guilty party. This means that they cannot take the sacraments in church. They will be re-admitted after a service where they express their sorrow over their part in the breakdown of the marriage. Orthodox Christians can re-marry in church, but without the full marriage ceremony.

Muslim view

Rather than condemn people to a life of misery Islam makes allowance for legal divorce although it is discouraged. In the Hadith it is written:

> 'The most detestable act that God has permitted is divorce.'

Muslims see divorce as the last resort. However if a marriage becomes destructive then a divorce is permitted. There has to be a period when the couple try and work out their problems themselves. If they fail then family members will try and help them settle their differences. If these attempts fail then divorce is granted. Islamic Law requires that both man and wife have to agree to a divorce. After the divorce takes place there is a waiting period called **Iddah** (normally lasting between three months to a year) when the woman is supported and maintained by her former husband. This waiting period gives the couple another chance to think about whether they really want to go ahead with the divorce.

By allowing divorce Islam recognizes that destructive marriages are more harmful than divorce:

> 'Either keep your wife honestly, or put her away from you with kindness. Do not force a woman to stay with you who wishes to leave. The man who does that only injures himself.'

Qur'an, Surah 2: 231

A divorce is acceptable if: the partners are sane, conscious, not under pressure from some outside party, are not under the influence of alcohol or drugs, or so angry that they do not know what they are doing. A wife may divorce her husband if: he refuses to maintain her, abuses or mistreats her, is impotent or insane, deserts her, is away for long periods without contacting her, is imprisoned, or deceived her when they were first married.

Hindu view

In Hindu law marriage is for life. High class or caste Hindus could not divorce their spouses, but divorce or separation was practised among the lower castes in rural areas. Since the Hindu Marriage Act of 1955, marriages can be ended by divorce, but traditional Hindus do not accept the idea. Divorce is not common in Hindu society and it can be a social **stigma**. Re-marriage after divorce is difficult.

FOR DISCUSSION

A Write down why you think marriages sometimes break down. What problems can divorce cause?

B Do you think that a couple, if they have children, should stay together whatever the state of their marriage, 'for the sake of the kids'?

C Do you think modern pressures of work have led to a reduction of 'quality time' people spend together?

D Increased divorce rates has meant that the stigma of divorce is not as influential as it once was. Do you think this a good or bad state of affairs?

Launching your learning

Using some or all of the words and phrases below, write an essay on attitudes to divorce in world religions.

Stigma, lifelong commitment, irretrievable breakdown, spouse, committed adultery, desertion, reconciliation, separation, sacrament, annulment, consummated, excommunicated, Iddah.

11 Relationships: CONTRACEPTION

If a fertile couple have regular unprotected sex there is a considerable chance that the woman will get pregnant. Using a method to reduce the chance of pregnancy is called contraception. Contraception, or birth control, may be used for a variety of reasons:

- to help couples plan their future and the approximate ages of their children

- to allow married couples to have sex without worrying about pregnancy

- to help control the population

- to allow couples who are not married to avoid unwanted pregnancy

- a married couple may not wish to have children

- a couple may decide that they should not have another child for emotional, psychological or financial reasons.

Roman Catholic view

The various Christian Churches have different views on contraception. While Protestant churches see contraception as a responsible way of arranging a family, the Roman Catholic Church teaches that the use of contraception is not in keeping with human nature. (See Unit 14.)

This is the official teaching of both the Roman Catholic and the Orthodox Churches. In 1930 Pope Pius XI said contraception was wrong in the following statement:

'Any use whatsoever of any method that stops the natural power of sex to generate life is forbidden.'

It is natural that conception may happen with sexual intercourse and therefore this should not be prevented. The only form of contraception permitted is the rhythm method where intercourse takes place at a time when the woman is not fertile. For many years in the Roman Catholic Church the primary purpose of sex was for procreation. Pleasure was a secondary process. Some Catholics even argued that if couples did not want to have children then they should not have sex at all.

Islam

In recent years the **Conference on Islam and Family Planning** agreed that contraception can be used if:

- the mother's health is threatened

- there is a chance of a child being born mentally or physically disabled

- the family does not have the money to bring up a child.

Humanist view

Unlike some opponents of birth control, humanists do not believe that contraception is wrong because it 'interferes with nature'. Humanists do not believe that interfering with nature is in itself a bad thing, particularly if the consequences are good. If contraception results in every child being a wanted child, and in healthier lives for women, it must be a good thing. Young people should be fully informed about contraception and a range of methods should be available to all, although people should also think carefully before embarking on sexual relationships. No one should have a child until they are ready and able to take on the responsibility. However, contraception should be voluntary, not enforced by the state or by doctors, which would be an offence against *personal autonomy*.

▲ Discussing condoms in an African college

Methods of contraception

'Natural' methods

- **The rhythm method**. For a few days of the menstrual cycle a woman is not fertile so a couple can have sex during those days. However keeping track of the 'safe period' is very tricky so this method is not reliable.

- **The withdrawal method**. The man removes his penis from the woman just before ejaculation (coming). This is very unsafe since sperm is often released during sex.

'Unnatural' or artificial methods

- **The pill**. This alters the balance of hormones in the woman's body. The long-term effects of taking the pill are not known. It must be taken regularly and forgetting to take the pill can make having sex unsafe for 28 days. If used properly it is 99% safe, the safest method.

- **A barrier method**. There are two of these. The woman may use a **diaphragm** or the man a **condom**. This is a rubber barrier that stops the sperm from entering the womb (diaphragm) or the vagina (condom). These are fairly safe but there is a danger of them breaking and so failing.

- **The IUD (an inter-uterine device)**. This is a small coil or wire with a piece of copper attached. It is placed inside the woman's womb and is believed to work by preventing the egg from attaching itself to the uterus wall. It is fairly safe but can cause heavy periods or cramps.

Launching your learning

- What are the advantages and the dangers of the above types of contraception?

- Why do some people believe that contraception 'interferes with nature'?

- What do you think humanists mean by 'an offence against *personal autonomy*' – when they say that contraception should be voluntary, not enforced by the state or by doctors?

- Why do humanists hold different views to Roman Catholics regarding contraception?

- Do you think that there is enough information on contraception made available to young people today?

12 Life and death issues:
INTRODUCTION TO ISSUES OF LIFE AND DEATH

It is possible to do things today in medicine that, a generation ago, would have seemed to belong to the realm of science-fiction. Tomorrow who knows what humans will be capable of? But we must prepare for the future by considering the issues today. New medical and reproductive advances increasingly catch the attention of the media, religious leaders and politicians.

Medical ethics – a definition

These issues of human health, technology, medicine, and right and wrong are called **medical ethics** or **bioethics**. Bioethics or medical ethics is a very fast growing subject and one that more and more people do as part of their training in the medical profession.

'Do no harm'

In the Western world, medical ethics traces its roots back to an early **Code of Ethics**, requiring physicians, above all, to 'do no harm'. This was created about 2,500 years ago in Greece and is known as the **Hippocratic Oath**.

Doctors practising today in the twenty-first century still abide by the Hippocratic Oath which states:

> 'Life is short, the art long, opportunity fleeting, experience treacherous, judgement difficult. The physician must be ready, not only to do his duty himself, but also to secure the cooperation of the patient, of the attendants and of externals.'

KEY IDEA

It would not be right to use medical technology to harm others. The discipline of medical ethics imposes constraints on its abuses.

CITIZENSHIP CHALLENGE

- Most people today believe it is their right to good health care and that governments have a responsibility to provide a fair and accessible health service. But the costs are high, and who is going to pay? Should taxes be raised to pay for the increased pressure on the National Health Service?

Society versus the individual
Conflict between society's priorities and individual needs can sometimes lead to conflict.

- If a Jehovah's Witness refuses a life saving blood transfusion for her child because of her beliefs, have doctors the right to intervene to save that child and therefore go against the parent's wishes?

- Has a hardened life-long 40-a-day smoker dying of lung cancer as much right to a hospital bed as a teenager suffering from alcohol poisoning? Have they as much right to medical care as a mother suffering from breast cancer?

What issues should we be talking about?

Questions about medical ethics were at one time thought to be for doctors alone to answer; for example should a patient's family be told if the patient were suffering from a transmittable, condition, and the patient did not tell them himself? Although dilemmas about **rights** and **responsibilities** like this arise all the time for doctors and nurses, advanced medical technologies raise even more complicated questions.

Possible abuses

Some new technologies could possibly lead to abuses. For example, the prospect of slavery combining with **breeding technologies** is a terrifying thought. There are fears that in extremely poor countries big businesses may deliberately create a steady supply of child labourers by forcing women of a low socio-economic status into having fertilized eggs implanted in them, to provide businesses with a new generation of slaves.

KEY IDEA

New technologies in medicine have created new demands. A fifteen-year-old boy with heart disease in the sixteenth century, or even later, would most likely die, given the medical knowledge of the day. Today that boy, if he had access to the right treatment, would probably survive.

This new demand is *not*, however, a *new* right.

The sixteenth-century child had the right to life just as the twenty-first-century child does. In the sixteenth-century the right could not be protected. The twenty-first-century child lives in a time when he can be protected from disease.

Consent

In 2001, it was revealed that some British hospitals had cut out and stored the organs of deceased babies without telling the child's parents (see Unit 25). This raised issues about the importance, the meaning and the practicality of obtaining **consent** – permission to carry out surgery from research subjects or their next of kin if the subjects could not provide consent themselves.

Launching your learning

Write an article entitled 'Medical ethics today' using the following words and phrases: **Bioethics, Code of Ethics, Hippocratic Oath, rights and responsibilities, breeding technologies, consent.**

▲ Playing God?

13 Life and death issues:
MIRACLE BABIES 1

Infertility

There is something deeply ingrained in most people that makes them want to be parents. However between ten and fifteen per cent of heterosexual couples are **infertile** and cannot have children. Infertility can cause much sadness.

New technologies of assisted reproduction

Over the last 25 years new technologies of 'assisted reproduction' have offered hope to childless couples, as well as single women, post-menopausal women, lesbians or women wanting a dead partner's child. These techniques include:

- **Artificial insemination (husband) (AIH)** – live sperm are injected into a woman's uterus at the time of ovulation.

- **Artificial insemination (donor) (AID)** – the semen (seed) is provided by an anonymous donor and not the husband. **Muslims** condemn **AID** since procreation is legitimate only within marriage. Likewise many Christians, particularly in the **Roman Catholic Church**, argue that AID violates the dignity of the person and the sanctity of marriage. It is condemned because a third party is involved – the donor fathers a child with his sperm yet he has no responsibility to the child. Any process that isolates the sacred act of creating life from the marriage union is a violation of that marriage union. However, if the marriage act is preserved, then various clinical techniques designed to help create new life are not to be condemned.

- *In vitro* **fertilization (IVF)** – sometimes called 'test tube babies'. *In vitro* means the fertilization takes place 'in glass' – the ovum is withdrawn from the woman and fertilized with a man's semen under laboratory conditions. The embryo is then transferred to the womb.

- **Egg donation** – a woman donates an ovum, which is then fertilized with the semen of the husband of the woman into whose uterus the resulting embryo is transferred.

- **Embryo donation** – similar to egg donation, except the ovum is fertilized by semen from a donor because both partners are infertile or both carry a genetic defect.

- **Surrogacy ('womb-leasing')** – a woman bears a child for a woman who cannot become pregnant and hands the child over after birth. Surrogate motherhood is a commercial transaction in which a couple, and sometimes a single person, buy the services of a woman to bear them a child. It is unacceptable to **Islam** as it entails a pregnancy outside the legitimacy of a marriage contract. Likewise many **Christian Churches** condemn surrogacy because 'it violates the dignity of motherhood' when a women is paid for bearing a child.

- **Research on human embryos** – research ranging from a simple study of early embryos to increase knowledge about infertility, to testing new drugs on embryos.

The law

These techniques raise many moral issues. To protect people from abusing the new technologies, **The Human Fertilization and Embryology Act** was passed in 1990:

- there should be complete **anonymity** for semen, egg or embryo donors

- both partners should give written consent to treatment

- a woman giving birth as a result of egg or embryo donation should be regarded in law as the child's mother, and the donor should have no rights or duties relating to the child

- surrogate motherhood 'rent-a-womb' agencies are illegal

- no human embryo should be kept alive outside the womb or used for research beyond fourteen days after fertilization

- it is a criminal offence to transfer to a woman any embryo used for research, or to place a human embryo in the womb of another species.

Who is the 'real' Mum or Dad?

It is now possible to create a normal baby with no fewer than five 'parents'. One would be the woman who actually bears the child. Two others, its genetic parents, would supply the sperm and the egg implanted as a living embryo in a surrogate mother's womb. Finally come the infertile couple who will take the baby home and call it theirs.

In 2001, a 62-year-old British woman went to an American fertility clinic where she had an egg implanted from an American donor and sperm from her brother. She gave birth to a baby boy in June 2001.

Launching your learning

A Find out the meaning of the following words and phrases:
Genetic parents, procreation, IVF, AIH, AID, surrogate mothers, commercial surrogacy, embryo research, anonymity, selective abortion.

B Write an article entitled 'Babies in the Front Line of Medical Technology'.

Concerns

- For many women IVF treatment means doctor's appointments, hospital visits, tests, repeated examinations, surgery, anxiety, depression, disruption of work, strain on personal relationships, disappointment – often without a baby at the end of it.

- While scientists scramble to develop wonderful technology to 'solve infertility', the environmental causes of infertility can be overlooked.

- It is now possible to create embryos in test tubes for research purposes. Embryo research is allowed for up to fourteen days after fertilization. Is it right that in law an embryo is seen as rather less than a living child?

- The combination of slavery and breeding technology could lead, in some parts of the world, to babies being produced for child prostitution or child labour.

- Children put up for adoption might lose out if more and more infertile couples use IVF.

- Fertility drugs are an essential part of IVF but they increase the chances of a multiple pregnancy from 1–2 per cent to 25 per cent. One way round this is **selective abortion** – where one or more of the foetuses is aborted to give the remaining ones a better chance. But has the aborted foetus equal rights with the foetus allowed to live?

- Online auctions in which egg donations from young models were offered to the highest bidder through a website have raised concerns. Many scientists were outraged about the false advertising associated with a promise of 'beauty' from 50 per cent of a baby's genes. Is it wrong to search for eggs from the 'beautiful'?

14 Life and death issues:
MIRACLE BABIES 2

CITIZENSHIP CHALLENGE

Do all couples have a right to have children?

Does a 'genetic parent', like a sperm donor, have any rights, or duties, towards the eventual offspring?

What are the dangers of 'rent-a-womb' agencies? What problems might face:

1 the surrogate mother

2 the parents who commission her

3 the child when it grows up?

Why do you think many religious believers argue that surrogacy treats the baby as a 'commodity' and reduces motherhood from a 'value' to a 'price'?

The Natural Law Theory

Do modern medical technologies follow natural laws? Or do some **violate** – cruelly disregard – natural laws?

To try and answer the question 'What is natural?' Christians, particularly Roman Catholics, have looked to the **Natural Law Theory**. This is an interesting theory to apply to today's dilemmas about medicine.

The Natural Law Theory sees everything as being created for a particular purpose and fulfilling this purpose is the good to which everything aims.

St Thomas Aquinas (1225–74), regarded as one of the greatest Christian philosophers, argued that things are as they ought to be when they are fulfilling their *natural purpose*, and *unnatural* when they are not. Some ways of behaving are 'natural' but some are 'unnatural' and go against the natural order of things and are therefore morally wrong.

▲ A gay couple with their twins born from a surrogate mother

The Jewish, Muslim and Christian traditions teach that human beings are made in the image of God (Genesis 1: 26). We have a unique status in creation. To treat ourselves and others, not as persons to be *respected*, but as things to be *manipulated*, is to violate this God-given nature.

Islam and IVF

In vitro fertilization (IVF) is acceptable as long as it is within marriage. Since divorce or widowhood in Islam brings a marriage contract to a conclusion – and they are then no more husband and wife – it follows that a woman may not be impregnated by the sperm of her ex-husband kept in deep freeze in a semen bank. Intervention of a third party, other than husband and wife and the bearers of their genetic material (sperm and ovum), is not permissible because this would be an intrusion into the marriage contract binding the pair. 'Alien sperm,' or an 'alien egg,' or an 'alien womb' (to carry a couple's embryo) is not allowed.

Hinduism and artificial insemination

Artificial insemination by donor, where the wife's egg is fertilized in the laboratory using the sperm of an anonymous donor, is difficult for Hindus to accept because of the importance of the male ancestral line in matters of inheritance and the need to establish caste and family background at marriage. The identity of the donor, and thus his caste and family background, is unknown and this would be unacceptable to a Hindu family.

Traditionally, in an Indian extended family with its numerous aunts and uncles and cousins, Hindu law allows the adoption of children from relatives in cases of infertility. This means that inheritance still goes through the male ancestral line and the caste and background of the adopted child is known.

FOR DISCUSSION

When does life begin? Has an embryo the same rights as you or me?

In what ways might assisted reproduction techniques be exploited for the wrong reasons?

With only limited money available in the health service, should infertility treatments be widely available?

How far should science be allowed to use embryos for experimentation in order to push back the frontiers of medical knowledge?

In 2001, a child was born from sperm harvested from a dead man. Is it wrong that the dead man had no say in the matter?

Is it acceptable that to be sure of fertilizing an egg, several eggs have to be fertilized? This method creates **spare embryos**, which have to be thrown away or used for experimentation.

Sperm banks are clinics where men, specially selected for their genetic quality, donate sperm. Do these men have any **responsibilities** towards their offspring?

Is it 'natural' for scientists to pursue new technologies, or is there a point where science becomes 'unnatural'?

15 Life and death issues:
EMBRYO RESEARCH

Embryo – a definition

In popular usage the term **embryo** is often used to refer to any stage of pre-natal mammalian development from 0–8 weeks after fertilization. From nine weeks after fertilization until birth, it is called a *foetus*.

Embryology – a definition

Embryology is the study of the changes that occur to an organism from its earliest stages.

Embryo research

Embryo research helps detect and treat many diseases and disorders. However, there is much controversy about when life actually begins and whether research on embryos should be carried out.

Arguments against

- Life becomes human life at the time of fertilization of the ovum. Thus, an embryo is a human being with all of the rights that this implies.

- Experiments that subject an ovum to any significant risk are the ethical equivalent of Nazi medical experiments in the death camps, in that they, too, were inflicted on unwilling and uninformed victims. **Ends do not justify the means**.

- Individual human beings must not be used or abused for some grand scheme promising '**the greatest good for the greatest number**'.

Arguments for

- A fertilized ovum is not human life; it is rather *potential* human life. Human life begins either when the foetus can live independently, or when the foetal brain develops to the point where it experiences self-awareness, or at some other stage of pregnancy, or at birth.

- Creating embryos and/or performing experiments on existing embryos is justified if the research has a reasonable potential of advancing medical knowledge.

KEY QUESTION

Although embryos have no brain, central nervous system, or internal organs; no organs to see, hear, touch, taste; lack a body, head, arms, legs and have no thought processes or consciousness, do they still have rights?

TALKING POINT

'It is wrong to create human embryos for the purpose of experimentation and destruction. This is biotech cannibalism, consuming our young for the sake of our own potential prosperity. It does not matter whether she is five days old or fifteen days old, a human embryo is a human being. That is just what human beings look like at that age. That is what all of us looked like at that age.'

C. Ben Mitchell – biomedical consultant

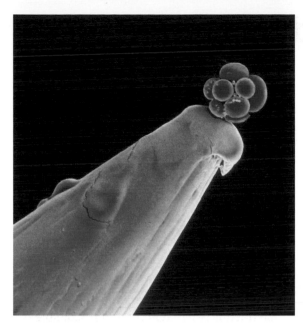

▲ Stem cells like these ones could be used for transplants

Stem cell research

Stem cells are primitive cells. They are usually extracted from 'unwanted' human embryos. Scientists believe that these cells have the capacity to develop into different cell types, such as blood, brain, heart tissue, nerve cells, bones and so on. Researchers are confident that they could lead to treatments to many diseases.

Methods may even be found whereby stem cells could be formed into replacement tissue and human spare parts for transplants (see Unit 24). They may eventually be used to repair injured or poorly functioning brains and nervous systems.

This they believe would provide the key to an unlimited supply of spare human cells for grafts and transplants. At present, research is being hampered by the poor quality of embryos available.

Supporters of stem cell research argue that these embryos are extras; that they will never be implanted and they are destined for destruction anyway, so they might as well be used for the benefit of others. Supporters regard a young embryo as not a full organism, at most they can become an organ not a complete living organism. They cannot be considered a form of human life. They argue that stem cells have an enormous promise to benefit humankind and these possibilities should be explored.

Critics, however, argue that:

- an embryo is a human being, so the act of extracting stem cells from an embryo is murder

- it is possible to 'adopt' those embryos – called 'rescue surrogacy' – and so embryos are not necessarily destined for destruction. They can be implanted, and a healthy baby can be born

- other methods of obtaining stem cells without 'killing' an embryo should be employed. *Advanced cell technology* has been able to extract human stem cells from brains of cadavers – dead human bodies – and from bone marrow. However, research to date indicates that these stem cells are very limited in their potential, compared to cells taken from embryos.

CITIZENSHIP CHALLENGE

A 'Ends do not justify the means' – is often used in discussions about what is right and wrong. What do you think this means? Can you think of examples where the end does not justify the means? Apply this idea to the issues covered in Units 13–16.

B 'The greatest good for the greatest number' – is another idea used in discussions about right and wrong. What do you think this means? Can you think of examples? Apply this idea to the issues covered in Units 13–16.

16 Life and death issues:
ABORTION 1

Abortion is a highly emotional subject. In the USA violent protests by **anti-abortionists** against abortion clinics have erupted over recent years. There have been cases involving the assassination and attempted murder of abortion providers.

▲ Abortion – a controversial issue

Abortion – a definition

Abortion is defined as 'the premature expulsion of the **foetus** from the womb' and 'the operation to cause this'. The word 'abortion' comes from the Latin word *aboriri*, meaning 'to fail to be born'.

Abortions may be carried out for a number of reasons: to preserve the life, or physical or mental health of the mother; to prevent a pregnancy brought about by rape or incest; to prevent a child being born severely mentally or physically disabled; to prevent a birth because, for example, the mother is very young.

Doctors have a range of opinions on abortion. Generally, however, they tend to give the medical interests of the mother – which may include her mental health – the most weight when making decisions. Modern medicine can keep very **premature** babies alive, changing ideas about when foetuses become human beings with rights. Very ill babies who would probably once have died before or shortly after birth can now be kept alive. Babies in Britain have been known to survive outside the womb as early as 23 weeks into pregnancy.

KEY QUESTIONS

A If a woman finds herself pregnant, what is the best, or least bad, solution for her and the potential newborn that she is carrying?

  1 To do nothing, have the baby and raise it herself, hopefully with help from others.

  2 To do nothing, have the baby and give it up for adoption.

  3 To have an abortion.

B If a pregnant woman discusses her options with her doctor and decides to have an abortion, should the law override her decision and prevent her from having an abortion?

C Who should make decisions about abortion? Doctors? Religious leaders? Individual women? Their partners? Politicians?

The law

Abortion has been legal in England, Scotland and Wales since 1967 when **The Abortion Act** was passed. Changes were made under **The Human Fertilization and Embryology Act** of 1990, bringing in a new upper time limit, allowing most abortions to take place only up to 24 weeks.

The law in England, Scotland and Wales states that *an abortion can be performed before the 24th week of pregnancy if two doctors agree that there is a risk to the life or the mental or physical health of the mother if the pregnancy continues; or there will be a risk to the mental or physical health of other children in the family.* However, there is no time limit if there is a large risk that the baby will be born severely disabled or there is a grave risk of death or permanent injury, mental or physical, to the mother. In effect, this means that almost every woman who wants an abortion and is persistent in seeking one before the 24th week can obtain one. However, some women who do not realize that they are pregnant until it is too late may not be able to have abortions though they would have qualified on other grounds.

Viable

The law in England, Scotland and Wales is based on the fact that after 24 weeks the foetus is often **viable** – with medical care it can survive outside the womb. Before 24 weeks there are no specific legal requirements governing the disposal of foetal tissue. If no personal wishes have been expressed foetuses are incinerated. Foetuses terminated after 24 weeks gestation are registered as stillbirths and must be buried or cremated.

Abortions in Britain

Up to 31 March 1997, nearly 4.7 million abortions had been performed in England and Wales since the 1967 Abortion Act was passed. In 1968, there was a total of 23,641 abortions performed in England and Wales. By 1999 the figure had risen to 183,250 abortions.

Figures for Scotland show a similar rise from a total of 1,544 abortions in 1968 to 12,144 in 1999.

Single women make up the largest group having abortions – in 1999 they accounted for 70 per cent of abortions.

Global statistics

An estimated 46 million women around the world have abortions each year. Of these women, 78 per cent live in developing countries and 22 per cent in developed countries. The reasons women give for choosing to have an abortion include: they have had all the children they want; they want to delay their next birth; they are too young or too poor to raise a child; they are separated from or on uneasy terms with their sexual partner; they do not want a child while they are in school or working. About 26 million women have legal abortions each year, and 20 million have abortions in countries where abortion is restricted or prohibited by law.

Abortion at sea

To overcome anti abortion laws in some countries, for example Ireland, doctors have set up private abortion clinics on ships moored outside of a country's territorial waters.

'Back street abortions'

Some people argue that the way to prevent abortion is *not* to make it illegal. Whenever governments have made abortions illegal they have not stopped them. When women have felt abortion to be their only option they have had them whether they were legal or not. Women go 'underground' and have illegal operations, known as 'back street abortions'. These are often dangerous and women can die or become seriously ill from lack of medical care. Also women are forced to behave as if they are criminals in order to do what they feel is right for themselves.

17 Life and death issues:
ABORTION 2

Opposing views

The pro-life movement

The pro-life movement generally argues that life becomes human life at the moment of conception, when a unique DNA is created. To deliberately stop the developing process from conception to birth is considered by the pro-life movement to be murder. **Pro-lifers** argue that life is sacred. Abortion is immoral and should be outlawed.

Almost all, however, would allow abortions if continued pregnancy would cause the death of the woman. A few radical pro-lifers would outlaw abortions under all conditions, even if it were necessary to save the life of the woman. Many would permit an abortion if the pregnancy resulted from rape or incest.

The pro-choice movement

The pro-choice movement generally argues that life becomes human life much later in pregnancy, or at birth. There are many variations in views among **pro-choicers**. Many would argue that a woman should have full control over her body. If she is convinced that she wants to end her pregnancy – after discussing her options and their consequences with a doctor – she should be allowed to have a safe abortion at any stage in pregnancy.

▲ A pro-choice rally

The media often emphasizes the difference between the pro-life and pro-choice movements. However, there is one major point on which they agree: pro-lifers *and* pro-choicers generally believe that when the embryo or foetus becomes a human person, women should not seek an abortion for themselves, except under very unusual circumstances. However, pro-lifers and pro-choicers differ greatly about *when* personhood happens.

The egg

Life and personhood are two very different matters. The human ovum (egg) is already clearly alive when it enters the fallopian tubes, many hours or days before it has the opportunity to be fertilized. Women release one each month between puberty and menopause – a few hundred in a lifetime. Almost all of these will die and be ejected from the body. Although the ovum is a form of life, there is agreement that it is *not* a human person.

The sperm

Hundreds of millions of male sperms are released during sexual intercourse – enough to theoretically double the earth's population in a week or two if they were all used to fertilize a separate ovum. Sperm are also clearly alive. If we watch sperm under a microscope we can see that they are energetic swimmers. All of these will die within days. An average man produces thousands of sperm a second. Very few during his lifetime may contribute to the formation of a baby. The rest will die. Although sperm are very much alive there is general agreement that they are *not* human persons.

When does human personhood begin?

The meeting of sperm and ovum often causes conception. If all goes well, the single cell divides in two. This process of division continues. About 72 hours after conception, the **embryo** has reached the seven-cell-stage. However, there is no general agreement as to *when* human personhood starts.

The soul

The idea of a soul is a religious one; it cannot be located, weighed, seen, smelled, felt, measured or otherwise detected by any known instrument. The famous Greek thinker, Aristotle (384–322BCE), argued that the male embryo develops a human soul about 40 days after conception, whereas a female embryo acquires its soul at about 90 days. For much of its history, the Christian Church believed in this and allowed abortions up to 90 days into pregnancy. Arguments that refer to the existence of a soul are not convincing to atheists, humanists and others who do not believe that souls exist.

FOR DISCUSSION

So when does personhood begin?
Look at the stages of embryo/foetal development below and discuss when *you* think the transition to personhood takes place.

1 A few hours after conception, when the ovum splits into two cells. Some regard human personhood as being defined by the act of cell splitting.

2 About twelve days from conception, when pregnancy begins, that is, when the fertilized ovum has attached itself to the lining of the uterus.

3 Three weeks from conception, when the embryo is about two mm long and has started to develop visible external body parts.

4 Four weeks from conception, when the heart starts to beat.

5 Six weeks from conception, when brain waves can be first sensed and bones begin to appear.

6 Two months from conception, when the foetus and the face resembles that of a primate.

7 Three months from conception, when the foetus begins to 'look like' a baby. Its vocal chords and sexual organs begin to form.

8 Four months from conception, when the foetus' face has developed to the point where one can tell one foetus from another. At this stage it is roughly half its birth length.

9 About six months from conception, when the foetus becomes **viable** (able to live outside the womb).

10 Six months or later, when its brain has developed to a particular degree. Scientists have measured brain wave patterns like those during dreaming at eight months.

Some people might argue that the foetus becomes a human person only after it has been delivered and is breathing on its own. There is some Biblical justification for this belief. Genesis 2: 7 states that God made Adam's body from the dust of the ground. But it was only after God 'breathed into it the breath of life' that 'man became a living person'.

18 Life and death issues:
ABORTION 3

Christian view

The sixth Commandment is: 'You shall not kill'. In the Tenakh it appears to say that life begins when the baby is in the mother's womb:

> 'Before I formed you in the womb I knew you, before you were born I set you apart.'

Jeremiah 1: 5

This is supported in the New Testament in the experience of John the Baptist's mother Elizabeth:

> 'When Elizabeth heard Mary's greeting, the baby leaped in her womb and Elizabeth was filled with the Holy Spirit.'

Luke 1: 41

Early Christian philosophers believed that abortion was an act of murder. Barnabas in the first century CE wrote:

> 'You shall not kill the foetus by abortion.'

Some Church writings of this period also condemned abortion. *The Didache* (also known as *The Teaching of the Twelve Apostles*) dates from the first half of the second century CE. It refers to:

> 'child-murderers, who go the way of death, who slay God's image in the womb.'

St Augustine (354–430CE) reversed centuries of Christian teaching and returned to Aristotle's idea of 'delayed ensoulment'. He argued that a human soul cannot live in an unformed body. Thus, early in pregnancy, an abortion is not murder because no soul is destroyed.

By the twentieth century a different view had developed within Christian Churches. While some churches promote a woman's **right to choose** an abortion, other churches are generally opposed to all abortions, from conception to birth, although some would permit it in the event of rape, incest or extreme danger to the woman's life. None of the Christian Churches believe that abortion should be encouraged and all agree that it should only be used in the most serious circumstances.

The **Roman Catholic Church** and **Orthodox Church** (see Addresses/websites) believe that all abortions are a form of murder. The Roman Catholic Church only makes an exception when it is the inevitable result of necessary life-saving treatment given to the mother (called the **Principle of Double Effect**). The Roman Catholic Church teaches that the foetus is a human being from the moment of conception and that its rights to life are equal to those of the mother:

'From the time that the ovum is fertilized a new life is begun which is neither that of the father nor the mother. It is the life of a new human being with its own growth. It would never become human if it were not human already.'

Document on Procured Abortion (1974)

The Church of England agrees with the Roman Catholic and Orthodox Churches in principle, but they also teach that each case is different. The Church of England has spoken out against the rising number of abortions in Britain, but has left the final decision on the issue up to the people involved. Therefore, while abortion is generally not accepted, especially as a method of birth control, it may be permitted if there is a serious risk to the mother's life, if conception takes place as a result of rape or if there is a grave risk that the baby will be born severely disabled:

'We affirm that every human life, created in the divine image is unique ... and that this holds for each of us, born or yet to be born. We therefore believe that abortion is an evil ... and that **abortion on demand** would be a very great evil. But we also believe that to withhold compassion is evil and in circumstances of extreme distress or need ... Christians need to face frankly the fact that in an imperfect world the 'right' choice is sometimes the acceptance of the lesser of two evils.'

Muslim view

Abortion is not generally permitted within Islam unless it is to save the mother's life. Generally, Islam is opposed to abortion. The Qur'an teaches:

'Slay not your children ... the killing of them is a great sin.'

Qur'an, Surah 17: 31

Launching your learning

A Look at the Key Questions in this Unit. What are your views? Try and give reasons for your answers.

B Write a short essay on Christian views on abortion. Why are there different views among Christians do you think?

C Some Muslims believe that for the first four months of pregnancy the woman has greater rights than the foetus but that after this time they are equal. Why would some people disagree?

KEY QUESTIONS

Science can tell us, with increasing detail, the processes that start with a sperm and ovum and end up with a newborn baby. But it cannot answer the following questions:

1 A fully grown baby emerging from the womb is alive in its own right, but is the **zygote** – the union of sperm and ovum – a 'person'?

2 Does a developing foetus have human rights?

3 Should we consider the moment that the foetus can survive outside the womb as the moment it becomes alive?

4 Is abortion murder?

5 Does the foetus have a soul?

19 Life and death issues:
ABORTION 4

Uniqueness

Some **pro-lifers** point out that shortly after conception a unique DNA code is formed which will remain unchanged throughout the life of the foetus and throughout the potential life after birth. They might say that the presence of a unique DNA code converts the egg into a human person. But others disagree. A skin scraping of a child or adult contains a very large number of living, single cells; each has the same unique human DNA code, as does the human from which it came. We do not consider hair follicles, skin scrapings or swabs from mouths to be a human person.

Some **pro-choicers** feel that this transition to personhood does not happen at conception. They state that the newly fertilized ovum has no limbs, no head, no brain, no ability to see, hear, smell, taste or touch, no internal organs, no self-consciousness, no ability to think, reason, sense its environment, and so on. Even one month after conception, it cannot be distinguished from the embryo of a cat or dog.

Hindu views

According to the Hindu law books, human life is sacred and abortion is a sinful act. However, a distinction is made between the killing of an embryo and the killing of a 'still-indistinct' embryo, the latter being considered a lesser offence. This is similar to the distinction between the developing embryo (before thirteen weeks), and the fully-formed, though tiny, human embryo that develops after this time.

Strict Hindus still believe that deliberate wilful abortion is a sin, though this is largely ignored in modern India, where abortion is legal if carried out in government clinics. Many Hindus clearly support abortion, both as a method of ending unwanted pregnancies and as a method of birth control. It has been estimated that 5 million abortions are performed every year in India.

Amniocentesis: a definition

Amniocentesis is a scientific method developed to detect any abnormalities in the foetus.

Amniocentesis in India

However, one form of the test can also be used to identify the sex of the foetus and since 1986, when the test became widely available in India, many women have had abortions after learning that their unborn babies were female. Because the test is so cheap even poor families can afford the fee, and today both rich and poor routinely use the test mainly to find out the baby's sex.

In parts of modern Indian society, girls are considered a drain on the family's resources, especially the large **dowry** payments which will have to be made upon their marriage, whereas boys will bring money into the household and support the parents in their old age. This is because traditionally, brides move to their husband's home.

From a financial point of view, many parents think it is better to spend 500 rupees on an abortion in order to save thousands on a marriage. The custom of terminating female foetuses also occurs among Asian families in Britain, as they are still subject to cultural pressure to pay a large dowry to the bridegroom's family at the marriage of a daughter.

Humanist view

Generally, humanists are more concerned with the *quality* of life than the *right* to life, if the two come into conflict. The probable quality of life of the baby, the woman, the father and the rest of the family, would all have to be given due weight.

Most humanists would probably put the interests of the woman first, since she would have to complete the pregnancy and probably care for the baby. They believe, however, that all possible options should be explored. Adoption of the unwanted baby might be a better solution in some cases.

Sex education

For society as a whole, as well as for the children themselves, the existence of unwanted children cannot be a good thing. However, abortion is not the best way of avoiding unwanted children and improved sex education and easily available contraception can all help to reduce the number of abortions. But as long as abortion is needed as a last resort many people would argue that society should provide safe legal facilities because the alternatives, including illegal abortions, are far worse.

FOR DISCUSSION

A Either the doctors who perform the abortion operation are removing an unthinking, unfeeling bundle of protoplasm from the mother's womb or they are killing a human being capable of experiencing sensations. What do you think? Give reasons for your views.

B Some people believe that a woman has rights over her own body that override those of any unborn foetus. What do you think? Give reasons for your views.

C All religions teach that human life is sacred and that life begins at conception. But if a woman has to choose between risking her own life or the life of the unborn foetus, how might she go about deciding what to do?

Launching your learning

After reading Units 16–19 on abortion, prepare a project on some of the difficult issues that this subject raises. Conclude your project with your own reflections on abortion. Remember always to give reasons for your personal views.

20 Life and death issues:
GENETIC ENGINEERING 1

Learning about myself

Science, at its most basic level, is about observing.

It is this curiosity that marks a person out as having a scientific mind and it is the desire to find ways of understanding and controlling things that makes a person a scientist.

Many scientists dream of working at the 'cutting edge' of new research and technology – where people pave the way for humankind, but only a few can ever mark their place in history.

What is it that drives these men and women to dedicate their lives to understanding the unknown? Why do people dedicate their lives to any search for truth and a goal?

TALKING POINTS

'Science and technology by themselves cannot disclose the meaning of human existence and human progress.'

Catechism of the Catholic Church

'Everyone who is seriously involved in the pursuit of science becomes convinced that a Spirit is manifest in the Laws of the Universe – a Spirit vastly superior to that of man, and one in the face of which we, with our modest powers, must feel humble.'

Albert Einstein, scientist

New frontiers

Food producers dream of crops that flourish year after year.

Parents of children with inherited diseases dream of a day when doctors might be able to heal them.

AIDS patients dream of a cure for HIV infection.

These 'new goals' and dreams of humanity seem ethically noble in their aim to feed, heal and protect humankind. But are there dangers?

Scientific knowledge is accelerating at a remarkable pace. The computer you buy today will be 'prehistoric' within five years. Computer programming promises to develop into every part of our lives, and genetic engineering seems set to develop at a similar rate. In both fields of science, the tools and equipment available are developing considerably faster than our thinking about how to use them. However, there is one big difference: computers may make people redundant in some jobs, but they do not alter life itself. **Genetic engineering**, on the other hand, by definition alters the very substance on which life is based.

Genetics is the great new frontier of science. Already it helps with diagnosing and curing genetically linked diseases. However, there are also concerns about where genetic engineering might lead us.

Genetic engineering – a definition

The purpose of genetic engineering is to introduce *desirable* properties from one organism into another, and/or to remove *undesirable* properties from an organism. Genetic engineering is defined as '**the deliberate modification of the genetic code of an organism by the manipulation of genetic material**'.

Since the 1970s, scientists have learned how to introduce new genes into plants and animals, and even into human cells kept alive in the laboratory. Already, farm animals have been genetically engineered to make them larger and plants have been genetically engineered to resist diseases or insects (see Unit 75). This means that very soon scientists will be able to introduce new genes into a human organism to change it for better or for worse.

The unknown

Genetic engineering is at the frontier of knowledge – an unknown future. As with any exploration into the unknown, there are dangers:

- The possibility of grafting new genes into germ cells (see Unit 21) and affecting coming generations could later be associated with **mutants**.

- The introduction of genetic material from one species into another practically means the creation of a new species with mixed features.

- Science's desire to seek the unknown until it is known and the unachievable until it becomes achievable may discover patterns of life yet to appear on the biological stage. Science might think that everything is under control while it is not really so.

- The technology itself is attractive to multinational companies. It could attract large capital for investment and its investors will seek maximum profits. Some scientists have already exchanged their 'ivory towers' for golden ones and already exchanged the spirit of openness and cooperation for trade-secrecy and patenting forms of life (see Unit 21).

Robots

Nanotechnology is 'the science of the tiny'. Structures, the size of atoms, are programmed to do what scientists want. Scientists have already created atom-sized switches and collections of molecules with 'on' and 'off' positions. Once the realm of science fiction (explored in Hollywood films, such as *Blade Runner*), the prospect of **artificial intelligence** is a distinct possibility in the next fifteen years.

FOR DISCUSSION

A When the atom was split in 1933 people thought it was a move forward for the human race. The knowledge however was abused and led to atomic weapons being used twelve years later (see Unit 69). How could genetic engineering be abused do you think?

B Give examples of:

1 science helping humanity, and

2 science harming humanity.

21 Life and death issues:
GENETIC ENGINEERING 2

Germline gene therapy

Germline gene therapy involves altering the genes of an embryo so that both it and its descendents are permanently changed. At the moment human germline therapy is both technically impossible and illegal. There are good reasons for banning it. The moment scientists are allowed to tinker permanently with the **genetic code** is the moment we begin to guarantee that children will be 'beautiful', 'intelligent' or 'heterosexual'. Only the rich would be able to afford such treatment. In laboratories around the world, scientists are working on technologies that bring such possibilities closer.

Designer babies

Could we eventually find the very rich designing their 'perfect baby' and then going shopping in **genetic supermarkets** on the Internet?

The inequality and racism we suffer from today would look insignificant beside the '**geneticism**' this would inevitably unleash if genetic engineering was not controlled.

Eugenics

Once the technology is there, there is always a danger that the people who could afford it would use it, leaving the rest of us 'sub humans' in the control of a group of cruel fascists who think they are the 'genetically elect'. Maybe it could lead to the manipulation of human sperm or eggs for **eugenic** purposes – improving the hereditary 'qualities' of a race. Hitler manipulated and controlled breeding in slave camps in an attempt to create a **genetic elect**.

Embryos

Recently there have been much publicized cases in which parents have been able to choose between embryos to produce a second child whose cells could be transplanted to their seriously ill first born. The embryos are chosen to make sure that the second child is not born with the same life-threatening disease as the first. The practice of choosing between embryos to cut out an inherited disease is already a well-established practice in Britain.

Patenting genes

Commercially useful genes taken from human populations and from plants are being sold. Multinational pharmaceutical firms buy up and **patent** genes giving themselves total control to sell a new drug. Animals can be patented too.

Transgenic technology is capable of transferring DNA from one species to another. In 1988, the US Patent and Trademark Office issued the world's first patent on a mammal, a **transgenic** mouse known as the '**oncomouse**'.

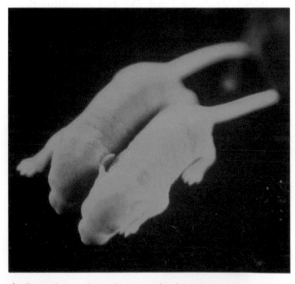

▲ Genetic engineering manipulates genetic material

Fighting disease

By the 1970s, enough was known about genetics to make it possible to manipulate genes in simple organisms, such as bacteria. For practical purposes, genetic engineering began when scientists added the gene for human **insulin** to the DNA of a bacterium so that it could then produce insulin. Insulin is an important hormone in the human body and the lack of insulin causes a form of **diabetes**, which can only be treated by regular injections of the hormone. Genetic engineering has made it possible to manufacture human insulin in large amounts simply by growing the bacteria in tanks and removing the hormone. In effect, the bacterium becomes a factory for producing human insulin.

Today, many other human proteins (hormones, enzymes, and other biological chemicals) are made in the same way and used in the treatment of diseases, such as **multiple sclerosis**.

In the near future, once the genes that cause an inherited disease, such as **haemophilia**, have been identified, it will be possible to remove them from the genetic code of a human embryo and to replace them with the code taken from a healthy organism. As the embryo grows all its cells would now have the healthy section of DNA code and haemophilia would be eliminated from that person.

CITIZENSHIP CHALLENGE

A Examine closely the following statement:

'The benefits of genetic engineering may seem attractive but have we the right to interfere with the natural world and its organic processes?'

B Discuss the following questions:

1 What do you think are benefits and dangers of genetic engineering?

2 Is it a blessing or a curse to possess a technology that identifies inherited diseases?

3 Is it a blessing or a curse that one day some parents may be able to design their 'perfect baby' and then go shopping in **genetic supermarkets** on the Internet?

4 What might be the concerns of a technology that is moving so fast that rules have difficulties in keeping pace?

5 Have parents a *right* to use technology so that their children are not born with hereditary diseases?

6 Should parents be allowed to produce an embryo just for tissue transplants for themselves?

7 Do you think that genetic engineering and manipulation of human cells breaks:

  a natural laws?
  b moral laws?
  c religious laws?
  d no laws?

8 Who do you think owns my genes:

  a only me?
  b banks?
  c the security services?
  d employers?
  e governments?
  f God?
  g nobody?

22 Life and death issues:
GENETIC ENGINEERING 3

The human genome – a definition

The human genome is essentially a scientific 'map' of the human gene, or of the smallest parts of us that make us what we are. The 'plotting of' this map of the human genome aims to understand the biological 'code' that is used to make an individual human being.

With the understanding of this code, scientists may then proceed to use it almost like an **assembly guide** to making a human being, with the genes themselves being the 'assembly parts'. These parts can be 'mixed and matched' to produce a unique human being, like you or me, or a certain combination can be isolated and reproduced resulting in a clone (see Unit 23).

Nature versus nurture

The Book of Humankind, known as '**The Human Genome Project**', was set up in 1990 to identify and map the genes in the human body. In February 2001, scientists informed the world that there are not enough genes in the human make-up to programme us. We are more likely to be formed by our experiences (nurture) than our genetic make-up (nature). This will have massive implications on the way we think. For example, we now know that criminals are made and not born (see Unit 46).

Genesis and genes

The extraordinary thing about the code of life is that it is so constant: the smallest most primitive living organism to the largest, has a code written in exactly the same language and structured in an identical way.

For evolutionists this comes as no surprise, neither does it to those who believe the meaning behind the **Genesis** account is true (not necessarily literal timings or order) and that when God spoke the language of Creation he spoke the language of life, or genetic code.

> **TALKING POINT**
>
> 'And the Lord God commanded the man, saying, "You may freely eat of every tree of the garden; but of the tree of the knowledge of good and evil you shall not eat, for in the day that you eat of it you shall die".'
>
> Genesis 2: 16, 17

A Muslim view

Genetic engineering has attracted lengthy discussions amongst Islamic scholars because of a phrase in the Qur'an about 'changing God's creation'. According to the Qur'an, after Satan tempted Adam and Eve to sin by eating from the forbidden tree, he was dismayed to see them repenting and being forgiven. Satan asked the Lord to give him another chance to prove that humans are not that trustworthy after all.

If allowed to test them on earth, Satan disclosed some of his plots:

> 'Verily of Thy servants I shall most certainly take my due share, and shall lead them astray and fill them with vain desires. And I shall command them so that they cut off the ears of cattle (in idolatrous sacrifice), and I shall command them and they will **change God's creation**.'
>
> Qur'an, Surah 4: 119

This verse cannot be interpreted as a total ban on genetic engineering because many forms of curative medicine involve some *changes in God's creation*. Applications, such as the diagnosis, cure or prevention of genetic disease, are beneficial and can open up tremendous possibilities in the treatment of many illnesses.

But the development of genetic engineering raises serious concerns if it is used to create new deadly bacteria for use in biological warfare (see Unit 66) or to clone humans (see Unit 23). Such applications are clearly wrong.

Protection or prediction?

In 1997, The United Nations made a **Declaration on Human Dignity and the Genome**, including the following six Articles:

- The human genome underlies the fundamental unity of all members of the human family. In a symbolic sense, it is the heritage of humanity.

- Everyone has a right to respect for their dignity and for their rights regardless of their genetic characteristics. That dignity makes it imperative not to reduce individuals to their genetic characteristics and to respect their uniqueness and diversity.

- The human genome, which by its nature evolves, is subject to mutations.

- The human genome in its natural state shall not give rise to financial gains.

- No research concerning the human genome should prevail over respect for the human rights, fundamental freedoms and human dignity of individuals or, where applicable, of groups of people.

- Practices contrary to human dignity, such as reproductive cloning of human beings, shall not be permitted.

The Declaration not only sets out an ethical guideline for today, but also for the future. Many issues the Articles cover are a sort of prediction about how genetic engineering appears set to affect our society.

Launching your learning

Write an article for a teenage magazine using the following words and phrases:
Genetics, genetic elect, eugenics, genetic code, gene therapies, 'The Human Genome Project', change God's creation, geneticism, mutant, nanotechnology, artifical intelligence, assembly guide, genetic supermarkets, patents, transgenic, insulin, oncomouse, inherited diseases, Declaration on Human Dignity and the Genome.

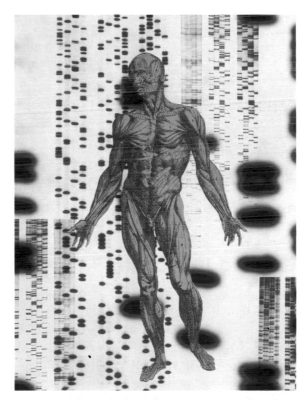

▲ The human genetic code

23 Life and death issues:
HUMAN CLONING

Introduction

In recent years scientists have developed a way of 'cloning' plants and animals. They usually do this by taking the DNA from one animal or plant and transferring it to another of the same kind. Soon it might be possible to do this with human beings to make a new person! Is this a wonderful breakthrough in scientific knowledge – or is it a case of science gone mad?

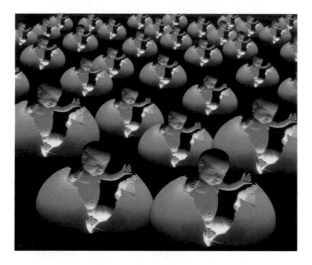

▲ Science: breaking through or cracking up?

Cloning in action

Cloning was first brought to media attention in 1997, when scientists in Scotland announced that a sheep called 'Dolly' had been cloned using DNA from another sheep. Dolly was 'made' from the cells from two different sheep. No ram had anything to do with it. Some newspapers commented that if the technique were perfected in humans the time would come when there would be no need for men to keep the human race going!

Cloning a sheep was a significant step, but soon things became more controversial. In December 1998 a report by scientists in Britain said that it was acceptable to clone human material for medical purposes – but that producing a fully-formed human clone should not be allowed. Cloning as a means of obtaining replacement tissues and organs was permitted. Cloned tissue could be used for transplants, benefiting the patient and cutting down on animal experiments.

Controversy erupted too in the USA, in 2001, when a couple paid $300,000 to a religious group, called the *Raelians*, to clone their dead daughter. Her parents had cells from her body removed and stored in the hope of producing an identical twin of her in the future.

Brave new world?

With developments in science taking place almost daily, the possibilities for cloning are becoming enormous. Such possibilities could:

- benefit infertile couples
- produce greater understanding of the causes of miscarriages
- offer ways of curing diseases
- help with treatments for brain damage
- improve scientific understanding about how organisms develop over time
- provide children who need organ transplants to have a clone born to donate organs and so reduce the chances of organ rejection

help lesbian or gay couples who want children – DNA from a woman's ovum could be removed and replaced with the DNA from a male. The ovum could then be fertilized with the sperm of the first male's partner. The fertilized 'male egg' could then be implanted into the womb of a surrogate mother. This could produce a child whose DNA came from both of its fathers.

So why do some people object to cloning?

- **Playing God** – Religions teach that humans have souls and all individuals are valued for their unique worth. Cloning is 'playing at God' and will ultimately destroy the natural order forever. Roman Catholics for example believe that the soul enters the body at the instant of conception and the fertilized ovum is in fact a human being: dividing that 'baby' in half would interfere with nature. They also argue that the cloned 'materials' destroyed in the process would be lost human beings. The world religions believe that human cloning is morally wrong and would like to see an international treaty to ban it worldwide.

- **Health risks** – Cloning techniques are still very risky. Many attempts at animal cloning have produced animals with severe abnormalities. There is no guarantee that the first cloned humans will be normal.

- **Emotional risks** – Cloning may lead to devastating psychological problems and emotional difficulties; for example, a child born from adult DNA cloned from her father or mother would in effect be a delayed twin of one of her parents. Emotional problems may also arise later if a child were to find out that he or she was cloned.

- **Abuse** – A dictator could finance a programme to breed humans with certain characteristics. Once the 'perfect human' was developed, cloning could produce unlimited numbers of clones.

The same approach could be used to create a 'genetic underclass' for exploitation: for example, individuals with sub-normal intelligence and above normal strength. Those of you who have studied Hitler's terrible racial beliefs might wonder what he would have done if cloning had been available in the 1930s.

- **Depletion of genetic diversity** – Humankind exists and evolves because of diversity. Small communities where inter-breeding takes place soon suffer major problems. Large scale cloning could deplete the human gene pool. If everyone has the same genetic material, what could happen if we lose the ability to clone? We would have to resort to natural reproduction, causing us to in-breed, which will cause many problems. Also, if we all had the same genetic make-up then it would be easier for a killer disease to wipe out the entire population.

Launching your learning

Write an article for a magazine on *either*:

A the benefits of cloning

B the dangers of cloning.

Give reasons to support your arguments.

FOR DISCUSSION

1 Should cloning be used to change what children might look like – or even behave like?

2 'Just because some people might misuse the results of scientific advances (for example, by making atomic bombs) we should not stop those advances happening.' Discuss with reference to cloning.

24 Life and death issues:
TRANSPLANT SURGERY 1

Introduction

The world's first successful kidney transplant took place in 1954, as a live donation from an identical twin. Liver transplants began in the early 1960s and in 1967 a South African surgeon, Christiaan Barnard (1922–2001), made a huge medical advance by performing the first successful heart transplantation.

In the 1980s, with progress in understanding of the immune system and the availability of new drugs to prevent rejection, organ transplants have become a *potentially* routine form of therapy in modern medicine; 'potentially' routine because transplant surgery is severely limited by shortages of organs.

Transplant surgery saves lives and improves the quality of life insofar as it spares many from a life linked to a dialysis machine or scarcely able to move from bed. The technique of transplanting human organs allows over 3,000 people in the UK every year to take on a new lease of life – a full and healthy lifestyle replacing a terminal illness. These organs come from around 900 donors each year, whose families have agreed that the donors' deaths should be turned into something positive.

The law

The Human Organ Transplants Act of 1989 made it illegal for any commercial transactions to take place in respect of transplantation and for anyone to advertise to supply human organs for payment. In 1990, it became illegal to remove a human organ from a living person intended to be transplanted into another person. It is also illegal to transplant an organ removed from a living person, unless the persons giving and receiving the organ are genetically related.

Life giving

In principle, there is much that is right about transplant surgery. It is life giving. Jews, Christians, Muslims, Hindus, Buddhists, Sikhs and humanists have no objections to them provided they are not bought and sold. So what are the moral issues surrounding transplant surgery?

Resources

Ideally everyone should have the operation they need. However, resources are limited and demand can outstrip available funds. Transplants are expensive. They involve long operations and many staff. Drugs have to be provided on a life-long basis to prevent the patient's body rejecting a donated organ. The money used for transplants could provide many smaller operations that would improve many other lives.

CITIZENSHIP CHALLENGE

1   A four-year-old girl has a life-threatening kidney illness and has only a limited chance of survival if she has a kidney transplant. An organ becomes available. The transplant can go ahead. However, this will be the little girl's second operation. The first one was unsuccessful because the organ was rejected. The operations cost as much to perform as 100 routine operations for children – all of which have an almost 100 per cent chance of success.

The girl's second operation has little chance of success because the child is very sick indeed. There comes a time when doctors have to write off a patient's chance of survival when they just cannot be healed. Usually this is in old age, but there are times when it has to be done with a child. Should doctors write off the child in this case? Are they right to perform the transplant or should the money be allocated to other procedures to help people with less life-threatening illnesses?

2 You are a surgeon with the money for one transplant operation, but there are four patients who would benefit from the donor organ. They are: a brilliant scientist working on a cure for cancer; a fifteen-year-old girl; a father of two small children; and a single mother with one child. To whom would you give the operation? How do you decide which person benefits the most? Give reasons for your choice.

Who should have the right to take organs for transplant?

There is a shortage of donor organs. The eyes, heart, liver, kidneys, pancreas, lungs, and so on, of people killed in accidents can be used to give life or provide a better quality of life for others. However, many people do not carry **donor cards** which would allow doctors to cut out the organ they need. They will contact the bereaved families who may give permission, but this takes time. But have people the right to refuse their organs to those who desperately need them?

Should we then refuse to give our organs? This raises an important question: 'Who owns my body?'

When someone dies they obviously cannot own their body. So who does? Is it the State or the family? In Britain it is the family. However bearing in mind the acute need for organs, should not the State be allowed to take organs as it needs them? There might be abuses, particularly if big businesses became involved. Some people, especially those in prisons, psychiatric hospitals, or the elderly or the poor, might be given less care so that organs become available to other people of more privileged classes.

Jews, Christians, Muslims, Hindus, Buddhists, Sikhs and humanists are aware of the human capacity for corruption and believe that laws are necessary to protect the powerless and prevent the greedy from exploiting other people's despair.

FOR DISCUSSION

A Would you be prepared to donate your organs for transplantation?

B Is an alcoholic patient a suitable candidate for a liver transplant?

C Is it worth giving a transplant to a person who will be bedridden for the rest of their life?

D Should an organ go to the sickest patient on the waiting list, or to a more robust patient who may live longer?

E Is it right to take a kidney from a living donor? If so, should living donors be compensated for the lost organ? Is it right to expose a healthy donor to any risk for a procedure that will not benefit him/her and could cause harm?

25 Life and death issues:
TRANSPLANT SURGERY 2

Autopsies

A scandal erupted in 1999 following revelations that children's hospitals in Britain had been 'harvesting' – storing – hearts, lungs, brains and other organs from dead babies without their parents' informed consent.

Postmortem examinations, called autopsies, are performed when there is doubt about the cause of death – especially important when young children have died. Organs and other tissues are removed and examined during autopsies. Doctors often feel that telling parents exactly what happens during and after an autopsy is too distressing.

Tissues

Parents had not realized that by signing a consent form for an autopsy – stating 'tissues may be retained for research' – they were allowing hospitals to remove or dispose of all their child's organs. They were misinformed as to the full meaning of the word 'tissues'.

The 'new cannibalism'

As the story broke it became clear that the organs of 170 children who died at Bristol Royal Infirmary had been kept without parental consent. 2,080 organs had been removed from 800 children at Alder Hey Hospital in Liverpool. Other hospitals had removed glands during heart surgery from live children, and 'given' them to a pharmaceutical company for research in return for financial donations. Alder Hey also stored, without consent, 1,500 foetuses that were miscarried, stillborn or aborted.

Organ harvesting

But 'organ harvesting' has been happening for decades and these organs actually saved countless lives during this time.

What has changed?

The public outcry about what had happened at these hospitals led to changes in practice. Hospitals in England must now give out information on whether hearts, lungs and other organs are removed from dead children or other relatives without their consent. Bereaved parents will be told if their dead children are stripped of vital organs. Hospitals will be required to tell parents exactly what autopsies involve and get their permission if there is any need to remove organs. The Human Tissue Act 1961, which regulates the keeping of organs, will be changed to make it illegal for staff to ignore informed consent. A new consent form will be introduced throughout the National Health Service, and a code of practice will be issued on the use of organs by pharmaceutical companies.

Do doctors always know best?

This scandal shook many people's faith in hospitals. An important organization concerned with medicine and morals, The British Medical Association (BMA) is now prepared to accept the 'doctor knows best' attitude is no longer acceptable and relatives should be fully briefed about informed consent.

'Spare parts'

In some parts of the world people are driven by poverty to sell their organs to wealthy patients from Europe or America. There have been reports that in China long-term prisoners have been 'killed to order' and their organs used for transplant surgery.

Human Rights organizations are concerned that the list of crimes punishable by death have been increased in China to accommodate the demand for organs. In India an underground market exists controlled by cash-rich crime gangs. Indians from the slums offer their kidneys for sale to rich foreigners. In Brazil 'organ trafficking' has become common.

Sex organs

Some commentators believe that technology, one day, might be capable of transplanting sex organs. This possibility raises many moral issues. Does the transplanted organ become 'your' own organ? This would be the case with a transplanted liver for instance, but would it be the case with the genetic material in the donated organ? The genetic material, except in the case of identical twins, is not the same genetic material as that possessed by the person who receives the transplanted organ. When a man fathers a child he is sharing with it some of his genes. However with transplanted testicles, it will always be another's person genetic material that he is giving. The child would never be his biologically as it would be if it were fathered by his own sperm.

Xenotransplantation – a definition

Xenotransplantation is the means by which animal organs are transplanted into humans.

Pig organs

The organs of some species, particularly pigs, and possibly apes, can be transplanted into humans. As there is a shortage of organs, xenotransplantation could save many lives and help solve the worldwide shortage of donor organs. However, Jews and Muslims regard pigs as unclean and xenotransplantation is forbidden by them. Vegetarians and vegans would also object to this technique if the animal organ was obtained cruelly. (See Unit 79.)

▲ Could these cloned pigs help solve the shortage of human donors?

Xenotransplantation – difficulties

Research published in 2001 suggests that the use of animals for transplantation has not lived up to its early promise. Animal to human transplants are dangerous because humans could become infected with animal viruses. Transplant patients who receive pigs' hearts and lungs risk passing an unknown number of animal viruses to the general population.

Many animal viruses have the ability to jump species barriers and kill humans. There are more than 25 diseases in pigs that can infect humans. The BSE crisis has illustrated the massive dangers to public health of misusing animals. Some scientists now argue that **stem cell technology** (see Unit 15) may provide alternatives to the shortage of organs.

Launching your learning

Find out the meaning of the following words and phrases:
Harvesting, informed consent, autopsies, consent form, tissues, parental consent, The British Medical Association, xenotransplantation, living donors.

26 Life and death issues:
EUTHANASIA 1

Introduction

In 1989, a disaster at Hillsborough football stadium in Sheffield claimed the lives of many fans. As a result of this tragedy, a teenager, Anthony Bland, lay in hospital in a coma – in a **persistent vegetative state**. He might have lived that way for 50 years, but he would never have recovered consciousness. In 1993, his family and doctors obtained permission from the courts to end his life by withdrawing the tubes through which he obtained food and water. In deciding Anthony's fate, the courts stated that in their view Anthony's life was not worth living. These developments indicate that a major transformation of Western medical ethics is in progress. A major factor in this change is our growing technical capacity to keep human beings alive. No previous generation had to consider the question of whether we should keep human beings alive when their brains had irreversibly ceased to function.

Sufferers sometimes wish to commit suicide but do not have the physical strength or the means to do it painlessly. A century ago most people died quite quickly, and probably painfully, if they had serious injuries or illnesses. Nowadays, they can be treated, sometimes cured, and often kept alive for many years.

Euthanasia – a definition

Euthanasia originally meant 'a gentle and easy death'. The word 'euthanasia' is now used to mean 'the act of *bringing about* an easy death'. Euthanasia is arranging for a person who is dying from an incurable disease to die as quickly and as painlessly as possible. It is sometimes called **mercy killing**.

Euthanasia is illegal in the UK. In the Netherlands in 2001, the Dutch government made it legal for doctors to help terminally ill patients to die as long as they follow strict rules. Belgium has also recently passed legislation legalizing certain forms of strictly controlled euthanasia.

Voluntary euthanasia

Voluntary euthanasia is sometimes called 'assisted suicide'. It is used in cases where the sufferer has made it clear that s/he wishes to die and has asked that this be brought about. Those who want to see voluntary euthanasia made legal accept that there must be safeguards, for example the prevention of pressure on patients; clear witnessed instructions from the patient who must have full information and sound judgement; the involvement of several doctors and no reasonable hope of recovery.

The **Voluntary Euthanasia Society** known as 'EXIT' (see Addresses/websites) campaigns for a person's right to seek an 'easy' death:

> 'An adult person suffering from a severe illness, for which no relief is known, should be entitled by law to the mercy of a painless death, if and only if that is their express wish … Doctors should be allowed to help incurable patients to die peacefully at their own request.'

Involuntary euthanasia

Involuntary euthanasia occurs when a patient does not give their **consent** – permission – to die. It is important to distinguish between cases where patients *cannot* express a wish to die (for example, patients in comas, infants, or cases of extreme senile dementia), called **non-voluntary** euthanasia, and those cases where they *can* express a wish to die but *do not*, called **involuntary** euthanasia.

Active euthanasia

Voluntary or **active euthanasia**, also called **direct euthanasia**, is when the person concerned asks someone else to help them die. They may persuade another person to help them die or they may refuse to have the medical treatment necessary to be kept alive.

Passive euthanasia

Passive euthanasia is the practice, widely carried out and generally judged to be legal, where patients are allowed to die by withdrawing treatment and/or nourishment. Passive euthanasia is when the person concerned is no longer in a condition where they can make a decision, for example being in a persistent vegetative state (PVS). The decision to bring about the death of the person is taken by relatives and/or doctors.

Indirect euthanasia

Indirect euthanasia – sometimes referred to as the **double effect** – is the practice of providing treatment, normally pain relief, which has the side effect of quickening death. This is also widely practised and generally considered legal if killing was not the intention.

What is 'death'?

This might seem like a strange question. However, huge advances in medical technology have complicated the issue. For centuries, if the pulse or breathing stopped working a person was regarded as being 'dead'. However, as new technologies, like the respirator and the heart-lung machine, allowed doctors to keep the heart and lungs functioning, the clear signs of death became more blurred. Death was defined in a new way so that the gravely ill would have the right to be kept alive by technology, while those who had technically died would not be kept alive on life-support machines.

The modern view is that 'the irreversible loss of brain activity is the sign that death has occurred' – **brain death**.

Even the 'brain death' definition has been challenged in recent years. While a person may be incapable of higher mental functioning, such as talking, lower-brain functions, such as breathing, can still continue. For this reason, some authorities now argue that death should be considered as 'the loss of consciousness or the ability to communicate'.

Living wills

Many people want to see an individual's 'right to die' established particularly through the legal means of '**living wills**' in which an individual gives family members or legal figures the right to withdraw life-sustaining treatment.

Launching your learning

A Explain briefly in your own words the different types of euthanasia.

B Write down your views on the following questions and then discuss them with your class:

1 If voluntary euthanasia was made legal would this give doctors too much power and responsibility?

2 Could it possibly lead to involuntary euthanasia for the old or handicapped?

3 Do you think life is always precious no matter what sort of life it is, that is the sanctity of life against the quality of life?

4 Can we always tell when a case is without hope especially as new cures are being discovered all the time?

5 What is death?

6 Is euthanasia necessarily helping people to 'die with dignity'?

7 Does someone in continuous terrible pain have a **right to choose** to end their own life, or is life God's alone to give and to take away?

27 Life and death issues:
EUTHANASIA 2

The case for voluntary euthanasia

- It is wrong to keep a human being alive against his will when all the dignity, beauty and meaning of life have vanished.

- If our pets are dying in agony we have them put down. Why should humans have to die long, undignified and painful deaths?

- Voluntary euthanasia can put an end to a patient's suffering quickly and humanely.

- Voluntary euthanasia can help to shorten the grief and suffering of the patient's loved ones.

- Everyone has the **right to choose** how and when they die.

- If the law in Britain was changed doctors could let patients who want to die, die without breaking the law.

- If voluntary euthanasia was legal people could face death, knowing they could die with dignity.

- Religious people often use phrases like the 'sanctity of life' to justify the view that life is valuable and must not be destroyed. However if an individual has decided on rational grounds that his life has lost its meaning and value, have they not **the right to die**?

The case against voluntary euthanasia

- There are many pain-killing drugs, which can help the patient die naturally with dignity.

- A patient might not be able to make a rational decision or might change their mind but be incapable of telling the doctors.

- Some people recover after being 'written off' by doctors.

- Old people might feel they are a nuisance to others and opt for euthanasia when in their hearts they want to continue living.

- The *slippery slope* argument or *thin end of the wedge* argument says that if you allow voluntary euthanasia, involuntary euthanasia will follow. Hitler's programme of euthanasia is often given as an example when he put to death disabled people.

- The relationship of trust between doctors and patients could be destroyed.

- Under the Hippocratic Oath doctors must try to preserve life.

- If there were better facilities for caring for the dying there would be less need for euthanasia.

- It is not for doctors to play God. Life is a gift from God and only God can take it away.

Humanist view

Humanists argue that the quality of life and respect for personal freedom leads to the view that in many circumstances voluntary euthanasia is morally acceptable. People should have **the right to choose** a painless and dignified end, either at the time or beforehand, perhaps in a 'living will'. The right circumstances might include: extreme pain and suffering; helplessness and loss of personal dignity; permanent loss of those things which have made life worth living for this individual.

Christian view

The Bible teaches that all life is sacred and comes from God. The sixth Commandment is:

> 'You shall not murder.'
>
> Exodus 20: 13

In the New Testament it says:

> 'Your body is a temple of the Holy Spirit.'
>
> 1 Corinthians 6: 19

It is clear from the Bible that human beings cannot choose when they die:

> 'For everything there is a season, and a time for every matter under heaven: a time to be born, and a time to die; a time to plant, and a time to pluck up what is planted.'
>
> Ecclesiastes 3: 1–4

The **Roman Catholic Church** teaches that euthanasia is 'a grave violation of the law of God'. However, if large doses of painkillers are used to help ease a person's suffering, and as a result of these the person ultimately dies, this is understood as the **double effect** and is permitted. The **Church of England** holds that although the deliberate taking of a human life is forbidden, there are strong arguments for people not to be kept alive at all costs when they are suffering intolerable pain.

Muslim view

Islam is opposed to euthanasia. The Qur'an says that Allah created all life. Life is sacred and everything belongs to Allah:

> 'To Allah belongs the kingdom of the heavens and the earth. He creates what He pleases.'
>
> Qur'an, Surah 42: 49

In the Qu'ran it is also written:

> 'Do not take life which God has made sacred except in the course of Justice.'
>
> Qur'an, Surah 6: 151

While Muslim doctors are not encouraged to artificially prolong the misery of somebody in a vegetative state, they are ordained to help those suffering. The Qur'an says:

> 'Anyone who has saved a life, it is as if he has saved the life of all mankind.'
>
> Qur'an, Surah 5: 32

It is clear from the Qur'an that human beings cannot choose when they die:

> 'When their time … arrives they cannot tarry for a single hour nor can they go ahead.'
>
> Qur'an, Surah 16: 61

The hospice movement

A **hospice** is a place where people who have a terminal (fatal) illness are treated until they die. Dame Cicely Saunders founded the first modern hospice in London in 1967. It was founded on the principles of caring for the sick, researching pain control, searching for cures for the diseases and teaching nurses and doctors how to cope with terminal disease. The hospice movement aims to give people with painful and terminal diseases the best possible quality of life. The staff help patients prepare for their deaths and also help the relatives prepare for the loss of their loved ones. Hospices are concerned not only with the physical health of their patients but also with their emotional, psychological and spiritual health.

CITIZENSHIP CHALLENGE

Look carefully at the arguments both for and against voluntary euthanasia. Organize a class debate on the following motion: 'This House believes that Everyone has the **right to choose** how and when they die.'

28 Life and death issues: *SUICIDE*

The UK has one of the highest rates of suicide in Europe. At least 160,000 people attempt suicide each year in England and Wales alone. The most commonly used method is self poisoning. *Attempted suicide* and *parasuicide* describe non-fatal acts of self-harm. Deliberate self-harm is most common among young women aged fifteen to nineteen.

But why do individuals feel that life is so bad that they need to end it? Suicide is devastating for 'those left behind', for family and friends.

People kill themselves for a variety of reasons: maybe they are suffering from an incurable illness; or they have lost a loved one; maybe they are lonely or have lost faith in the future; or have money worries, drink and drug problems or pressures at work and at school; or they may have suffered bullying or depression brought on by relationship difficulties. Many suicides are caused by treatable depression and could be avoided with counselling or medical or psychiatric care.

The law

In 1961, **The Suicide Act** was passed. Before this, attempted suicide could be punished, although it rarely was.

Assisting a suicide is still illegal and remains a criminal act, punishable by up to fourteen years imprisonment.

Youth suicides

Suicide accounts for over a fifth of all deaths of young people in Britain. 80 per cent of suicides are by young men. Every day, an estimated two young people under the age of 25 commit suicide in Britain. Alcohol and substance misuse are significant factors in youth suicide. Other factors include the prospect of no work or mindless employment; physical or sexual abuse; arguments with parents, peers or partners.

High risk

High stress, together with easy access to the means of killing oneself, contribute to the fact that some jobs put people at greater risk of dying by suicide. These include: the medical professions; female nurses and nurse administrators; male dentists and vets; farmers, horticultural workers and farm managers.

Responsibility

Religions have sometimes taught that if people commit suicide they will not have eternal life. In the past, societies based heavily upon such religious ideas, condemned those who took their own life. It was held to be a sin against God in renouncing His greatest gift to them.

Today, however, society is coming to terms more with its own **responsibility** for the conditions leading a person to such a low point in their life that they wish to end it.

Help!

Many attempted suicides are not intended to succeed – they are cries for help and it would be right to try to discourage these and offer the necessary help. Sadly, some cries for help go unheard or the attempts succeed better than was intended.

Few people need be as isolated and alone as they may feel – there will be others in the same situation and there are organizations that can offer help. It is right to do your best to dissuade a suicide – talk, friendship, practical advice and listening may all help.

The Samaritans

In 1953 Chad Varah, a Church of England priest, was appalled to discover that three suicides were taking place every day in London.

He installed a telephone in his church and publicized the fact that anyone thinking of committing suicide could telephone him and talk to him. This was the start of the Samaritans. The Samaritans is a registered charity based in the UK and Republic of Ireland that provides confidential emotional support to any person who is suicidal or despairing. It increases public awareness of issues around suicide and depression.

There are 18,700 Samaritans and over 500 telephone helplines open or available 24 hours a day, seven days a week, throughout the year. There are 203 Samaritans centres within the UK and Republic of Ireland. The Samaritans are busiest between 10pm at night and 2am in the morning. You can email the Samaritans in confidence at **jo@samaritans.org** (see Addresses/websites).

> **If you need to speak to a**
> **Samaritan call: 08457 90 90 90**

The way of the Samurai

In some cultures, people thought that in certain circumstances it was perfectly honourable to take one's own life. The way of the Samurai held that when defeated, suicide was a more honourable alternative to 'enslaving' oneself to the enemy. During World War II, 'kamikaze' pilots from Japan deliberately crash-dived their planes into enemy ships.

Suicide bombers

A martyr is someone prepared to give up their life for something they believe in. They sacrifice their life to their cause and become 'freedom fighters', arguing that the 'freedom' they are fighting for is an ultimate justification of taking the 'enemies' lives by acts like suicide-bombing. On 11 September 2001, the world watched in horror as suicide bombers used hijacked aircraft to kill nearly 3000 people in New York. (See Unit 70.)

FOR DISCUSSION

1 Suicide has been called 'a selfish act'.

2 'People who feel their quality of life has reached rock bottom have the right to end their own life.'

3 Is life such a precious gift that nobody should be allowed to take it away?

4 Have doctors a right to revive or force-feed would-be suicides?

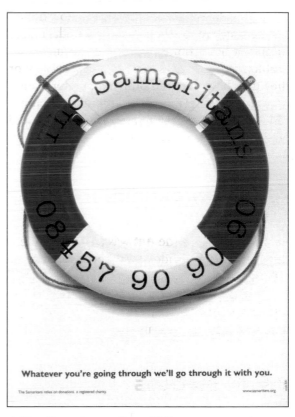

Whatever you're going through we'll go through it with you.

The Samaritans relies on donations. A registered charity.   www.samaritans.org

▲ The Samaritans offer a lifeline to anyone in despair. You can phone them in strictest confidence, day or night, 365 days a year.

29 Life and death issues:
HIV AND AIDS

HIV – a definition

HIV stands for Human Immuno-deficiency Virus. Several distinct varieties of the virus have been found in humans. HIV attacks the immune system which protects the body from disease. HIV does not just affect particular groups of people. It can affect anyone, woman or man, straight or gay, black or white, young or old. It is found virtually everywhere in the world.

People who have come into contact with HIV may be shown to have formed antibodies to the virus – this is known as being 'HIV positive'. People who are HIV positive may live healthy lives for many years without developing serious symptoms; different people respond in different ways, as with many viral infections.

AIDS – a definition

AIDS stands for Acquired Immune Deficiency Syndrome. Death from AIDS is actually death from a range of infections or cancers, when HIV has seriously affected the immune system.

The toll – so far ...

Every minute, worldwide, six young people under the age of 24 become infected with HIV.

The United Nations estimates that 36.2 million people worldwide were living with AIDS in 2001. 21 million people worldwide have already died from AIDS and 15 million children have been orphaned.

In Britain, by March 2001, there had been 44,988 reported cases of HIV of which 14,038 people had died of AIDS.

Ten myths exploded

1 *'AIDS can be transmitted by oral sex.'*
Although it is possible to become infected with HIV through oral sex, the risk of becoming infected in this way is much lower than the risk of infection by having unprotected sexual intercourse with a man or woman. When giving oral sex to a man a person could become infected with HIV if infected semen got into any cuts, sores or receding gums a person might have in their mouth. Giving oral sex to a woman is also considered relatively low risk. Transmission could take place if infected sexual fluids from a woman got into the mouth of her partner. The likelihood of infection occurring might be increased if there is menstrual blood involved or the woman is infected with another sexually transmitted disease.

2 *'AIDS can be transmitted by kissing.'*
Deep or open-mouthed kissing is a very low risk activity in terms of HIV transmission. HIV is only present in saliva in very tiny amounts, insufficient to cause infection with HIV alone. There has been only one documented case of someone becoming infected with HIV through kissing, a result of exposure to infected blood during open-mouthed kissing.

3 *'HIV can be transmitted through normal social contact/activities, such as shaking hands/toilet seats/swimming pools/sharing cutlery/sneezes and coughs.'*
HIV is not an airborne, water borne or food borne virus and the virus does not survive for very long outside the human body. Therefore ordinary social contact, such as shaking hands, coughing and sharing cutlery, does not result in the virus being passed from one person to another.

4 *'AIDS is a gay disease.'*
There are more straight/heterosexual people with HIV in the world today than there are gay/homosexual people with HIV.

5 *'AIDS is God's judgement on sinners.'*
HIV affects people from all religions, non-religious people, and people from all walks of life. Immuno-deficiency viruses can affect other animals, which are outside most religions' concept of sin. The major religions profess to care for others unselfishly, but sweeping judgements using God to justify prejudice does no credit to any religion.

6 *'Promiscuous people get HIV.'*
Promiscuous people increase their chance of exposure to the HIV virus, especially if they do not practice **safe sex**. *However, it is possible to have sex with only one person and still come into contact with HIV.* The most important thing is for people having any sort of sex to be aware of what safe sex means and to have the confidence to refuse to take part in unsafe activity.

7 *'You can get HIV through blood transfusions.'*
In the 1980s, before scientists had identified the virus and its means of transmission, some haemophiliacs and other patients received blood contaminated with HIV. Now, blood products are carefully screened for HIV, hepatitis and other infections.

8 *'Everyone should be tested for HIV.'*
Widespread anonymous testing programmes have been carried out, usually on people who are in hospital for other things or having a blood test for other reasons, but these do not identify the individual tested and there is no follow-up if a sample is found to be HIV positive. Enforced testing has been used in several countries and it has sometimes been used to take away the rights of people found to be HIV positive. Knowing who some of the people with HIV are does not in itself stop the spread of the virus. Have people who have engaged in unsafe sex a moral responsibility to get tested?

9 *'People with AIDS should be isolated.'*
People with HIV or who have developed AIDS have the same rights as everyone else. As well as denying people's rights, isolating groups of people simply drives others underground – making it even more difficult to tackle the transmission of HIV or to provide proper medical care for people who are ill.

10 *'Drug-users have all got HIV.'*
HIV can be transmitted in blood by needles used for injecting drugs and this is why needles must never be shared. If people who use syringes do not share needles they will not come into contact with other people's blood.

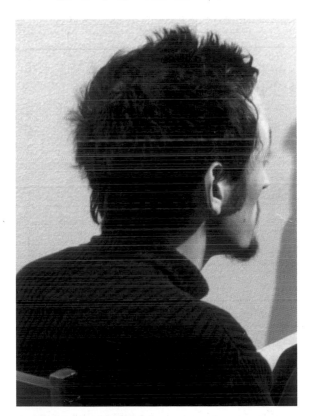

▲ AIDS is not prejudiced

CITIZENSHIP CHALLENGE

Look at the caption to the photograph. Design your own caption.

30 Life and death issues:
DRUGS 1

CITIZENSHIP CHALLENGE

Read and discuss the following passage.

Why do young people take drugs?

When we are young we are keen for adventure: we want to experience everything for ourselves. We do not want to hear of, or be guided by, other people's experience and advice. Of course, our parents are too old to understand, if they ever did. We are attracted to those of our peers who have been on the street, who know 'where it's at', and will follow them, even if our parents and teachers, and the news media, tell us we are being reckless and risk killing ourselves. We like risk and we like being 'bad' – it gives us self-esteem, it makes us feel good about ourselves.

It was always like this: this is the way every generation feels. But deep down we know that our parents' anxiety is not entirely stupid. If I drive my motorbike home without a helmet after drinking all night at the pub, I am almost certainly going to kill myself and that is not cool, it is just stupid. The fact is that without proper guidance we may damage ourselves, sometimes for life. So who do we listen to – the street gossip or our elders?

Risks

These days we may just want to have fun, and we do not want to think 30 or 40 years ahead.

We do not want to think about whether our liver, or our lungs, or our brain will be damaged.

Maybe we will not be able to work because of depression or chronic fatigue, or we will have become addicted to cigarettes or antidepressants. But who cares? It is not going to happen to me, and anyway I would rather take the risk and live a bit while I am young.

But what are the risks? We all know that some things are more risky than others: greasy burgers, though unhealthy, are less so than heroin.

What we need to do is get the right information about the risks we might be taking and think about providing a happy and productive future for ourselves.

Legal drugs

We can draw a distinction between illegal substances and those which are permitted in our society. Doctors prescribe drugs to their patients to alleviate medical conditions. These prescription medications are necessary for a person's treatment or recovery from an illness or condition.

Drugs such as alcohol, tobacco and caffeine, are legal in our society, but are also often abused. Over-drinking causes liver damage and can lead to addiction. The social problems caused by alcohol cause huge numbers of deaths a year: on the roads, in nightclubs, and in alcohol-fuelled domestic disputes. Smoking cigarettes can lead to a whole variety of life-threatening diseases.

Recreational drugs

The term 'recreational' is often confused. In describing the nature of a substance, a 'recreational drug' is simply one that is used by people for *purposes of pleasure or relaxation* of the body or mind, as a pastime, or for amusement. It does not necessarily mean that such substances are alright to use, nor does it make any claim on how harmful the drug is. Alcohol, tobacco and caffeine are recreational drugs because they are used for purposes of pleasure and relaxation. However, most other recreational drugs are not legal.

Cannabis

Cannabis is derived from *cannabis sativa*, a bushy plant found growing wild in most parts of the world and easily grown in Britain. Historically, it was used for its therapeutic properties.

Cannabis is not *physically addictive*, but if it is smoked all the time, the user can become **psychologically dependent** on the drug.

Almost everyone who takes cannabis has occasional unpleasant experiences from the drug. This is part of the process of learning how to use the drug, rather like getting drunk on alcohol and having a hangover the next day. However, an overdose of cannabis cannot kill you, whereas some teenagers die from alcoholic poisoning – a bottle of vodka can be a fatal dose.

The law on cannabis

Cannabis in its various forms is controlled under **The Misuse of Drugs Act 1971**. Herbal cannabis (everything except seeds and stalks) and cannabis resin are classified together as a **Class B** drug, though the law is currently changing, downgrading these forms of cannabis to **Class C**. Cannabis oil is classified as **Class A** and the penalties are higher. It is illegal to grow, produce, possess or supply the drug to another person, even if you are a doctor. It is also an offence to allow premises to be used for smoking or supplying cannabis.

Legalization of cannabis

Keeping drugs illegal might seem to be an effective way of stopping their use. However, millions of people use, or have used, cannabis in Britain. **The European Human Rights Act** may mean, in the near future, that possession of a small amount of cannabis could be **decriminalized**. Since the 1960s, many public figures have campaigned for the decriminalization of cannabis, claiming:

■ it is medically useful as an anti-depressant, as a natural sleeping aid, and as a painkiller, and is helpful to sufferers of painful illnesses such as multiple sclerosis

■ it is less harmful than legal drugs like alcohol and tobacco. Unlike alcohol use, cannabis users are not prone to violence

■ the current, illegal status of cannabis places the control of its commercial distribution in the hands of an underworld industry. Vast amounts of money spent on cannabis end up in the hands of international criminal organizations. Legalized cannabis could be taxed and the monies spent on health and education, and official standards would ensure cannabis was not adulterated with more harmful substances

■ 'bad' laws bring the law itself into disrepute, making it difficult for the police force to maintain good public relations.

Those who oppose legalization feel it would encourage more young people to take up smoking, which already takes enough lives. Some argue that cannabis can make people lazy, docile and lose their sense of ambition. Supporters of legalization claim that the development of these characteristics depends on the user, not cannabis.

Launching your learning

A Write down a list of legal drugs, recreational drugs and drugs that are both.

B Explain in your own words the arguments that have been put forward for the decriminalization of cannabis. What are your views?

31 Life and death issues:
DRUGS 2

Ecstasy in the UK

Ecstasy, or MDMA as it is properly known, is also classed as a recreational drug because of the way it is used. Its side effects have proven to be, in some cases, much more harmful than cannabis.

The drug is used recreationally as a stimulant of energy and **empathy** – emotional closeness with other people – to accompany long, energetic dancing sessions. Over the past fifteen years, the rise of the different forms of dance music has been reflected in the increase of ecstasy's popularity. In some dance cultures, the use of stimulants is regarded as a part of that culture.

Effects

The effects of ecstasy vary with the amount taken, the mood of the user, and the surroundings in which it is taken.

After a 'come up' lasting between 20 and 60 minutes, most users report a mild euphoric 'rush', followed by feelings of calmness, a general sense of enthusiasm, happiness and empathy.

▲ Ecstasy?

After the positive effects of the drug have worn off, users experience the 'comedown'; at its best, a feeling of tiredness and slight irritability, not dissimilar to a 'hangover'; at its worst, a stark and harsh 'return to reality', which may be made worse by lack of sleep, dehydration, over-drinking and the cocktail of unidentified substances often present in the dose. Heavy use of the drug can cause irregularities in eating and sleeping habits and can make reaction times slower.

Is it dangerous?

A recent survey of fourteen tablets and capsules sold as ecstasy from around the UK, found after laboratory analysis that none of them contained a psychoactive dose of MDMA! Two of the samples, large white 'doves', contained ketamine, an anaesthetic with hallucinogenic properties, which can produce horrific hallucinations, loss of feeling and movement in the limbs and sometimes even coma.

There have been over 80 reported deaths in the UK linked to the use of ecstasy by apparently healthy young people. The symptoms, generally the same in each case, include convulsions, dilated pupils, very low blood pressure, accelerated heart rate, high temperature and coma. Most of the deaths are due to respiratory collapse and haemorrhaging.

The relatively high number of deaths attributed to ecstasy use in the UK can be linked to its use in a 'rave' context. The symptoms are very like heatstroke. In a hot club environment the user may be dancing for hours and get over-heated and dehydrated, leading to a fatal seizure, while others have drunk as many as 26 pints of water, leading to kidney failure.

The advice given to users is to be aware of the dangers of dehydration, and not to drink more than one pint of water or non-alcoholic drink per hour in order to minimize the risk posed by water itself.

There is concern from doctors about the long term effects of ecstasy, possibly brain damage and liver damage. Ecstasy can also lower bodily immunity to a variety of colds and infections.

The law and ecstasy

Ecstasy is classified as a Class A drug under The Misuse of Drugs Act 1971, and it is illegal to possess, supply or manufacture the drug.

Hard drugs

The title of 'Class A' is reserved for those drugs considered to be the most harmful and imposes the highest penalties of the law. The maximum penalty for possession is seven years imprisonment and an unlimited fine. For dealing, the maximum penalty is life imprisonment and an unlimited fine. Sentencing varies according to the individual circumstances and possession of even quite small amounts can lead to charges of intent to supply.

There are some recreational drugs in this category, like ecstasy, although many people feel that despite the fatalities recorded with the use of ecstasy, the proportionally 'small' number of such cases makes the substance a *statistically* less harmful drug than cocaine, heroine and other physically addictive drugs.

Withdrawal symptoms

When a drug is 'physically addictive', it means that the user often suffers very unpleasant *withdrawal symptoms* when the body does not receive more of the drug.

These include: appetite loss, vomiting, nightmares and hallucinations, fatigue and physical pain, all of which can be alleviated in the short term by taking more of the drug.

Heroine and cocaine (particularly the purer and more dangerous 'crack' cocaine) are two such substances. The pleasurable experiences at first can turn into withdrawal symptoms felt after continued use and can make quitting the drug impossible for some addicts.

Heroine and cocaine, of course, could be described as *recreational* because of the feelings of relaxation and enjoyment they promote, but when using the drug becomes less of a leisure pursuit and develops more into a craving for relief, the user's *choice* becomes crushed. Addicts are often described as being 'slaves to the drug'.

Such drugs destroy lives through the user's loss of any sense of obligation other than to their habit, which if not escaped from, almost always causes their untimely death.

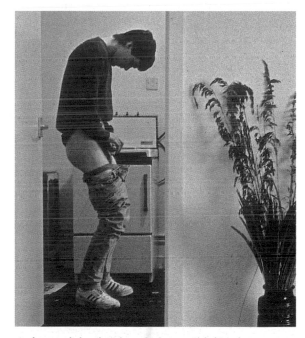

▲ A user injecting heroin into a thigh vein

Launching your learning

A Explain in your own words the dangers of taking ecstasy.

B Explain in your own words what 'hard drugs' and 'withdrawal symptoms' are.

32 Life and death issues:
DRUGS 3

DEATH

Amphetamine, or speed, kills eight times more young people per year in the UK than ecstasy in the same rave party context.

The leading cause of death among young people in the UK is car accidents involving the consumption of alcohol.

70 per cent of all drug-related deaths are due to smoking. 25 per cent are due to alcohol.

Three per cent are due to heroin and related compounds.

Religions

Drugs-related issues are important in religion and ethics because they concern the possible harming or ending of life, as well as raising issues around rights and responsibilities.

Christian views

'Your body is a temple of the Holy Spirit.'

1 Corinthians 6: 19

This is the key Christian teaching. The physical body is the natural home of the soul and is precious and sacred. Christians believe that drugs, especially hallucinogenic drugs, can alter the mind, making people incapable of praying, meditating or connecting with their spiritual lives. Wine is used as part of the communion ritual, but Christians condemn the overuse of alcohol if it impairs personal judgement or leads to an addiction that creates a priority greater than that of following God.

Smoking tobacco is not condemned by the churches although many Christians are concerned about the destructive effects it can have on people's health. The Roman Catholic Church teaches:

'The use of drugs inflicts very grave damage on human health and life. Their use, except on strictly therapeutic grounds, is a grave offence. Clandestine production of and trafficking in drugs are scandalous practices. They constitute direct co-operation in evil, since they encourage people to practices gravely contrary to the moral law.'

Muslim views

The Qur'an prohibits alcohol and gambling, which are linked to pagan rites:

'Wine and gambling, idols and divining arrows are only a filthy work of Satan; give them up so that you may prosper.'

Qur'an, Surah 5: 90

We might argue that a little wine can aid the digestion, that it helps people to relax and promotes friendship, and that alcohol can be used as a painkiller for such things as toothache, but the Qur'an reminds us that too much wine can also lead to violence, and so the bad outweighs the usefulness.

Islam is opposed to the use of any drugs except for those medically prescribed. Muslims consider that all recreational drugs cloud people's thoughts and actions and so they cannot serve Allah. Tobacco is not specifically mentioned in the Qur'an as being *haram* – unlawful or not permitted – but some Muslims say it is forbidden because it harms the body, while others simply say it is *makruh* – 'strongly disliked'. The Prophet Muhammad (pbuh) taught that all intoxicants are *haram*.

THE DRUGS INDUSTRY

HARD FACT

The income of the drugs barons is an annual $500,000 million greater than the American defence budget.

Drugs – The Phoney War Channel 4, 19 June 2001

Using drugs, illegal or legitimate, carries its own risks, and raises a variety of moral issues concerning a person's right over their own body, protection of the ill-informed or irresponsible, and the position of the law.

However, these should not be the only ethical considerations for the user, or indeed society as a whole, when looking at the bigger picture of the worldwide industry that has grown around drugs. The global drugs industry, legitimate and illegal, is responsible for many unfair, unethical and damaging practices.

Wrecking the joint!

On 2 December 1999, a military force made up of US Marines, and the US Drug Enforcement Agency launched a surprise attack on the tiny island of St Vincent in the Caribbean. Their aim was to destroy the marijuana crops that local peasant farmers were growing in a struggle against poverty on what is one of the poorest islands in the Caribbean.

For thirteen days, US Marine helicopters ferried heavily armed troops back and forth, scouring the island and burning the marijuana crops along with farmers' homes. At least one farmer was shot dead in the violence, and 250 families were left homeless that Christmas.

Every year, the US government deploys this task force to carry out the 'Marijuana Eradication Programme', publicly justifying itself by referring to the *violence and corruption* that the *evil drug* produces on American streets. The farmers of St Vincent, however, would argue that the US itself is the main cause of violence on their island!

Marijuana only takes between three and six months to grow back, so the annual 'eradication' is more of a cull to stem the outflow of US dollars than a fight against the 'immoral' nature of the drug. An unnamed US official quoted in the *Los Angeles Times* explained that, 'Operation Weedeater' is basically a training mission to help the US Marines brush up on their guerrilla warfare techniques.

Drug money

Poor tropical countries are often left with little choice but to produce illegal drugs for which there is a guaranteed market. The big money, however, is not in the production of the drug, but in the control of the drug's distribution. The same is true for the tobacco industry, with the distribution controlled primarily by tobacco companies – who reap the largest profits – then by governments through tax, leaving the smallest share to the poor farmers.

The drugs industry flourishes through a combination of greed, vested political interests and criminal operations; but most of all, by modern society's demand for drugs as a highly desirable form of recreation.

The black market

Throughout history, 'bootleggers', or smugglers attracted to 'easy money', have risked heavy jail sentences in attempting to secretly import large quantities of cigarettes and alcohol into Britain, evading heavy 'import duties' so that they might be sold for the profit of the smugglers. Such practice is damaging to a country's economy. The economic problem is that we will normally always buy something at the lowest possible cost. The ethical problem is that we often do this regardless of the reasons why something may be cheaper. Some members of society are prepared to pay a little more for their coffee if organizations, such as *CafeDirect*, guarantee that the plantation workers receive a fair price for their crop. Are people prepared to pay more for cigarettes and alcohol if it prevents damage to their own country's economy by way of money slipping into the hands of criminals?

33 Life and death issues:
DRUGS 4

Illegal drugs and 'mules'

Illegal drugs, like bootleg liquor and tobacco, are smuggled into the country and distributed by criminals to the wider public. They are also damaging to a country's economy, as enormous sums of money filter through many hands, into the pockets of criminals, out of the economy. The difference is, of course, that the substances themselves are illegal *under any circumstances* in this country.

The law is much stricter on sentencing for illegal drug traffickers – in some countries a death sentence is imposed – and the risk for smugglers is therefore much greater. However, the knock-on effect of this is that the harder it becomes to import illegal drugs into the country, the more smugglers can charge for their efforts. The riskier the business, the more lucrative it becomes. HM Customs estimate that the large majority of regular cocaine imports enter the country hidden in human body orifices or in the stomach. The people who engage in this highly risky practice are known as 'mules', and there have been many cases of people seizing up uncontrollably in mid-flight as they fatally overdose on a ruptured cocaine-filled condom in their stomach.

Cocaine and corruption

If we look at cocaine as an example of illegal drug trafficking, we must first establish who produces it. Colombia is responsible for producing most of the world's cocaine. Individual 'drug barons' have become so wealthy and powerful that they are often 'above the law', with money to hire the best lawyers in the world, 'buy' the protection of corrupt government, military and police officials, and even to build their own private armies. This is a very dangerous world, where no one can ever fully trust anybody else, and 'silence' is heavily guarded and enforced by violence and corruption. Murders and tortures are hidden from the public eye as members of this lawless industry establish their power and stab each other in the back. The super-rich in this business rarely come to harm as they indulge in many illegal spin-offs from their 'untouchable' status, including enslaved prostitution.

An individual buying a couple of grams of cocaine in Britain is making a person like this even richer.

When cocaine reaches Britain, criminal gangs take care of the larger imports. These powerful gangs, like the drug barons abroad, use violent means to ensure that their business is not hampered. As the cocaine becomes divided into ever-smaller amounts, it becomes 'cut', or mixed with other substances, so that smaller and smaller dealers can make more money. Dealers will often defend their own 'patch' in the same violent ways as the drugs barons, and will often give 'free samples' away to encourage addiction and hence encourage further trade.

By the time a gram finds its way into the hands of a small-time user, it will probably have been bought from a friend or close acquaintance and it is easy to simply not think about the sinister criminal practices that are being supported by the few notes that are being handed over.

Under the influence

Legitimate drugs industries will use these same practices of cheap labour, establishing and encouraging addiction in their attempt to make the biggest profit. In the 'legal' world, however, the aggressive pitch wars are not fought in the street, but on billboards, television and in newspapers and magazines.

▶ Drugs war over Colombia

Marketing is the weapon of the legitimate drugs company. The influence marketing has on the individual over a period of time in the legitimate world is as powerful a means of persuasion as any form of violence used by criminals in the illegal underworld. (See Unit 87.)

A cigarette smoker can be encouraged to stay 'loyal' to a brand if the 'image' the brand's marketing portrays is agreeable. Smoking a certain cigarette will identify you and your feelings with the people and feelings portrayed in an advertisement of that cigarette.

Similar to the illegal drugs industry, tobacconists are always looking for new markets and tobacco advertising repeatedly tries to give trading standards the slip and make campaigns that are aimed at children. In third world countries, where trading standards laws are more relaxed, tobacco companies demonstrate even less regard for ethical practice as cigarettes are handed out as 'free samples', just like addictive heroin and cocaine in the illegal drugs world.

Summing up

The global drugs industry, legitimate and illegal, is responsible for many unfair, unethical and damaging practices, and many people argue that looking at the bigger picture is the best way to evaluate whether a substance is 'evil' or not. In some cases it might be argued that it is a drug's legal status that determines whether or not the people in possession of it are criminals. In any case, it is the criminal practices *surrounding* drugs that form the most objectionable arguments against their position in a global society.

FOR DISCUSSION

A substance is not 'evil' in itself, it is the people who manipulate it for their own benefit, at the expense of others, who are evil.

CITIZENSHIP CHALLENGE

After reading about the drugs industry, work in groups of three or four and prepare a presentation on the issues involved particularly concentrating on how the global drugs industry, legitimate and illegal, is responsible for many unfair, unethical and damaging practices.

34 Social harmony: PREJUDICE AND DISCRIMINATION

Prejudice – a definition

Prejudice is defined as 'thinking badly about other people without sufficient reasons'. The word 'prejudice' means to prejudge. This means that we judge someone before we know them or before we even meet them.

Discrimination – a definition

Discrimination occurs when people are treated badly by others because of prejudice. **Discrimination = prejudice + power**.

Discrimination is not always a bad thing, however. It means 'careful judgement'. For example, if you are buying a new CD player, it is a good idea to be a bit *discriminating*, to look carefully, to choose something that you really like, not just the first thing you see. Discrimination becomes unfair when we make a big deal out of differences between people so that it affects their lives, education, employment, housing – their human rights.

Scapegoat – a definition

In the Book of Leviticus in the Bible, a goat was sent out into the wilderness after the Jewish chief priest had symbolically laid the sins of the people upon it. All the wrongdoings of the tribe were put on the goat. A scapegoat is someone who is blamed for the shortcomings of others.

Stereotyping – a definition

Stereotyping a person means conforming to an unjustifiably fixed, standardized, mental picture.

After World War I, Germany was in a dreadful economic mess. A group of brutal thugs led by the Nazi dictator Adolf Hitler (1889–1945) looked for scapegoats. By 1945 over 6 million Jews had been murdered in 'death camps' (sometimes called 'concentration camps') in what has become known as **The Holocaust**. Jewish men, women and children were forcefully transported in cattle trucks to these camps. They were stripped naked, given soap, and led into the 'showers' – showers of death – the gas chambers.

Hitler and the Nazis claimed that Jewish people were 'sub-human' and deserved to die quite simply because they were Jews.

There are Nazi groups in Britain today like the British National Front (BNF) who hold similar views about British Africans, Asians, Rastafarians, Muslims, Sikhs and Hindus.

The cost

Prejudice and discrimination continue to have a devastating effect today. Racism, tribalism, sectarianism, nationalism, and colonialism were responsible for the deaths of an estimated 65 million human beings in the twentieth century (more than today's population of Britain).

Asylum seekers – a definition

The word 'asylum' is a strange one. It can mean 'a mental hospital', or, 'a place where a person can be safe or looked after'.

People *seek asylum* in countries like Britain because they hope for a life free from grinding poverty (**economic migrants**) and they seek safety from governments that torture, rape and murder courageous people or their families who speak out against injustice and barbarism (**political asylum seekers**).

As the world globalizes (see Units 62–4), in terms of nations' trade and investment, borders are opened up more easily for 'freer' flow of goods and products. However, people are not allowed to move as freely as money or big business. There are enormous restrictions put on people's movements especially those desperate to escape from poverty and persecution in poorer countries.

This situation violates Article 14 of The Universal Declaration of Human Rights:

> 'Everyone has the right to seek and to enjoy in other countries asylum from persecution.'

Today there are an estimated 25 million refugees in the world, forced to abandon their homes essentially because of nationalistic wars. Millions of people seek safety, *seek asylum*, in Europe, Australia and America. These countries in the rich world are making it increasingly difficult for people from Africa, Afghanistan, Algeria and many other countries to escape torture, persecution and economic slavery.

Ethnic discrimination in Britain

In theory the **UK Race Relations Act 2000** bans **indirect discrimination** across both public and private services from the smallest nursery school to the grimmest prison. However, when it comes to immigration and asylum seekers, **ethnic discrimination** by public authorities is encouraged. Afghans, Albanians, Romas, Tamils, Somalis and Pontic Greeks, trying to immigrate to Britain – many of them escaping torture, poverty and persecution – are more likely to be detained, questioned and rejected than others. Britain's current process means that the prison-like asylum centres house people who may be waiting up to seven years before their case can be heard.

Launching your learning

Find out the meaning of the following words and phrases:
Prejudice, discrimination, concentration camps, The Holocaust, scapegoat, to violate, tribalism, sectarianism, nationalism, colonialism, economic slavery, economic migrants, political asylum seekers, seeking asylum, indirect discrimination, ethnic discrimination.

CITIZENSHIP CHALLENGE

A We can conform to prejudgements about lots of things: the way someone talks or looks; their race or religion; their age ... maybe you can think of more things? Who do you prejudge?

B Brainstorm on the words *injustice, prejudice* and *discrimination*. Discuss your findings with a friend. Pick out any two examples. Write a short press release of about 50 words.

C 'Putting someone in a box' is one definition of stereotyping; 'conforming to a *fixed mental picture*' is another definition. Give examples of 'stereotyping' in the modern world.

D What does it say about the world's priorities that people – unlike money, profits and big business – are not allowed to move freely around the world?

E 'Economic slavery caused by the policies of the rich world means that countries like Britain have a moral responsibility to help victims of poverty who seek asylum from slavery.' Discuss.

Racism – a definition

Racism is defined by the formula **prejudice + power = racism**.

Racism is when racial prejudice is turned into action that harms others.

Racism is the belief that one race of people is superior to another because of the race they are born into.

Racism is discrimination based purely on the colour of a person's skin. In this book the word 'black' is used to refer to any non-white group.

Slavery

It was only 150 years ago that Charles Kingsley, a famous Victorian Christian clergyman and author of *The Water Babies*, wrote that black people were from 'degenerate races' and not as good as pink people.

How could it happen that a Christian who followed Jesus Christ was so ignorant?

In the seventeenth century, after they had convinced themselves that black people were 'savages', British and other European businessmen became slave traders. They entered the slave trade not because they were prejudiced against Africans but because they were driven by greed. They saw, especially in Africa, profits and property not people with feelings. They hounded people, threw nets around them, ripped them from their homes, chained them neck to neck, and shipped them, like cattle, into a world of terror. They raped the women, abused the children, flogged the men, often to death, and became incredibly rich in the process.

All the ignorant rumours about black people became a set of beliefs. **Institutionalized racism** was spawned – a system justifying slavery and the building of empires. The British rulers argued that 'white supremacy' was necessary for human progress.

This belief spread across the world and, in time, led to the near extermination of the Native Indians in the Americas and the Aboriginal people in Australia.

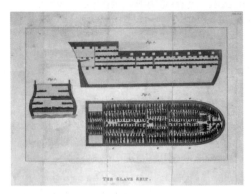

▲ Plan of a slaveship

Crime against humanity

A row erupted in 2001 between Britain and South Africa. South Africa called the slave trade a **crime against humanity** and argued that Africa should receive compensation from countries like Britain and Spain which grew wealthy from raping the African continent. The British Government, however, maintained that the slave trade *was* a tragedy but *not* a crime because 'international law at the time did not recognize slavery as a crime'. In effect, Britain is not prepared to link the question of development aid to past history. However, millions of Africans today still suffer widespread poverty because of a world economic system first founded on slavery.

The sword and the cross

Like all major institutions, the Christian Churches have been guilty of institutionalized racism. Alongside the slave-traders came the missionaries determined to convert millions of 'savages' to their way of thinking (see Unit 41). Black people were seen as 'uncivilized' and the existence of the great black civilizations was hidden from history.

Over recent years there has been increased awareness of **cultural diversity**. Today most churches speak out and work against racial prejudice. However, there is no room for complacency. In 2001 the Radio Authority found *Premier Christian Radio* guilty of insulting other religions; while in the US churches like the *Church of Jesus Christ Christian Aryan Nations* preach 'white supremacy'.

The MacPherson Report

In 1993 teenager Stephen Lawrence was brutally murdered in London by white racist thugs. It became clear that racist attitudes in the police force had prevented proper investigations into bringing the murderers to justice. The **MacPherson Report** in 1999 into Stephen's death confirmed what many black people already knew – that institutionalized racism existed in the police force as well as in other institutions.

Built-in racism

Not all black people come face-to-face with this intentional expression of racism, but all black people suffer the effects of the subtle institutional racism that exists in society. This is a racism that individual white people cannot avoid, for it has been *built into* British culture over several centuries.

One of the problems of looking at racism today is that people tend to think of it in terms of tragic stories like Stephen Lawrence's or think that strong personal prejudice exists only within certain neo-nazi organizations. However racism is deeply ingrained in institutions including the media, schools, religions and the immigration service.

Propaganda *(see Unit 91)*

When Britain needed cheap labour to rebuild the country after World War II, the Government organized a massive publicity campaign in India, Pakistan and the Caribbean colonies.

Adverts posted in these countries showed beautiful pictures of Kew Gardens. The reality was very different! New immigrants were forced to live in the most run down parts of post-war cities and given underpaid dead end jobs. By the 1960s there was no longer such a need for cheap labour and Tory politicians began inciting racial hatred by calling for repatriation.

The BNP

In Oldham in the 2001 General Election, the BNP, an ugly neo-Nazi party, deliberately fuelled racial tensions and obtained over 11,000 votes by making the Hindu and Muslim communities scapegoats (see Unit 37). A report into the riots concluded that many cities in Britain were dangerously **segregated**.

Launching your learning

A Explain the meaning of the following words and phrases:
   Prejudice, power and racism, institutionalized racism, crime against humanity, cultural diversity, repatriation, segregated.

B Imagine you are a slave (past or present) and somebody owns you and totally controls your life. Write a diary of a typical week. Express not only what happens to you but how you feel.

C In 2001 three damning reports came out documenting institutionalized racism in the National Health Service, the law and housing. This does not mean that all people in these institutions are racist but that racism comes in three main strands:

   ■ intentional

   ■ disguised but deliberate

   ■ unintentional but destructive.

   Using examples try and explain the difference between these strands.

36 Social harmony: *RACISM 2*

Leviticus

In the Jewish tradition, all human beings are neighbours:

> 'When a stranger sojourns with you in your land, you shall not do him wrong.'

Leviticus 19: 33

Jewish Scripture (the Tenakh) teaches that all human beings are made in the image of God (Genesis 1: 26). Human beings are made for each other; to live in community and to act responsibly towards creation (Genesis 2: 19–20). But unlike the rest of creation there are no separate species within humanity. There is only one human race. 'Races' are nothing more than slight variations of the basic human stock (Genesis 3: 20).

Jesus Christ

In the New Testament, Jesus taught we should love others as we love ourselves. When asked by a lawyer, '…and who is my neighbour?' Jesus relates the parable of the Good Samaritan (Luke 10: 25–37) – a story about a victim of a mugging helped by a Samaritan, a people who normally suffered from discrimination and prejudice.

Muhammad (pbuh)

Muslims believe that Allah has given every person on earth dignity, breathing into them His own spirit. We are all the same and no distinction can be made among us on account of our accidental differences, such as nationality, colour, race, religion or lack of it. We are all related to each other. In his Last Sermon, the Prophet Muhammad (pbuh) taught:

> 'All mankind is descended from Adam and Eve, an Arab is not better than a non-Arab and a non-Arab is not better than an Arab; a white person is not better than a black person, nor is a black person better than a white person except by piety and good actions.'

Guru Gobind Singh

Sikhs believe that we are created beings and God lives within us all. All humanity is one. We are interdependent and need each other to survive. A Sikh regards the world as a meaningful creation of God wherein noble, truthful and selfless actions can bring a person closer to God. Sikhism preaches universal equality, and therefore, regards all religions and people as equal before the eyes of God. Being a minority of about 20 million worldwide, and having been subjected to persecution throughout their 500-year history, Sikhs wish for a world order in which all minorities, whether racial, ethnic, religious or linguistic, or any other type are protected. Guru Gobind Singh, the last Guru, wrote in the Guru Granth Sahib:

> 'There is only one race, the human race.'

His Holiness, the Dalai Lama

> 'The main problems which humankind is facing today are basically created by ourselves … We must build a closer relationship among ourselves, based on mutual trust, mutual understanding, mutual respect and mutual help, irrespective of culture, philosophy, religion or faith.'

His Holiness the Dalai Lama, in *Voices of Survival in a Nuclear Age*

▲ Musician Nitin Sawney: 'My identity and my history are defined only by myself – beyond religion and beyond skin.'

Rasta

'The Rastafarian doctrine grew out of the realities of the African peoples over the past 500 years, and represents an African renaissance of human work and self-dignity in the face of slavery, brutality, discrimination, abuse, exploitation and colonial domination. One is born a Rasta and one becomes aware of divine status by the removal of the effects of Western brainwashing, distortions, lies, half truths, stereotyped self-images and propaganda, which cloud our inner vision of Jah, who is love. With such a foundation it is not surprising that Rastafarian doctrine has a ethos of respect for others.'

Testing the Global Ethic, The World Congress of Faiths

Nitin Sawhney

'I am Indian. To be more accurate I was raised in England, but my parents came from India … the BJP in India … the BNP in England! The first would define me by my religious heritage, the latter by the colour of my skin. I believe in Hindu philosophy. I am not religious. I am a pacifist. I am a British Asian. My identity and my history are defined only by myself – beyond politics, beyond nationality, beyond religion and beyond skin.'

Nitin Sawhney, *Beyond Skin*, Outcaste Records Ltd, 1999

CITIZENSHIP CHALLENGE

Write an article for a website, or write a text message using no more than 30 characters, or write a song, or design a poster expressing something of what has been said in this unit.

37 Social harmony: RACISM 3

After the defeat of the Nazis at the end of World War II, the German poet and writer Bertolt Brecht (1898–1956) said, 'The bitch is dead but the bastard lives on'. Nearly 60 years on we find that sadly he was right – fascism and racism still exist. In this unit we will find out where.

Xenophobia – a definition

Xenophobia – an irrational hatred of foreigners.

Europe

Europe has many cultures in a relatively small area of land and has seen many conflicts throughout history. Although most of these conflicts have been caused by trade and resources, national identities often add fuel to conflicts.

Today, Europe is seeing an alarming resurgence in **xenophobia** and racial hatred. Far from being a fringe activity, racism, violence and **neo-nationalism** have become normal in some communities. Ethnic minorities and different cultures in one country can often be used as a **scapegoat** (see Unit 34) during times of economic crisis. Today there is rising support for **populist anti-immigrant** parties in national, regional and local governments across Europe. For example, in Austria, the birthplace of Adolf Hitler, the so-called 'Freedom Party' was recently able to secure the majority of the cabinet posts. The party is an extreme far-right party, whose leader, Jörg Heider, has been accused of sympathetic statements towards the Nazis.

Britain

Britain has one of the highest rates of racial violence in Western Europe, and it is getting worse. In the 2001 General Election, the fascist BNP secured over 15,000 votes in Oldham and Burnley. An estimated 200,000 black people are attacked in Britain every year because of the colour of their skin. Many of these attacks go unreported to the police – those that were reported rose by 107 per cent in 2000. Beatings, fire-bombings, and excrement pushed through letter-boxes, are just some of the horrors that black people in Britain face today. There are terrible racist murders too. In 2001, Shiblu Rahman a 34-year-old Asian chef, and father of two daughters, was ambushed outside his home in East London by three white racists. He was brutally stabbed to death.

Australia

In 1998, 'One Nation', an Australian nationalist party in Queensland won 25 per cent of the votes with their promises to fight immigration by non-whites. In a speech the party leader Pauline Hanson said that Australia was 'in danger of being swamped' by Asians and she also questioned the special welfare benefits for Australia's **Aborigines**. Controversy erupted in 2001 when a boat of desperate and ill asylum seekers were refused permission to land in Australia.

Australia has a racist history where **apartheid** policies – separating people because of the colour of their skin – have been practised. Aboriginal people have lost almost all their land and suffered many prejudices. Today they are the poorest group in Australia. In the past, a notorious policy that led to the 'Lost Generation' was practised when whites tried to 'breed out' Aborigines. Until 1967, Aborigines were not even regarded by law as human.

Africa

A number of nations in Africa are at war or civil war only a few years after they have gained their independence from former colonial countries. While most of the conflicts have resources at their core, additional fuel is added to the conflict by the stirring up of **ethnic differences** and encouraging ethnic hatred. An example of this was in Rwanda (see Unit 86).

Asia

In **Cambodia** there has been a strong anti-Vietnamese sentiment. In **Indonesia** there has been violence against the affluent Chinese population who have been blamed for economic problems that have plagued the country in recent years.

North America

Racist government policies, under the guise of economic 'progress', have crippled the Innu of eastern Canada – a once self-sufficient and independent people. Racist attacks against peace-loving Muslims, including murders, rose sharply in 2001 after the terrorist attacks on 11 September. Despite the civil rights victories of 30 years ago, official racial prejudice is still reflected throughout the criminal justice system (see Unit 50). Skin colour can make you a suspect in America and makes you more likely to be stopped, more likely to be searched, and more likely to be arrested and imprisoned.

The lure of Adolf Hitler

Many people who join **white supremacist groups** do so at a young age, and a lot of recruiting by **hate groups** is targeted at children. On the anniversary of Hitler's birthday in April 1999, a killing spree in an American school by two teenagers involved in Nazi-related activities, claimed the lives of many teenagers.

The **Oklahoma City** bombing in 1995 – on the day before Hitler's birthday – triggered **anti-Muslim** sentiments (see Units 38 and 94)

and there was a 60 per cent increase in attacks on Muslims in the US, even though no Muslims were responsible.

The Internet and racism

While the world wide web can advance free speech it can also be a breeding ground for hatred and **bigotry**. This is very serious as the number of 'hate sites' that have sprung up in recent years is increasing at an alarming rate. Some groups such as **HateWatch** (see Addresses/websites) have gone as far as buying racist domain names so that real racists cannot buy these domains themselves!

CITIZENSHIP CHALLENGE

Begin a project on racism. For more information see Addresses/websites.

- The **Institute of Race Relations** (a very informative site about racism in Europe and UK in particular).

- A report from VSO's *Orbit* magazine looks at how poor and misrepresented press coverage of the developing world by the developed countries leads to stereotyping.

- Asiandubfoundation.com

- cyberace.com

Launching your learning

Write a series of sentences using the following words and phrases:
Xenophobia, neo-nationalism, populist, anti-immigrant, Aborigines, apartheid, ethnic differences, white supremacist groups, hate groups, bigotry.

38 Social harmony:
ISLAMOPHOBIA

'And they ill-treated them (Believers) for no other reason except that they believed in Allah.'

Qur'an, Surah 85–8

Islamophobia – a definition

Today, the West has coined a new phrase *Islamophobia* to describe an old phenomenon – the hatred of Islam and Muslims. This gives the impression that either it is a recent problem or that Muslims are to blame for generating the fear of Islam that Islamophobia implies. Islamophobia, however, existed even when there were no Muslims living in Europe. The history of Europe has been shaped by its interaction with Islam, its misrepresentation and prejudices about Islam and indeed, its wars against Islam.

KEY IDEA

To understand a prejudice you need to go to its roots.

Power struggle

Christianity was the major power in much of the world until Islam burst onto the scene. As Islam spread, reactions appeared from both Christians living under Muslim rule and outside it. Christianity feared a loss of its followers to Islam and felt a need to respond.

Christian spin

The response from Christianity was a military one. The **Crusades** (1095–1291) were brutal wars fought against Muslims. But even before the Crusades, the distortion of Islam by some Christian writers had begun by false propaganda and misrepresentation. This prepared the European masses for a '**holy war**'.

The West's current image of Islam is rooted in early themes developed by Christian writers and artists. These have survived to become popular stereotypes.

The media as it was then, in the form of Christian writers, focused their attack on the character of the Prophet Muhammad (pbuh). The Qur'an and the facts about the Prophet's life were distorted. If the Prophet's character could be destroyed, the Qur'an would be proved a forgery. Thus the revelations of the Qur'an are described as 'epileptic fits' of a man 'possessed by demons'.

Books about Muhammad (pbuh) were given titles like *Demoniacus* to reinforce this message. In most works he is described as a robber, adulterer, a murderer, who schemed himself into power and spread it through violence. Elsewhere, he is described as Satan or the Antichrist. This early tendency continued and found its way into popular medieval literature. One scene from Dante's *Inferno* sums up early European attitudes to Islam; in his 'vision', Dante is walking through the circles of Hell. Muhammad (pbuh) is placed in the circle next to Satan.

Attacks on Muslim morality

The Christian Churches could only accept their own view of marriage – one partner for life. Muslim views were deliberately distorted from verses in the Qur'an and the number of wives permitted was exaggerated. The general argument was that Islam permitted sin and could therefore not be a 'Godly religion'.

Today, similar themes have been re-worked. Islam is now criticized for its lack of flexibility on sin. Islam is 'harsh' on adulterers and has 'primitive' attitudes to sex before marriage and homosexuality. Islam 'oppresses' women, and 'forces' them to wear hijab (see Unit 57). Islamic punishment of criminals is 'savage'. Muslims are 'fanatics' or 'fundamentalists' intent on destroying Western civilization.

▲ 'Muslims have been demonised and attacked in Britain for 30 years'

Treason?

Christians who negotiated with Muslim rulers in the past, in England, were suspected and accused of treason. Contacts with Muslims and Jews were not allowed. Christians were forbidden to work in Muslim and Jewish households. Muslims and Jews could not hold any position of public authority. They also had to wear distinct clothing so that they didn't mix. They were forced to accept missionaries to be converted to Christianity.

The Religions of the Book

The truth is that Islam has much in common with Christianity and Judaism and indeed comes from the very same roots in the Tenakh. They are called 'the Religions of the Book'. Judaism, Christianity and Islam all look back to the Prophet Abraham (c. 1800 BCE) as their founder, and Islam reveres Moses and Jesus as prophets of God. Muhammad (pbuh) taught a return to the pure **monotheism** – the belief in only one God – originally taught by Abraham.

The problem arises over the recognition by Jews and Christians of Muhammad (pbuh) as a prophet of God. Islam teaches that Allah (God) communicates with humankind through a series of divinely guided messengers. Muslims believe that all nations and peoples have their own prophets and that Muhammad (pbuh) was the last messenger sent by God to the Arabs. But Jews and Christians do not accept that Muhammad (pbuh) was the last prophet and the Jews do not accept that Jesus was a genuine messenger of God either.

So in some sort of idiot 'Punch and Judy show', Jews, Christians and Muslims fight each other over nobody-remembers-what, each cycle of violence and killing storing up hatred and the desire for revenge, until the whole nightmare cycle starts up once again.

FOR DISCUSSION

'Muslims have been demonized, shunned, misunderstood and attacked in America and Britain for 30 years. White people have never really wanted to live near us. We haven't been "cool" in the way Afro-Caribbeans have. They say it's a tolerant society, but I don't want tolerance; that just means putting up with something, often reluctantly. I'd rather you learnt about Islam. The problem is that most of Britain doesn't understand Islam.'

Aki Nawaz, head of Nation Records and the man behind the band *Fundamental*

39 Social harmony: SEXISM

Introduction

Throughout most of known history we cannot examine the status of women because they have had none. Their achievements have gone unrecorded. Women have nearly always been dominated by men and regarded as men's personal property.

This has certainly been the case during the 3,000 years of Judaic-Christian civilization and is symbolized by Eve being created from one of Adam's ribs (Genesis 2: 20–3).

Men have wielded the power, shaped the values and controlled the wealth. Throughout history, men have treated women as second-class citizens.

Today, women all over the world are victims of domestic violence, sexual violence and sexual harassment, at home, at work, and on the streets.

The struggle for equal rights

In Britain the struggle for equal rights for women has been a long one. It was not until the mid-nineteenth century that women were legally allowed to own possessions. After a militant campaign by women's rights activists – the **Suffragettes** – women over 21 were finally given the vote in 1928. In 1975 the **Sex Discrimination and Equal Pay Acts** were introduced, and it was only in 1991 that rape within a marriage became a prosecutable offence.

TALKING POINTS

'The most important chores on earth that are done by women are regarded as being low. In our kitchens we raise all the future Jesus' of the world or all the future serial killers. And we send them out from our kitchens to be grown men and women. What greater work is there than that? A mother with a family is an economist, a nurse, a painter, a diplomat, a psychologist and much more. We are the guardians of tomorrow.'

Buchi Emecheta, author's interview

'How many complaints would there be if women breastfed their young openly on buses, trains, in pubs, offices, on the streets, and so on? Yet no one objects to naked women in newspapers, read and displayed in all these places.'

Quote taken from Clare Short's book, *Dear Clare: this is what women feel about Page 3*, 1991

'You start by sinking into his arms and end up with your arms in his sink.'

Graffiti

Christian attitudes

Although Jesus was born into a **patriarchal** society, women played an active role in his ministry and life. He always considered women as equals, as deserving of respect as any man.

St Paul on the other hand warned wives to '… be subject to your husbands' (Ephesians 5: 22–23) and the churches reinforced the general sexist attitudes of the day:

> 'Women should remain at home, sit still, keep house, bear and bring up children.'
>
> Martin Luther (1483–1586)

Women were allowed no positions of power within the churches.

Women priests

In recent years the more liberal faith groups have modified their practices and some now select clergy on the basis of the individual's intelligence, personality and knowledge – without regard for their **gender**. In 1992 the Church of England, and in 2000 the Church of Pakistan and the Mombasa diocese of the Anglican Church of Kenya, ordained women priests.

However, more conservative traditions like the Roman Catholic Church have not followed suit because sacred texts are interpreted as restricting positions of authority to men. To treat women equally in their churches would ignore the teachings of scripture, as they view it. They feel that their stance is not driven by a desire to oppress women. Rather, they feel that the Bible does not authorize their denomination to ordain women:

> 'I permit no woman to teach or to have authority over men; she is to keep silent.'
>
> 1 Timothy 2: 11–12

Launching your learning

Write an article for either a teenage boys' or teenage girls' magazine on the issues covered in this unit, using some of the following words: **Sexism, suffragettes, patriarchal, gender.**

CITIZENSHIP CHALLENGE

Discuss why women are still struggling today to be treated with respect and as equals in society. The following statements may help you in your discussion:

- 'If girls sleep around they are called horrible names, while boys openly boast about their sexual "conquests".'

- 'An erect penis has no conscience.'

- 'Language is often sexist, for example, *craftsman*, *masterpiece*, *statesman*, *forefathers*, *manpower*, *God the father*, and so on.'

- 'Advertising and tabloid newspapers exploit the female body to make money.'

- 'Women's work as wives, mothers and carers is often undervalued and under-rewarded.'

- 'On the one hand, women are trivialized and treated as sex objects but on the other they are idealized and sentimentalized.'

- 'Equality and sameness are two quite different things.' Discuss.

- Men often think that women 'are more intuitive, irrational, gentle, passive, selfless and sympathetic than men'. Do you think this is true? Why might these characteristics actually suppress and restrict women?

40 Social harmony: *HOMOPHOBIA*

▲ Love cannot be defined in terms of sexual orientation

Gay and lesbian

In the nineteenth century the medical profession first coined the term 'homosexuality'. Nowadays, most homosexuals prefer to use the terms 'lesbian' and 'gay' because the word 'homosexual' sounds rather like a psychiatrist's diagnosis. There is no general agreement about what causes homosexuality or whether it is just how people are born.

The psychologist Alfred Kinsey wrote a report on sexuality in the early 1950s. He concluded that we are all somewhere on a scale of sexuality, with total heterosexuality at one extreme and total homosexuality at the other. He believed that many people are capable of feeling attracted to someone of the same sex, and that the absolute division between heterosexual and homosexual is a false one. Although the reasons for our sexual preferences are not fully known, it seems unlikely that homosexuals could be 'cured', as some Christian groups believe, any more than heterosexuals could be.

It is estimated that around two per cent of the world's women and four per cent of men live exclusively with same-sex partners.

Homophobia – a definition

Homophobia is an irrational fear of, and discrimination against homosexuals.

Controversy – 'Section 28'

The British Conservative Government introduced Section 28 of the Local Government Act in the 1980s. It states that schools 'shall not promote the teaching in any maintained school of the acceptability of homosexuality as a pretended family relationship'. The present Labour Government is considering scrapping the regulation. Some Christian Churches and Conservative politicians believe that homosexual behaviour is unnatural, abnormal and condemned by God. Thus, any attempt to accept homosexuality as a normal, natural orientation is not acceptable. They feel that it will have the undesirable effect of increasing the number of young people who choose homosexuality.

Liberal politicians and theologians on the other hand, believe that homosexual behaviour is not chosen and is not changeable. It is a natural, normal sexual orientation for a minority of people. Thus, any attempt to accept homosexuality as a normal, natural orientation is to be supported.

Marriage and parenthood

Gay and lesbian couples, who are Dutch citizens, are able to marry and adopt, making the Netherlands the first country in recent history to have legalized gay and lesbian marriages.

CITIZENSHIP CHALLENGE

Devise an RE lesson – presentation and content – around the subject of homophobia. What would you talk about and how would you organize the class? Discuss how schools can deal with issues such as homosexuality sensitively and fairly.

Christian views

Christians currently hold a wide range of views on homosexuality. Discussion is more widespread in the churches in Europe and North America because of campaigns by organizations like the **Gay and Lesbian Christian Movement (LGCM)** for lesbian and gay rights (see Addresses/websites).

Some homosexuals find it very hard to match their sexuality with their faith. '**Coming out**' – declaring their sexuality publicly – may be very difficult when family or friends are the kind of Christians who believe that homosexuality is a sin. For someone brought up to take the Bible literally, it can be very painful to break these rules. It can also be painful for lesbian and gay Christians to be prevented from marrying their partner before God. Sometimes couples are able to arrange a 'blessing' ceremony with a sympathetic priest or minister. Some would like to see the Church of the future offering the marriage service to lesbian and gay couples.

Opposing views

'Tradition has always declared that "homosexual acts are intrinsically disordered". They are contrary to the natural law. They close the sexual act to the gift of life ... under no circumstances can they be approved.'

Catechism of the Roman Catholic Church, 1994

'Each individual's journey through life is unique. Some will make this journey alone, others in loving relationships – maybe in marriage or other forms of commitment. We need to think about our own choices and try to understand the choices of others. Love has many shapes and colours and is not finite. It can not be measured or defined in terms of sexual orientation.'

Quaker Statement of Affirmation and Reconciliation, 2000

Muslim views

As with the Christian Churches there are different views about homosexuality among modern Muslims. Many Muslims consider homosexuality to be sinful. Homosexuality is seen as being unnatural, caused by environmental factors, and people should steer themselves away from homosexuality. However, groups like **Al-Fatiha** (see Addresses/websites) – an international organization for lesbian and gay Muslims – work to, 'enlighten the world that Islam is a religion of tolerance and not hate, and that Allah loves His creation, no matter what their sexual orientation might be'.

Discrimination

Although in recent years there has been growing social acceptance of same-sex relationships between **consenting** adults, discrimination against gays and lesbians still occurs in many parts of the world. In eighteen countries, gays and lesbians can be imprisoned, sometimes for life, and around 60 countries consider same-sex relationships as illegal. China prosecutes gays and lesbians under 'hooliganism' laws. Iran, Afghanistan and Saudi Arabia have executed homosexuals for their sexuality during the past decade. Gays and lesbians are banned from the armed forces in some countries, including Japan, Brazil and Greece. In London in 1999 a packed gay pub in Soho was bombed killing three people and maiming scores of others.

FOR DISCUSSION

A What might the problems be for a Christian who 'comes out'?

B Should lesbian and gay couples have the right to marry in church?

C Why do some people want to get rid of Section 28?

41 Social harmony:
MULTICULTURAL BRITAIN

Conversion

During the seventeenth, eighteenth and nineteenth centuries, Britain began to colonize and carve up large parts of the world. Businessmen and soldiers went arm-in-arm with missionaries who often forcibly converted 'unfortunate pagans' to become Christian. It is a bitter joke that in places like Africa, the missionaries taught people to pray with their eyes closed and when they opened them the missionaries had taken their land and given them the Bible.

Exclusivity

Many Britons who lived and worked in the British Empire had a standpoint of **exclusivity** towards other religions: the idea that only Christianity is the 'true' religion and all other religions are *excluded* from the truth. Followers of other religions were often regarded as 'heathens', 'savages' or 'pagans'. This attitude amounted to little more than a blanket condemnation of other faiths.

Multi-faith Britain

By the 1950s many people from the former British Empire were living in Britain. They brought with them their own customs and beliefs. Today modern Britain is a **multicultural** society (sometimes called a **multi-faith** or **pluralist** society) with people of different cultural and religious beliefs living together. Alongside the long-established Christian and Jewish communities are Muslims, Hindus, Buddhists, Sikhs, Jains, Baha'is, Zoroastrians and Rastafarians, making Britain one of the most religiously diverse countries in the world.

Religious freedom

In some parts of the world people suffer persecution because they belong to a certain religion. An organization that works to protect people's rights to follow their own religion freely is the International Association for Religious Freedom (see Addresses/websites).

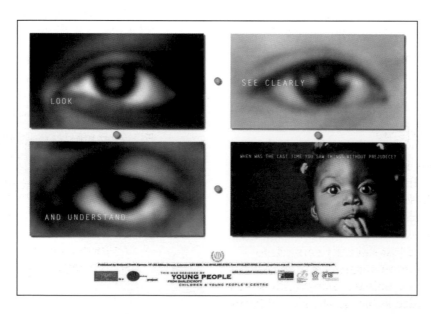

Inter-faith marriage

An inter-faith marriage occurs when two spouses follow different religious traditions. Marriages between persons of different religions can be called: **inter-faith**, **mixed**, **mixed-faith**, or **inter-religious** marriages.

Inter-faith marriages can take many forms. For example, the partners may be:

- one a member of a specific religion and the other an atheist, agnostic or humanist

- from two religions that are different – as in one Western and one Eastern faith (for example, Christianity and Hinduism)

- from two religions that have some points of similarity – as in two **Religions of the Book** (Unit 38) which share Abraham as a Patriarch (for example, Christianity and Islam)

- from different major divisions within the same religion (for example, Roman Catholic and Protestant)

- from different wings within the same religion (for example, two Protestants – one Evangelical and one Liberal).

Attitudes towards inter-faith marriage

The attitude of faith groups towards inter-faith marriage is largely derived from their belief about other religious traditions. While some groups value religious diversity and see great merit in other religions, others place restrictions on inter-faith marriages.

Muslim view

A Muslim male is permitted to marry a person of 'the Book' – in other words, a Jew or Christian. A Muslim woman is not allowed to marry outside Islam. However, a non-Muslim male who wishes to marry a Muslim woman could do so if he first sincerely converts to Islam. If a Muslim man agrees to allow some of his children to be raised as non-Muslims then he will be regarded as having abandoned Islam.

Hindu view

There are very different attitudes to inter-faith marriages within Hinduism. In rural India, mixed marriages are generally still **taboo**, but outside India they are becoming more acceptable. While some Hindus in Britain might see mixed marriages as a betrayal by both parties' families, others have no problems with such marriages.

Sikh view

A Sikh Code of Conduct known as the **Rahat-namas** teaches that a Sikh should only marry a Sikh and the couple should teach their children to read the Guru Granth Sahib, the Sikh Holy Scriptures.

Launching your learning

What do the following words and phrases mean?
Conversion, exclusivity, pluralist, multi-faith, multiculture, persecution, religious tolerance, inter-faith marriages, Religions of the Book, taboo, Rahat-namas.

FOR DISCUSSION

A 'Like different photographs of a building taken from different angles, different religions give us the pictures of one truth from different standpoints.' Discuss.

B What are the advantages of living in a multicultural society?

C What do you think have been the reasons that the number of inter-faith marriages has increased over recent years? (CLUE: increased attendance at colleges and universities.)

42 Social harmony:
INTER-RELIGIOUS DIALOGUE

▲ Hindu extremists destroy a mosque in Ayodha, India, in 1993, resulting in thousands of Muslim and Hindu deaths in years of riots

'In the name of religion'

In many parts of the world people kill, rape and maim others in the name of their religion. Religious and **sectarian** hatred sometimes spills out into open warfare. Untold millions throughout the ages have been killed in the name of religion.

Although all world religions teach that life is sacred, some politicians and religious leaders use religious differences as an excuse to divide people against one another in order to gain or retain their own political and material power. Terrible acts of cruelty have recently been carried out in the name of religion. In 2002 hundreds of Muslims were burned alive by mobs of so-called 'Hindus', after 'Muslim' extremists had firebombed a train killing 59 people.

TALKING POINT

'It's not religions which inspire hatred, it's human error.'

Aki Nawaz, head of Nation Records and man behind the band *Fundamental*

One world

Communication, trade and travel have made the modern world into a **'global village'**. We eat food and buy clothes from Australasia, Africa, Asia, America and Europe. We can travel across the world in a matter of hours, switch on the television or log onto the Internet and see events unfolding before our eyes. We have more information about cultures in other parts of the world and more contact with people from other parts of the world than any previous generation in history.

Respect

There will be no world peace until there is peace between the world religions. Today most reasonable followers of the world religions realize that it is only through talking, listening and learning about and from each other, that there is any real chance of peace. They recognize that listening as well as speaking is necessary for a genuine conversation. This process is called **inter-religious dialogue**.

Dialogue

Inter-religious dialogue is a process of the coming together of people committed to their own religions for the purpose of mutual understanding and respect. It is about offering space, openness and respect, rather than confrontation. It can be between neighbours, among community groups, or even large international gatherings. Through dialogue, followers of different religions have a lot to learn about their own and other faiths.

The Golden Rule

If we look at the scriptures of Judaism, Hinduism, Buddhism, Christianity, Islam and Sikhism – originating in different places and at different times – we find similar teachings:

'What is hateful to you, do not do to your neighbour; this is the entire Torah; the rest is commentary.'

The Talmud, Judaism

'Do not to others what ye do not wish done to yourself.'

Mahabharata, Hinduism

'Since to others, to each one for himself, the self is dear, therefore let him who desires his own advantage not harm another.'

Udana – Varqa, Buddhism

'So whatever you wish that men would do to you, do so to them.'

Matthew 7: 12, Christianity

'None of you truly believes until he wishes for his brother what he wishes for himself.'

The Hadith, Islam

'Do not create enmity within anyone as God is within everyone.'

Guru Arjan Devji 258, Guru Granth Sahib, Sikhism

CITIZENSHIP CHALLENGE

Dialogue

Why do you think listening as well as speaking is necessary for a genuine conversation? While discussing the quote below, concentrate on listening to what your classmates are saying. Spend five minutes trying to write down as accurately as possible what any particular person said in the class discussion.

'It is important for governments and politicians to understand that igniting and exploiting religious sentiments for reasons of political power is the most dangerous legacy that they can bequeath to any people – including their own. People who live in societies ravaged by religious or communal bigotry know that every religious text – from the Bible to the Bhagwad Gita – can be mined and misinterpreted to justify anything, from nuclear war to genocide to corporate globalization.'

Arundhati Roy – Indian writer

Launching your learning

1 Write an article entitled 'Listening' using some or all of the following words and phrases.
Global village, evangelize, convert, inter-religious dialogue, the Golden Rule.

2 Imagine you are asked to lead a dialogue between warring factions. Write an **Agenda** of the topics you would want discussed.

43 Social harmony: WEALTH AND WANT 1

The **Universal Declaration of Human Rights** states that:

> '...freedom from fear and want has been proclaimed as the highest aspiration of the common people.'

KEY QUESTION

Have rich people responsibilities towards the poor?

Jesus on wealth and want

> '"Good master, what must I do to win eternal life?" ... He said, "Go, sell everything you have and give to the poor and you will have riches in heaven".'
>
> Mark 10: 17–21

> 'Beware. Be on your guard against greed of every kind, for even when a man has more than enough his wealth does not give him life.'
>
> Luke 12: 15

> 'What will it profit a man if he gains the whole world and loses his soul?'
>
> Matthew 16: 26

> 'It will be hard for a rich man to enter the kingdom of heaven ... it is easier for the camel to go through the eye of a needle than for a rich man to enter the kingdom of God.'
>
> Matthew 20: 23, 24

The needle and the rope

One explanation for the last passage in Matthew 20 states that the word 'camel' is really a mistranslation for 'rope', and that Jesus was really saying that it would be easier to pass a rope through a needle than for a rich man to enter the spiritual world. Jesus was saying that it is people's **attachment** to riches that draws them away from God and truth.

He did not teach that all wealth is bad, but rather that it is our greed and selfishness and our identification with our material possessions which cuts us off from each other and from the spiritual dimension which Jesus calls the **Kingdom of Heaven**.

Many early Christians shared their wealth and lived a communal lifestyle, believing that this was in the spirit of the teachings of Jesus.

Capitalism

Capitalism has been the strongest economic influence in Britain for hundreds of years and as Christianity became the religion of the rich and powerful, ideas about wealth changed.

Many Protestant Churches began to argue that wealth was a sign of God's favour and a reward for hard work.

Critics reply that much of this wealth came from the profits of the slave trade, the Industrial Revolution and the British Empire, all of which involved brutal exploitation and terrible human suffering (see Units 34–5). They argue that because this money was immorally obtained, Christianity and the law should not support rich landowners and landlords, who use their inherited family wealth to exploit the poor and pile up yet more money and power for themselves and their families. Christianity should reflect the teaching of Christ and provide opportunities for the poor to raise themselves up from poverty.

Greed

'Woe to those who add house to house, and join field to field until everywhere belongs to them.'

Isaiah 5: 8–9

'People who want to get rich fall into temptation and a trap and into many foolish and harmful desires that plunge men into ruin and destruction. For the love of money is a root of all kinds of evil.'

1 Timothy 6: 10

Almsgiving in Islam

'Allah commands justice, the doing of good and liberality to kith and kin.'

Qur'an, Surah 16: 90

'He who eats and drinks while his brother goes hungry, is not one of us.'

The Hadith

The Qur'an stresses that people with more wealth must use it for the benefit of those in need. The fourth Pillar of Islam is **Zakat** or **Almsgiving**. Muslims must donate at least two and a half per cent of their income to the needy. This teaching is designed to help even out inequalities in wealth and to prevent personal greed. Its literal meaning is 'purity', for it purifies the distribution of money helping to keep it in healthy circulation.

Charities

Christian charities like **CAFOD** and **Christian Aid**, and Muslim charities like **Islamic Relief**, **Muslim Aid** and the **Red Crescent** (see Addresses/websites) support orphans and refugees, sponsor education and health, sink wells and erect water pumps for pure drinking water, provide funds and training to enable small farmers to set up cooperative businesses

and educate people in the so-called developed world about the causes, consequences and solutions to **want**.

TALKING POINTS

The South African Archbishop, Desmond Tutu, who has fought all his life for justice for the poor once said:

'A church that is in solidarity with the poor can never be a wealthy church. It must sell all, in a sense, to follow its master. It must use its wealth and resources for the sake of the least of Christ's brethren.'

'The Gospel is war to the death against the motive of acquisition.'

Jose Miranda – South American Theologian

Launching your learning

Write a paragraph on Christian and Muslim attitudes to wealth and want.

FOR DISCUSSION

Would it not be a far fairer and happier world if charities no longer needed to exist and every man, woman and child on the planet had a secure existence, free from fear, oppression and exploitation?

Many Christians are concerned about poverty yet they belong to one of the richest institutions on earth. What do you think the Christian Churches could do to improve the state of the world?

44 Social harmony: WEALTH AND WANT 2

Want is a strange word. It can imply two things: **need** or **greed**.

Winners take all

An auxiliary nurse, performing the most crucial and **needed** work, like bathing and toileting incontinent patients in under-funded hospitals, earns just £4.60 an hour.

▲ Worth £130,000 a week?

At the end of the 2001 football season, Sol Campbell, the Tottenham defender and English international footballer, told his club that unless they paid him £130,000 per week he would leave them and kick a ball somewhere else. The ex-Tottenham star Jimmy Greaves called him 'greedy'. In 1999 the Manchester United captain Roy Keane had threatened to leave the club unless he was paid £50,000 a week.

It would take an auxiliary nurse about six years to earn what the likes of Keane, Michael Owen or David Beckham make *in one week*; and twelve years to earn as much as Sol Campbell **wants** to earn.

The two richest people in the world in 2001 were Americans: Robert Walton's retailing business has brought him $453,000 million – $45.3 billion – and Bill Gates of *Microsoft* is worth $37.5 billion. The average wage of a black worker in America in 2001 is $29,000 – about £20,000. A factory worker in Indonesia will work 60 hours a week for just £15.

Walton and Gates, Beckham and Owen work hard for their money. But so do the workers in America, Indonesia, and auxiliary nurses.

Stinking rich

The rich often indulge in lavish and bizarre lifestyles. The younger brother of the Sultan of Brunei, Jefri, had a $28 billion, ten-year spending spree. He handed over huge sums of money for playboy toys that included amongst other things: 2000 of the world's most expensive cars that were kept in a climate-controlled garage; a solid gold tissue dispenser worth $500,000 and a $5 million bedside rug made from gold thread. He wasted enough money to have built a hospital in every developing country in the world.

Usury – a definition

One form of greed is **usury**: 'earning any **interest** on loaned money.'

Usury is condemned in the Tenakh:

> 'If you lend money to any of my people … you shall not exact interest from him.'

> Exodus 22: 25

Usury and Islam

The Arabic name for usury is **Riba** meaning 'any unjustified advantage in trade dealing' – a deeper meaning than the English term 'interest'.

Usury is forbidden by the Qur'an. Muslims believe that money is not a commodity to be used for gain but a facility to help others. Charging interest forces others into debt and dependency:

> 'If a debtor is in difficulty, give time in which to repay. If you could only accept it, it would be far better if you cancelled the debt altogether.'

> Qur'an, Surah 2: 280

'It could be you'

- Modern society is awash with opportunities to 'make a quick buck'; after all 'it could be me, one day'. Meanwhile the bookies become extraordinarily rich at the expense of other people's longing and greed.

- Gambling is on the increase, especially among young people.

- Gambling gives people a false sense of excitement – it always promises but very seldom delivers. People can lose their homes, destroy their personal honesty or be exposed to loss so great as to jeopardize themselves, their families and society at large.

- The Western economic world – stocks and shares, Wall Street, 'The City', 'The Dow

Jones', the Stock exchange – is all about gambling in the global financial systems – the biggest casino the world has ever seen.

CITIZENSHIP CHALLENGE

A Brainstorm: think about injustices around the world today that are caused by greed. Make a list. Discuss your findings with a friend. Pick out the two examples that interest you most. Write a short press release highlighting the issue.

B Mahatma Gandhi (see Unit 67) highlighted five problems:

1 Politics without principle.

2 Pleasure without conscience.

3 Wealth without work.

4 Knowledge without character.

5 Business without morality.

Brainstorm for three minutes and try and think of examples. In small groups discuss your findings.

C Discussion:
'Wealth is like muck. It is not good but it be spread'.

Francis Bacon (1561–1626) philosopher

'There is enough for each man's need but not each man's greed.'

Mahatma Gandhi

'One per cent of the British population own twenty per cent of Britain's wealth'.

'Usury is the abuse of a certain superiority at the expense of another's necessity.'

Dr Funk – German Theologian

45 Social harmony: WEALTH AND WANT 3

'Central to Christian belief is the fact that we are all one body, one creation. Social and economic division, therefore, is an affront to God as well as to our human dignity.'

Church Action on Poverty
(see Addresses/websites)

Breadline Britain

- Poverty is the core problem of British society. Its consequences spill over into crime, social instability, racial tensions and alcohol and drug abuse.

- Over 50 per cent of Britain's total wealth is owned by less than ten per cent of the population.

- Between 1979 and 2000, people living on a **low income** in Britain (below half of the average income) increased from 5 million to over 14 million people.

- An estimated 60,000 households, equivalent to the number of homes in a town the size of Brighton or Milton Keynes, join the poor each year.

Unemployment

Unemployed people can feel that they are not needed or wanted; their sense of belonging can disappear – they can feel humiliated, angry and worthless. Their local communities can become shattered. As local shops, post offices, garages, bus services, surgeries and schools close, depression, violence, suicide, alcohol and hard drug abuse increase. The numbers living in poverty have continued to grow despite the reduction in unemployment over the last few years. That is because many of the new jobs are part-time and low paid.

Child poverty in Britain

▲ Millions of British children are trapped in poverty

A report in 2000 by UNICEF, a wing of the United Nations, found that in a league table of 23 industrialized nations, Britain was 4th worst in terms of the proportion of children living in poverty. Millions of young people in Britain are trapped in conditions among the worst in Europe. Many live in terrible surroundings, with damp running down the walls and inadequate heating and poor nutrition. Parents often cannot afford to buy new clothes as the little money they have is spent on food.

'Everyone has the right to work, to free choice of employment, to just and favourable conditions of work and to protection against unemployment.

Everyone, without any discrimination, has the right to equal pay for equal work.'

Article 23, the Universal Declaration of Human Rights

A **vocation** is both a way of life and a job. Usually it involves serving. Nursing, teaching and working with disabled people are vocations. Some people may even experience a calling: 'This, I must do!'

Re-creation

For Muslims, Friday is a day of rest; for Jews, Saturday, and for Christians, Sunday. However over the last few years in Britain, more and more people find themselves working on Sundays. Increasingly psychologists are telling us that we all need a publicly expressed day of rest and 're-creation' – when people can re-create themselves and relax. Sunday has become as busy as any other day.

IMMORAL OCCUPATIONS

All the world religions believe that any work that brings suffering to others, or involves dishonesty, exploitation, unfair trading, violence, corruption, bribery, sexual degradation or fraud, is immoral.

Muslim views

For Muslims, work is **halal** if it is fair and benefits others. If someone's means of earning a living hurts another it is **haram** – forbidden. Work that is haram includes any activity involving sexual exploitation like the porn industry or prostitution or any form of dance or drama that is deliberately erotic; the manufacturing of intoxicants; working in an organization that supports injustice; or being involved in armed forces fighting against Islam. Islam views all work that benefits others as dignified. There is no room for snobbery. Society needs street cleaners as much as it needs doctors and nobody need regard any useful employment as being beneath them.

CITIZENSHIP CHALLENGE

Look at the following statements and discuss them in relation to the issues outlined in the Units on Wealth and want. Afterwards, write down your thoughts.

1 'Work is necessary for human survival. If everyone stopped working society would break down.' Would society break down if footballers or pop stars stopped working?

2 'Work is creative. There is joy in doing work well.' Is working in a supermarket or at McDonald's creative?

3 'Work brings us into a relationship with other people. It helps us to belong. It gives us a place, a status and a value.' Is this true of all work?

4 'Work is a way of obtaining the necessities of life and enriching our lives with beauty and enjoyment.' Or is it that today most people work just to pay the bills and keep their heads above water?

5 'Work is an essential part of being alive. It tells you who you are.' But many people do not work for the sake of working; they are working for a car, a new house, or a holiday.

6 'Work can be dangerous, exhausting, boring, repetitive, meaningless, monotonous, nerve-wracking, and soul destroying. It can make people feel like servants to some machine or system.' Give examples.

46 Social harmony: *CRIME AND PUNISHMENT 1*

The media often portrays a society where criminals prowl the streets looking for trouble. While many people call for extra policing and stricter forms of punishment, humanists and others feel that the root causes of crime ought to be looked at seriously.

Nature or nurture?

Ever since scientists began studying genetics (see Unit 22), many have argued that criminal behaviour could be explained by the presence of certain genes programming those who break the law to behave in the way they do. However, in February 2001 scientists working on the 'Book of Humankind' (called The Human Genome Project) – the study of the human genetic code – informed the world that there are not enough genes in the human make-up to programme us. We are more likely to be formed by our experiences (nurture) than our genetic make-up (nature).

This scientific discovery supports those who believe that 'criminals' can change because 'they were not born like that'. It throws us back on ourselves to be responsible to create a crime-free society.

Street crime, muggings, violence, gangs, juvenile crime, murder and theft have always existed, and some crimes are actually less common than they used to be. For example, murder has been declining steadily since the Middle Ages. In the thirteenth century, the murder rate was twenty per 100,000 of the population, now it is one per 100,000.

Murder rates

In modern Britain *fear* of crime, encouraged by a sensation-seeking media, is probably more common than crime itself. Crime does undoubtedly cause a great deal of suffering and unhappiness, but so do irrational fears about crime, which sometimes get in the way of sensible discussion about the issue. The quality of our life as individuals and as a community is diminished by these fears. The occasional religious leader or politician who tries to discuss the issue coolly is often criticized for being 'soft on crime'. For example, they suggest that a major source of crime is drug addicts stealing to pay for their habit. They argue that curing and rehabilitating them, or decriminalizing drugs might be the best way to deal with the problem. This is usually hailed as irresponsible and dangerous by the tabloid press.

▲ Criminals are made, not born

Slogans from politicians and media hysteria about crime are not nearly as useful as proper research into the causes of and cures for crime.

Crime figures

Crime figures need very careful analysis:

- Do some crimes, such as rape, child abuse and domestic violence, appear to be rising simply because people are more willing to report them?

- Do crime figures fluctuate because the police change the ways they record them?

- Do crime figures rise when the numbers of young men rise?

- Do crime figures rise in wealthier societies just because there is more to steal?

Inequality

Most 'criminals' are young men from the lower socio-economic groups. Many have been brought up in run-down inner-city areas, where dreadful housing, under-resourced schools and hospitals, organized crime, unemployment, homelessness, poverty, drug abuse and violence are the order of the day.

More crime is committed in very unequal societies where some groups are discriminated against or feel that they have little to lose by embarking on a life of crime. On the other hand, most people from relatively deprived backgrounds are honest and law-abiding – it would be useful to know why some people are like this but not others.

It is true that some crime rates are rising, but the increases affect the poor much more than the wealthy. For instance, in some parts of London an Asian person is 50 times more likely to be attacked than a white person. So the people most likely to be victims of crime are the inhabitants of run-down inner-city areas, especially if they are black. Most crime involves poor people robbing other poor people.

KEY IDEA

The links between crime and poverty are important and solving the crime problem means closing the gap between rich and poor (see Units 43–5). Our society encourages people to think of themselves as successful if they possess the trappings of wealth. Yet the same society prevents everyone from legally achieving this level of consumption by creating economic structures in which millions of people are poor.

The 'bang up' culture

Britain imprisons more of its people than any other country in Western Europe. In 2001 there were 64,600 prisoners in England and Wales but this number is expected to soar to 83,500 by 2007.

In 2001 the Chief Inspector of British Prisons condemned the 'degradation' and 'immorality' of the way British prisons were run, saying he was no longer prepared to keep apologizing for 'the hell holes' of modern prisons.

CITIZENSHIP CHALLENGE

1 Try and imagine a crime free society. Could it ever be possible?

2 How has genetics thrown the responsibility back on us to create a crime-free society? Is it possible?

3 Explain the link between crime and poverty.

47 Social harmony: CRIME AND PUNISHMENT 2

Why do laws exist?

Communities can only survive happily and harmoniously if the people who live in them accept certain rules and duties. Laws exist for the common good. Societies have to decide what to do with those who break the law.

From retribution to reform

There have been many different forms of punishment over the ages. Each form of punishment reflects that age's attitude to the criminal. Ideas behind punishment have changed from **retribution** to **reform**.

Public torture

The idea of public torture is as strange to us as the idea of reforming criminals would have been to the medieval spectator watching a drawing and quartering. Vicious methods of execution – such as the guillotine, hanging, drawing and quartering – were normal punishments in Europe right up until the nineteenth century.

But punishment was not limited to those guilty of theft or murder. The idea of a division between body and soul enabled the Church to torture and burn so-called heathens in South America – not to mention an estimated nine million peasant women in Europe accused of being witches. The pretext of destroying bodies to save souls thinly masked the theft of the victims' land and livelihoods.

Public execution was a grand dramatic symbol – a theatrical confrontation between the law-breaker and the forces of justice controlled by the monarch.

India

Elsewhere in the world, the authority to carry out punishment was not always vested in those who were distant from everyday life. In many areas of pre-colonial India, for instance, the local community assumed the right to judge its own offenders, collectively deciding which form of punishment would be appropriate. Families would meet and if they were unable to reach an agreement with the aggrieved person's family, then a court of older, respected members of the community would be called together. This ensured that legal power was not concentrated in the hands of a few people.

Psychiatry

Modern psychiatry refuses to put moral responsibility on the individual. Peter Sutcliffe, the 'Yorkshire Ripper', murderer of thirteen women and attacker of seven others, was able to plead **diminished responsibility** as a schizophrenic and so was found guilty of manslaughter rather than murder.

The aims of punishment

What is society trying to do when it punishes an offender – somebody who has broken the law and therefore 'offended' society? The aims of punishment today are defined as protection, retribution, deterrence, reformation and vindication.

- **The theory of protection**
  Punishments are used to protect society from somebody's anti-social behaviour. This punishment takes many forms, the most obvious being imprisonment. Also this type of punishment can be designed to protect the offenders against themselves.

- **The theory of retribution** If somebody does something wrong, then they should receive a punishment that is fitting for the crime they have committed. 'An eye for an eye.'

- **The theory of deterrence** If a person who commits a crime is punished then they will not (hopefully) commit such a crime, or any other crime, again. Also the punishment they receive will put others off (deter them from) committing crimes.

- **The theory of reform** People who commit crimes often need all sorts of help. The punishments that they receive should be of a kind that will prevent them from committing further crimes, and make them responsible citizens who have something to offer society.

- **The theory of vindication** In order that society is able to function securely, crime must be punished so that the law is respected.

Prison *(see Units 49 and 50)*

Prison is still central to our system of dealing with offenders. Historically, prison has functioned in three ways:

- **Custodially** To hold prisoners awaiting trial.

- **Coercively** To secure repayment of a debt.

- **Penally** As a punishment.

Launching your learning

Find out what the following words and phrases mean:
Retribution, reform, diminished responsibility, custodial, coercive, penal, deterrent, probation, community service.

CITIZENSHIP CHALLENGE

A Some people argue that victims should have more say in the sentencing of criminals. If the criminal is hurt as much as he has hurt his victim – 'an eye for an eye' – is this justice?

B Can very harsh punishments rehabilitate a criminal?

C Can education, training and counselling, act as **deterrents**?

D Did you know that prison costs more than **probation** which costs more than **community service**? Why is this so do you think?

E If we cannot cure criminals, should we lock them away forever?

F How important is it to treat criminals fairly? Is the policy in some American states of 'three strikes and you are out' – life sentences after a third offence, however trivial – fair?

G Some criminal behaviour begins very young, particularly in sectors of society where it is tolerated, or even a source of status. 80 per cent of prisoners are men under 30, who have few qualifications with little if any stable family background or upbringing. Nearly half have spent some time in care. Their crimes are very often associated with drink, drugs or cars. Discuss.

H If criminals are made by their environment and have had little or no choice, should this alter the way we treat them?

48 Social harmony: CRIME AND PUNISHMENT 3

Hindu justice

Dharma – a definition

The proper name for the Hindu faith is *Sanatana Dharma*, which can be translated as the 'Eternal Religion' or as the 'Universal Moral Law'. **Dharma** is a central idea in Hinduism, but 'dharma' is difficult to translate into one English word; it means all of these things: religion, justice, moral law, duty, right, the natural order of things.

Dharma, in the sense of moral duty or responsibility, is the core of Hindu moral law. Dharma is universal and therefore applicable to all people, but an individual's **responsibilities** will vary according to age, gender, social position, education and occupation. The duties of the different classes of society differ, but there is a general code of behaviour, called **sadharana dharma**, applicable to all Hindus, regardless of their social status. This code stresses the importance of truth, non-violence, honesty and respect for all living beings.

There are three forms of moral duty: to the outside world, to the family and to the self. Carrying out these various duties involves actions. Actions result in **karma**.

Karma – a definition

Karma, the law of action and reaction, determines the future life of a Hindu; thus a good life will create good karma and a happy future life, while a sinful life will create bad karma and result in an unhappy life to come.

Indian law

In ancient India, kings and judges were guided by the law books and other Hindu scriptures, which set out the rules of behaviour for all classes and gave guidelines for punishment and correction for different crimes.

They say that rulers have a duty to protect their subjects and punish offenders so that the population could carry out its lawful business without fear of crime. Rulers controlled criminal behaviour by punishments, including the death penalty. Punishment had three components: **retribution**, **restraint** and **reformation**.

In India, the law as it is understood in the West cannot be separated from the wider context of dharma. Hindus see crime as a sin. It is an act against dharma and the natural order of creation.

However, Hindus believe that the rules of moral conduct laid down in the law books are subject to change over time, as society itself changes over the centuries. Hindus consider that in the present age, called **Kali Yuga** or the **Dark Age**, the ancient rules of morality are no longer valid or useful. Thus the ancient rules of the law books have slowly been modified to meet changing circumstances. When India was a part of the British Empire, the British imposed their own laws on the country, but also made use of the ancient law books in settling many of the civil disputes which were brought before them. Today, Indian law, which affects all Indians whatever their religion, is based on English Common Law, as well as the Indian Penal Code of 1896, revised in 1961.

Islamic justice

The shari'ah: a definition

Although the Qur'an stresses forgiveness and reconciliation, the actual penal code of Islam, the **shari'ah**, is based on the doctrine of **retaliation**.

The punishment for murder is beheading; for theft, amputation of the right hand; for adultery and blasphemy, stoning to death; for drunkenness, flogging.

▲ The shari'ah is based on retaliation

These punishments have to be seen in the context of the society in which the Prophet Muhammad (pbuh) lived. His was a tribal society and one in which disputes over adultery, murder or the theft of a camel could end in a bloody feud which could last for generations.

Some of these punishments seem very harsh to us today, but we should remember that they were set down in the seventh century, when human rights were unheard of. Also there were no prisons in the Arabian desert and so wrongs had to be punished either by a fine or by corporal punishment of some kind.

In creating the Islamic state, the Prophet Muhammad (pbuh) abolished the **blood-feud** and replaced it with the principle of **retaliation** against the guilty parties; it was thought to be better to mete out swift and severe punishment for a crime than to allow rival tribes to exact revenge on each other in an endless cycle.

When the European empires took over large parts of the Islamic world, they imposed European-style systems of criminal law, and the traditional forms of Islamic justice only survived on the Arabian Peninsula. Since the end of the colonial period, a number of Islamic countries, such as Iran, Pakistan and the Sudan, have returned to the traditional Islamic punishments.

'An eye for an eye'

Muslims believe that God first sent down the Tenakh to the Jews, which contained 'guidance and light' in the form of clear teachings on justice:

> 'A life for a life, an eye for an eye, a nose for a nose, an ear for an ear, a tooth for a tooth, and for wounds retaliation.'

> Qur'an, Surah 5: 49

Later, God sent down Jesus, who confirmed the Tenakh, but also brought the Gospel, 'wherein is guidance and light, and confirming the Tenakh before it.'

The Law of Love

The Gospel of Jesus is the **Law of Love**; Jesus taught his followers forgiveness and mercy, and to see God in every man and woman, however humble. Islam thus teaches both the Law of Retaliation of the Tenakh and the Law of Love of the New Testament.

Justice must be done, as the law of nature cannot be violated, but mercy is better than revenge, and forgiveness is better than retaliation:

> 'The reward for an injury is an equal injury back; but if a person forgives instead, and is reconciled, that will earn reward from Allah.'

> Qur'an, Surah 42: 40

Launching your learning

Write notes on either Hindu or Muslim views on punishment using some of the following: **Dharma, sadharana dharma, karma, shari'ah, retribution, restraint, reformation, Kali Yuga, blood-feud, retaliation, Law of Love.**

49 Social harmony: PRISONS 1

'Keep in mind those who are in prison as though you were in prison with them.'

Hebrews 13: 3

The Prison Reform Trust

The Prison Reform Trust (see Addresses/ websites) is an organization that works to create a just, humane and effective penal system. In this unit we will explore why in 2001 it described British prisons as 'the most shaming of all our public institutions'.

The hard facts

- Half of all prisons in England and Wales are overcrowded.

- On average, one prisoner commits suicide every five days.

- People who should be cared for by the mental health system wrongly end up in prison. Up to one-third of prisoners have some identifiable psychiatric disorder.

- Many prisoners have time on their hands. There is insufficient work and education and not enough is done to stop them returning to crime.

- Only one in three prisoners is in prison because of an offence involving violence, sex or drugs. Many of the remainder have committed only minor property offences. The attitudes of minor offenders may harden as they mix with those convicted of more serious crimes. This often leads to minor offenders committing more serious crimes after they are released from prison. Many inmates come out fitter and more skilled criminals. **Recidivism** – relapsing into crime – is common amongst ex-prisoners.

- Every prisoner costs about £25,000 a year to keep in custody. A night in a police cell costs more than a night in London's Dorchester Hotel. The cost of locking people in prison is a tremendous burden on society. For instance, millions of working days every year are lost by men in prison and families are broken up through the imprisonment of men and women.

- Prison is ineffective at reducing crime. Half of all prisoners and nearly two-thirds of young prisoners re-offend within two years.

- Seven out of ten young offenders (sixteen to twenty-one-year olds) have reading ages of a seven-year-old or below.

- One-fifth of all prisoners have not been convicted of any offence. Remand prisoners, who have not been found guilty of any crime, suffer the worst conditions.

- Although only five-and-a-half per cent of the population is from an ethnic minority, they account for over twenty per cent of prisoners. Racism is rife in prisons. Racist murders have recently occurred where young Asian men have been made to share cells with prisoners known to hold extreme racist views.

- There is a small number of people who present such a danger to other people or to themselves that they need to be detained. However, for most offences, imprisonment is not an effective penalty. Many countries which have very high prison populations have very high crime rates.

Prisoners and rights

The **Human Rights Act** confirms that human rights do not stop at the prison gate.

Prisoners remain members of society and are legally entitled to the protection of their fundamental rights. Many of the Prison Service's policies and practices are in danger of breaching the Human Rights Act, and the Prison Service is likely to be challenged under almost every Article of the Human Rights Act. Probable challenges include:

- **Article 2 – The right to life.** The Prison Service will have an obligation to prevent suicide and the transmission of diseases. Prisoners should have access to condoms to prevent the spread of HIV/AIDS.

- **Article 3 – Freedom from torture, inhuman or degrading treatment or punishment.** Courts will have to decide if prison overcrowding is inhuman or degrading.

- **Article 5 – The right to liberty.** This may be used by life sentence prisoners seeking regular reviews of their detention.

- **Article 8 – The right to private and family life, home and correspondence.** Prisoners held a long way from their homes might argue that this disrupts family life. At present, 25,000 prisoners are held over 50 miles from their homes, 11,000 of whom are held over one hundred miles away.

- **Article 9 – The right to freedom of thought, conscience and religion.** The Prison Service may have to improve facilities for religions other than the Church of England or Roman Catholic – particularly Hindus, Sikhs and Muslims. For example, Rastafarianism may have to be recognized as a legitimate religion.

- **Article 10 – Freedom of expression.** Prisoners may challenge restrictions on the use of computers and the Internet. Prisoners may also argue that they should have access to the media and the right to write articles.

- **Article 11 – Freedom of association.** This may lead to prisoners forming a trade union.

- **Article 14 – Freedom from discrimination.** This will impact upon race relations issues, the treatment of disabled prisoners and equal treatment of men and women in prison.

- **Protocol 1, Article 3 – Free elections.** Sentenced prisoners are disqualified from voting for the duration of their imprisonment. The Government may find it difficult to justify the ban, which is neither a deterrent nor an effective punishment.

FOR DISCUSSION

A Is prison always the most appropriate punishment? Could community penalties work better?

B Most prisoners do not remain in prison forever. Only a tiny handful will never be released. Those who are released can be 'damaged' and disillusioned by their time in prison. What effect might this have on their attempts to return to 'normal' life?

C Why do you think the UK imprisons more people than in other European states? Are they more law-abiding than us?

D Do you think that prisons protect society in the long term?

E Home Office statistics show that about half of released prisoners were convicted again for crimes within two years. Does this mean that prisons do not work?

F Can a long prison sentence – removing the prisoner from family and society – prepare someone to become a useful member of society?

50 Social harmony: *PRISONS 2*

'No one shall be subjected to torture or to cruel, inhuman or degrading treatment or punishment.'

Article 5 of the United Nations Declaration on Human Rights

Prisons worldwide

Most countries fail to meet their international human rights obligations when it comes to their prison systems. Worldwide there are 8.6 million people in prison. The USA accounts for a quarter of these. Many prisons are overcrowded, dilapidated, filthy and cruel places where corporal punishment, torture and sexual abuse are commonplace. Many prisoners are innocent. Some are prisoners of conscience (see Unit 54).

▲ Prisoners have a right to be treated humanely

In extremely overcrowded and unhealthy conditions, diseases, such as tuberculosis and dysentery, spread very rapidly and without medical treatment can be fatal.

In many countries prisoners are held awaiting trial for many years – often longer than the maximum sentence for the charge faced.

Alternatives

Most countries spend large amounts of money on locking people up. A lot of this money could be better spent in other ways:

- introducing penalties, such as community service, for less serious offenders

- targeting scarce resources towards speeding up trial processes, so reducing numbers of pre-trial prisoners

- treating prisoners more humanely without vast expense or risk to security

- tackling poverty – the main cause of crime.

TALKING POINT

'If prison worked we would be shutting prisons not opening more.'

Chief Inspector of British Prisons

Prison reform

Many organizations are working towards trying to reform the criminal justice system so that more offenders repay society through community service, compensation and probation. See Addresses/websites.

- **RAP (Radical Alternatives to Prison)** – an organization that believes that prisons do more harm than good.

- **The Prison Reform Trust** (see Unit 49), works to create a just, humane and effective penal system.

- **Howard League for Penal Reform** – puts pressure on the Government to make prisons more humane places.

- **PROP (Preservation of the Rights of Prisoners)** – organization of prisoners and ex-prisoners trying to improve their rights.

- **The Prison Phoenix Trust** – The Prison Phoenix Trust, based in Oxford, helps prisoners and young offenders to see that being shut up in their cells for long periods gives them a unique opportunity for change. The cell is no longer seen as a prison, but as a place of spiritual retreat. The Trust introduces prisoners and young offenders to **yoga** as a means to exercise and bringing control to tense bodies, often misused through drugs and other forms of self-abuse. It then teaches **meditation**, directing the prisoner towards a silent mind.

  The Trust believes that there is a spiritual being inside everyone, no matter how 'hard', fearful, dangerous or lost a person is, and whatever their faith or lack of it. The Trust is in regular contact with 2,000 inmates in prisons and young offender units around Britain, and corresponds with over 5,000 prisoners. Many prison chaplains support the aims of the Trust, finding that its work supports their own work, counselling and helping prisoners.

  The Director of the Trust is Sister Elaine MacInnes, a Catholic nun. While working as a missionary in Japan she began to practise Zen meditation. After seventeen years of study she became a Zen master.

She was then sent to the Philippines for twenty years, where, as well as helping the poor, she taught meditation, at their request, to prisoners who had been badly tortured. Sister Elaine found that her own faith as a Catholic nun deepened when she studied and practised Zen Buddhism.

One prisoner had this to say about his experiences:

'If I could say just a few words to prison inmates I would say, "Surrender". You do not have to be an informer or kiss ass with prison officials. Just let go of the past and escape from the real prison, yourself. My prison door was always open but I didn't know it. Every day I practise letting go of the mind stream. It is a fiction, that mind stream. When you sit quietly and let go you will find the Pearl of Great Price of Jesus; the Buddha nature … or wherever you want to go. I wouldn't tell you if it weren't so. I have nothing to gain; no axe to grind. I only know I was in prison. I was in an impossible life situation with no hope. And it was through meditation that the prison doors opened me to a new unknown freedom.'

Launching your learning

A After reading the units on prison, write an article of at least 200 words entitled 'Prisons in Crisis'.

B Look at the five aims of punishment in Unit 47. Write down how far you think prisons go in meeting these aims.

C Considering that prisons are expensive places to run and that the crime rate is rising, how do you think society should deal with offenders?

D Contact one of the above organizations to find out about their work (see Addresses/websites).

51 Social harmony: THE DEATH PENALTY

Capital punishment – a definition

The word 'capital' in 'capital punishment' refers to a person's head because in the past people were often executed by the severing of the head from the body.

Capital punishment today

Although over half the countries in the world have now abolished the death penalty, it is still practised in 90 countries. During the last decade of the twentieth century, 547 prisoners were executed in the US, and another 3,500 are today waiting on death row. Many Muslim regimes practise the death penalty; for example in Iran there are public hangings and in Saudi Arabia there were 113 public beheadings in 2000.

The death penalty was last used in Britain in 1964 and was finally abolished in 1973. However, today there are some people who would like to see it reinstated for crimes like child murder or murderous acts of terrorism.

Abolitionists

People who wish to abolish the death penalty are called abolitionists. They argue that the death penalty increases people's tolerance of and tendency toward violence.

Defenders

Defenders of the death penalty argue that because taking an offender's life is a more severe punishment than any **prison term**, it must be a better **deterrent**. Without capital punishment there is no adequate deterrent for those already serving a life term who commit murder while in prison.

Moral considerations

The classic moral arguments in favour of the death penalty have been Biblical and **retributive**:

> 'Whosoever sheds man's blood, by man shall his blood be shed.'
>
> Genesis 9: 6

'Let the punishment fit the crime' is the secular equivalent. Both ideas imply that the murderer deserves to die. Defenders of capital punishment claim that society has the right to kill in defence of its members, just as the individual may kill in self-defence. However this is a weak argument as long as the effectiveness of the death penalty as a deterrent to violent crimes has not been proved.

Critics of the death penalty have always pointed to the risk of executing the innocent. The finality of the death penalty demands the perfect judgement of the people involved in the legal system. However human beings make mistakes and innocent people have been executed.

Deterrence

The **Deterrence Theory** is that any would-be murderer is less likely to kill if they know they will be punished by death. On the surface the argument makes sense – a fear of death or the possibility of death affects the behaviour of most reasonable people. People who murder, however, are rarely rational at the time they commit the crime. The threat of execution at some future date does not enter the minds of killers acting under the influence of drugs and/or alcohol, in the grip of fear, rage, or jealousy, or panicking while committing another crime.

Does capital punishment work?

The US, which is one of the few democracies to retain capital punishment (see Unit 52), has one of the highest murder rates in the world: one per 1,000 of the population. In Britain it is one per 100,000.

Therapeutic vengeance

Increasingly the argument of *therapeutic vengeance* is being voiced – the right of the victim's loved ones to gain peace of mind through the killer's death. Opponents view this kind of personal revenge as essentially barbaric, arguing that the mark of a civilized society is the ability to maintain a system of justice based on laws not emotions.

Seven methods of execution

1   **Hanging:** the neck is broken and death comes quickly unless the free-fall distance is inadequate when the prisoner ends up slowly being strangled to death. If it is too great, the rope will tear the prisoner's head off.

2   **Electric chair:** nobody knows how quickly a person dies from the electric shock, but cases have been reported where prisoners apparently suffered for four to ten minutes before dying.

3   **Firing squad:** the prisoner is shot through the heart by multiple marksmen. Death appears to be quick, assuming the killers do not miss.

4   **Lethal injection:** lethal drugs are injected into the prisoner who is strapped to a table. If carried out properly the prisoner fades quickly into unconsciousness. If the dosage of drugs is too low, the person may linger for many minutes, experiencing paralysis.

5   **Beheading/guillotine:** a famous French invention severing the neck. Death comes quickly.

6   **Stoning:** the prisoner is pelted with rocks until they eventually die.

7   **Crucifixion:** Jesus was brutally put to death by crucifixion, a Roman form of capital punishment, also used by the Japanese during World War II and the Chinese in Tibet (see Unit 92).

Compassion

Jesus consistently taught **compassion** and **forgiveness**. When an adulteress was about to be stoned to death, he said:

> 'He who is without sin among you, let him throw a stone at her first.'

John 8: 7

FOR DISCUSSION

A   Do you think that the death penalty is an effective deterrent to violent crime?

B   Has society the right to kill in defence of its members just as the individual may kill in self-defence?

C   What does 'retribution' mean?

D   What is 'therapeutic vengeance'? Why do many people disagree with this idea?

E   'Whosoever sheds man's blood, by man shall his blood be shed.'

F   'He who is without sin among you, let him throw a stone at her first.'

52 Rights: *HUMAN RIGHTS 1*

In December 1948 the United Nations produced its **Universal Declaration of Human Rights** (see Addresses/websites).

- All human beings are born free and equal.

- Everyone has the right to life, liberty and freedom from fear and violence.

- Everyone has the right to protection of the law without discrimination.

- No one shall be subjected to arbitrary arrest, detention or exile.

- Everyone has the right to a fair and public trial.

- Everyone charged with a penal offence has the right to be assumed innocent until proven guilty.

- No one shall be subjected to arbitrary interference with his privacy, family, home or correspondence, nor to attacks on his reputation.

- Everyone has the right to freedom of movement within his own country and abroad.

- Everyone has the right to a nationality.

- Adults have the right to marry and found a family regardless of race or religion.

- Both men and women are entitled to equal rights within marriage and in divorce.

- Everyone has the right to own property. No-one should be arbitrarily deprived of his property.

- Everyone has the right to freedom of thought, conscience and religion and the right to express their opinion both privately and publicly.

- Everyone has the right to attend meetings and join associations.

- No one should be forced to join an association.

- Everyone has the right to take part in the government of his or her country.

- Everyone has the right to work and to just and favourable conditions of employment.

- Everyone has the right to equal pay for equal work.

- Everyone has the right to fair pay to enable him and his family to live with self-respect.

- Everyone has the right to join a trade union.

- Everyone has the right to rest and leisure, including reasonable working hours and holidays with pay.

- Everyone has the right to a standard of living adequate for their health and well-being, including housing, medical care and social security in the event of unemployment, sickness, widowhood and old age.

- Everyone has the right to an education.

- Everyone has the right to enjoy the cultural life of the community and to share in its scientific advancements and benefits.

- Everyone has duties to the community to ensure the full recognition and respect for the rights and freedoms of others.

Human rights are the basic guarantees for every human being to be able to achieve happiness and self-respect. It has been over 50 years since the Universal Declaration on Human Rights, yet abuses continue to grow.

Human rights in the United States

The US is the most powerful nation in the world and its policies affect everyone. During the American election in 2001 a Ugandan citizen commented that it was unfair that he did not have the right to vote in the US elections because the US influences his country more than his own government!

The United States claims to be the beacon for the promotion of human rights around the world. If this is the case it is only fair that it must be subjected to detailed analysis and criticism itself, especially if all other nations are to follow its example.

However all is not as it seems and **Amnesty International** (see Addresses/websites) has called for the US to have a greater respect for human rights.

In May 2001, the US lost its seat on the **United Nations Human Rights Commission** for the first time since the panel's founding in 1947. The Human Rights Commission investigates abuses around the world.

The US was voted off because of their 'go-alone' stances on many international human rights issues, such as: not supporting the international criminal court; not supporting the International Landmine Treaty; its stance on the death penalty; not paying its dues at the UN (see Unit 54); and backing down from the Kyoto Accord on the environment (see Unit 76).

Admittedly the US has been more vocal than many nations on some human rights issues, but when it has come to substantial changes to promote and support human rights, the US has often acted purely out of its own self-interests.

The death penalty

Amnesty International campaigns for the abolition of the death penalty. In 2001 it condemned the use of the death penalty (see Unit 51) in the US:

'The US is engaged in a cruel, brutalizing, unreliable, unnecessary and hugely expensive activity for no measurable gain. There is no evidence that the US authorities have prevented a single crime with this policy. They have diverted countless millions of dollars away from more constructive efforts to fight crime. The death penalty is a symptom of a culture of violence, not a solution to it. The sooner US politicians begin to find the political courage to educate public opinion rather than hide behind it, the better.'

CITIZENSHIP CHALLENGE

Choose any three articles from the Universal Declaration on Human Rights and, using this textbook, try and give examples of where and how these rights are being broken.

53 Rights: HUMAN RIGHTS 2

▲ Religions teach respect for all humanity

Respect and religion

Over 2,500 years ago **sacred texts** like the Hindu *Vedas* and *Upanishads* and the Judaic *Torah* emphasized the importance of equality and responsibility to help others. These same principles are found in the Buddhist *Tripitaka* and in the Confucianist *Analects, Doctrine of the Mean* and *Great Learning*; and again **2,000 years ago** in the Christian New Testament; and again 600 years later in the Holy Qur'an; and 500 years ago in the Sikh Guru Granth Sahib.

Religion has been a powerful force through the ages reaffirming the dignity of the individual and of social justice. Religious leaders and institutions have often brought about reconciliation and healing within communities where there is tension. Despite this, however, acts of religious intolerance and discrimination based on religion or belief are common. Many acts of violence have been committed in the name of religion.

World Peace Summit

At the Millennium World Peace Summit of Religious and Spiritual Leaders in August 2000, religious leaders from around the world committed to work together for world peace. Leaders pledged to use their capacity to exercise moral authority to influence reconciliation and to accept diversity. They signed a **Commitment to Global Peace**, which recognizes that every religious tradition teaches that one must treat one's neighbour as one's self, regardless of racial, religious, ethnic, national, economic, age and gender differences.

Torture

In Western Europe we have a fair idea that if we are arrested, we will not be tortured, we will not be imprisoned without a trial, we will not be murdered. But this is not the case in some parts of the world.

According to the United Nations, more and more countries are torturing prisoners despite a commitment by 105 governments to outlaw one of the world's cruellest and terrifying forms of human rights violations. Torture has become an instrument of power used 'to break, terrify and devastate people', said the UN High Commissioner for Human Rights, 'and it does not spare either women or children'.

Children's rights

- Children make up over half of the world's refugees.

- Physical abuse, sexual violence, sexual abuse and trafficking are the norms in many impoverished places.

- Millions of abandoned children, orphans, victims of war, of AIDS, of filthy drinking water or no sanitation, struggle to survive without adequate care. Millions lack access to education, or have to endure substandard education.

Child soldiers

- Children as young as ten are recruited as child soldiers and put in the most life-threatening situations because they are 'expendable'.

- The easily available small arms make it easier for children to use weapons.

- These children are often severely **traumatized** after a conflict has ended.

- During the last decade, it is estimated that child victims have included:

  - Two million killed

  - Four to five million disabled

  - Twelve million left homeless

  - Some ten million psychologically traumatized.

▲ Millions of children are traumatized by war

Street children

There are almost 100 million 'street children' in the world. Most of the children have contact with their families who depend on them to supplement their income.

In countries like Brazil, Columbia, Guatemala and Venezuela, children are being murdered in an effort to 'clean' the streets. In Brazil some eleven-and-a-half million children live in poverty and are the targets of night 'death squads' who 'clean' the streets.

In recent investigations, a number of off duty police have been found to be involved in these death squads.

Child slavery

Child labour affects over 250 million children. However, it is not an easy problem to solve: while it seems noble to immediately withdraw investments and cooperation with firms and factories that employ child labour it may do more harm than good. Many of these children are from very poor families and work to pay for their family and/or their education.

CITIZENSHIP CHALLENGE

Find out more about children's rights by contacting the following organizations:

- Save the Children Fund UK.

- The International Coalition to Stop the use of Child Soldiers website (see Addresses/websites). They have databases on country by country, information on child soldiers and extensive reports on a number of issues.

- UNICEF – the United Nations Children's Fund have a vast amount of information available online, including the **Convention on the Rights of the Child**.

- Amnesty International.

FOR DISCUSSION

'To guarantee the human rights of children is to invest in the future.'

Amnesty International

54 Rights: HUMAN RIGHTS 3

'Everyone has the right to freedom of thought, conscience and religion and the right to express their opinion both privately and publicly.'

United Nations Declaration of Human Rights

CITIZENSHIP CHALLENGE

The British government declares itself committed to restoring a vibrant, civil society. The human rights group **Liberty** (see Addresses/websites) is concerned that New Labour has **disempowered** ordinary people, while officials have even more power to increase surveillance, intrude into people's privacy, detain people without trial, increase state secrecy and suppress **dissent**. For example, information from a wide range of sources (The Office for National Statistics, the National Health Service, the Inland Revenue, the Benefits Agency, school reports) can now be collated into a file on a citizen without a court order showing cause why.

Habéus Corpus has been abolished in the Anti-Terror Bill. People may now be locked up without trial. If tried, the court proceedings may be in secret. European ministers have agreed on a definition of terrorism. It includes people 'who hoped to seriously alter the political, economic or social structure of the EU'. This will include marxists, hunt saboteurs, peace campaigners, GM crop activists, anti-road protestors and Carnivalists against Capitalism.

Write an article for a teenage magazine illustrating how the government is stealing our freedom.

Freedom fighters or terrorists?

Between 1945 and 2000 an estimated fifteen million people were killed in Africa and South America in the struggle to be free of colonial and minority rule. These people are often called '**freedom fighters**'.

Nelson Mandela was a freedom fighter. He belonged to the ANC (African National Congress Party) and was involved in the struggle to bring democracy to South Africa, a country under minority rule. The ANC was declared 'a **terrorist** organization' by the American and British governments in the 1970s. Today Nelson Mandela is respected around the world and the ANC is the democratically elected party in South Africa. Freedom fighter or terrorist?

The dissident – a definition

A dissident is a person who openly and strongly disagrees with a political system that in his or her view ignores human rights. The word 'dissident' comes from the word 'dissent' meaning 'to disagree'.

The revolutionary – a definition

A revolutionary is a person who tries to bring about complete change in a society or system that is, in his or her opinion, corrupt and unjust.

Prisoners of conscience – a definition

Prisoners of conscience are people imprisoned because of their political, religious or other conscientiously-held beliefs, and who have not used or encouraged violence.

The detention of any prisoner of conscience violates the Universal Declaration of Human Rights (see Unit 52). In many countries people are thrown into prison for trying to exercise their basic human rights. Some are imprisoned because they or their families are involved in political or religious activities; or because of participation in strikes or demonstrations, or because of their connection with political parties or national minority movements that oppose government policies. Often people are imprisoned simply because they disagreed or questioned their government or tried to publicize injustice in their own countries.

Amnesty International

Founded in 1961 by a British lawyer called Peter Benenson, Amnesty International (see Addresses/websites) is the world's largest voluntary body working for human rights today. It has over one million members in 150 countries. Amnesty International is independent of any government, political faction, ideology, economic interest or religious creed. Amnesty aims to:

■ seek the release of all prisoners of conscience

■ obtain a fair and prompt trial for all political prisoners detained without charge or trial

■ abolish torture and the death penalty in all cases.

The United Nations

On 24 October 1945, 51 nations formed the United Nations, an association of states working together for international peace, security and cooperation. The UN aims to:

■ develop friendly relations among nations

■ cooperate internationally in solving economic, social, cultural and humanitarian problems, and in promoting human rights and fundamental freedoms

■ make nations think 'globally' not nationally

■ secure a world of peace and progress

■ promote social progress for all the nations of the world.

The UN has many political issues and problems to contend with. But, despite this, it is also performing some crucial tasks around the world. Unfortunately though, it is not perfect and is often negatively affected by the self-interests of powerful nations such as the US (see Unit 52).

▶ The UN aims at world peace and security

TALKING POINT

'In Germany, the Nazis first came for the Communists and I did not speak up, because I was not a Communist. Then they came for the Jews and I did not speak up, because I was not a Jew. Then they came for the trade unionists and I did not speak up, because I was not a trade unionist. Then they came for the Catholics and I did not speak up, because I was not a Catholic. Then they came for me ... and by that time, there was no one to speak up for anyone.'

Martin Niemöller, pastor, German Evangelical (Lutheran) Church

'Terrorists' or 'freedom fighters'?

The terrorist – a definition

A terrorist is someone prepared to use force – or threaten to use force – to bring about a change to what they believe to be an unjust system. Terrorists can use politics, propaganda, and/or violence to achieve their goals. Like generals in war they can use violence as a means to an end. Terrorism is primarily the weapon of the politically weak or frustrated, those who are, or who believe themselves to be, unable to exert their grievances through conventional political or military means.

The objectives of terrorist groups are self-advertisement – to show the world that the group exists and is ruthless in its determination to achieve its ends and demoralize governments; and to provoke governments into such savage acts of suppression that they lose public support, thereby awakening public and international sympathy for the revolutionary cause. Terrorism then, achieves its goals not through its acts, but through the response to its acts.

Unlike war, terrorism has no boundaries and no obvious beginnings and endings. Terrorist targets include cities, international airports, major international events, military establishments, financial centres, holiday resorts and high-profile landmarks.

While the issues behind terrorism are usually national or regional, the impact of terrorist campaigns is often international. Advances in global communications have given some small groups international standing. Terrorists in one country frequently use other countries as 'safe havens' or for fund-raising and training.

State sponsored terrorism – a definition

The FBI defines terrorism as 'the *unlawful* use of force or violence against persons or property to intimidate or coerce a government or the civilian population, in furtherance of political or social objectives'. This definition, however, ignores the other form of terrorism – 'state-sponsored terrorism' – equally unlawful and equally murderous, but with state approval.

Since 1946 the American government has been running a terrorist training camp at 'the School of the Americas' in Georgia, US (it changed its name to *Whise* in 2000 after its activities were brought to public attention).

Among its 60,000 graduates are some of Latin American's worst torturers, mass murderers, dictators and state terrorists. In 2001 Guatemalan Bishop Juan Gerardi was brutally murdered for protesting against the destruction of 448 Mayan Indian villages and the massacre of tens of thousands of Mayan people by government forces. The man who murdered him and many of the government officials who ordered the destruction of the Mayan Indian villages had been trained in 'the School of the Americas'.

▲ If the rich world supported human rights and international justice, 'terrorists' would have no reason to operate

Government ministers too, in Guatemala, El Salvador, Chile, Argentina, Peru, Honduras, Colombia and Panama have trained in 'the School of the Americas'/Whise. 'Top tips' in the training involve blackmail, torture, execution, the intimidation of witnesses' relatives and the arrest of ordinary men and women struggling for their rights: teachers, labour leaders, cooperative leaders, priests, nuns, church leaders.

KEY QUESTION

Is the US and Britain opposed to terrorism in general or specifically to terrorism that threatens their own political and economic interests?

The real war on terrorism

The rich world fears that democracy for the impoverished world could lead to the loss of cheap labour and natural wealth for the rich developed countries (see Unit 63). Western governments and their 'intelligence agencies' have been, and are still in, the business of **destabilizing** some undeveloped countries. The poor remain poor as their wealth is siphoned to the rich world.

Terrorism feeds off such injustice and greed. If the rich world, particularly the US, Israel and the Gulf States, supported democracy, disarmament, justice, human rights and economic development, terrorists would have no sound reasons to operate.

FOR DISCUSSION

A By simply addressing the security aspects of terrorism at airports and other possible targets, governments merely confront the *symptoms* of terrorism rather than its *causes*.

B World leaders have not always actively encouraged the development of democracy, human rights and economic justice across the world. In a fair and just world there would be less potential terrorist recruits.

C One country's terrorist is another's freedom fighter.

D However illegitimate terrorism itself is, the concerns that spawn violence often have a reasonable basis.

E Terrorism feeds off injustice.

F Nothing can excuse or justify an act of terrorism, whether it is committed by religious fundamentalists or dressed up as a war of retribution by a recognized government.

Arundhati Roy, Indian writer

G British human rights lawyers are worried about the British government's Anti-Terror Bill in 2001, which abolished **habéus corpus**: the right to demand a written order as a protection against unlimited imprisonment without charges (see Unit 54).

Discrimination on grounds of gender

Although a number of countries have adopted International Human Rights treaties and have laws banning discrimination on grounds of gender, women are still treated as second-class citizens all over the world.

- At the beginning of this century women made up two-thirds of the world's one billion illiterate population.

- Today, 50 per cent more women are living in poverty than 30 years ago. This is tragic since the well-being of children depends more on the income available to mothers than to fathers.

- Women and girls make up half the world's population yet they do two-thirds of the world's work.

- Women earn one-tenth of the world's income yet own less than one hundredth of the world's property.

- Women are often excluded from making decisions that affect the way society is organized or even decisions over their own bodies.

- Discriminatory laws and practices, often in the name of religion, tradition or culture, preserve the idea that women are inferior to men and do not deserve equal rights or equal protection. In some societies women are still seen as the property of their husbands or fathers. In Bangladesh, women who want to be free to choose when and whom to marry or are involved in dowry disputes have had acid thrown in their face.

- Half a million women die in childbirth every year – leaving millions of motherless children.

- Women in many parts of the world suffer sexual abuse at the hands of the very authorities whose duty is to protect them. These violations often go unreported.

Migrant workers

Poverty forces hundreds of thousands of young girls to migrate from their countries seeking work often as domestic workers without government protection from abusive employers. Many end up as sex slaves.

In Saudi Arabia, one of the major destinations of migrant women employed as domestic workers, harsh Islamic law restricts their freedom of movement.

Female genital mutilation

In some parts of the world there are also socially acceptable forms of violence. The **World Health Organization** (see Addresses/websites) estimates that 90 million girls have been subjected to genital mutilation, usually performed without anaesthetic, on girls and babies aged between seven days and fifteen years old.

Female genital mutilation is practised in parts of Asia and the Middle East and in more than 25 African countries, in both Islamic and Christian societies – though neither the Qur'an nor the Bible mentions it.

The operation is forced on approximately 6,000 girls per day, worldwide. Around 10,000 children from minority groups in Britain are also at risk. It was, and remains, a cultural, not a religious practice.

The mutilation of female genitals can take a number of forms. The least dangerous involves the cutting of the hood of the clitoris. In its worst form – *infibulation* – the circumciser scrapes away the entire genital area, removing the girl's clitoris and the inner and outer labia. The vaginal opening, save for a small hole, is then sewn up with catgut. Many girls die from excessive blood-loss, tetanus, septicaemia and bladder or kidney infection.

The description of children being mutilated – the panic and shock from extreme pain, biting through the tongue, convulsion and death – indicate a practice comparable to torture.

In some cultures the practice is not seen as cruelty, but considered a necessary operation to make a girl 'more attractive for marriage'. Intercourse brings no pleasure – only pain. On her wedding night an infibulated girl must be 'cut open' to allow intercourse. Organizations like **Womankind Worldwide** (see Addresses/websites) campaign to rid the world of the evil of sexual control.

Refugees and rape

Refugees often have to care for the very young and the sick and elderly in unfamiliar and dangerous surroundings. At the same time they are extremely vulnerable to rape.

In West Timor, Indonesia, there were reports of widespread rape of refugees fleeing the violence in neighbouring East Timor in 1999. Thousands of women were abducted from refugee camps and forced to work as prostitutes or regularly taken from camps and raped.

Reproductive rights

Without fair sexual and reproductive rights, women can never achieve equality with men. The World Health Organization states that:

> 'Reproductive health implies that people are able to have a responsible, satisfying, and safe sex life, and that they have the capability to reproduce, and the freedom to decide if, when and how often to do so.'

Human rights defenders

Education paved the way towards gender equality in Europe. Women around the world today are at the front line of the struggle not only for their own rights but also for those of their communities. In the midst of these struggles, many of women's human rights defenders are at risk of becoming victims of human rights abuses themselves.

FOR DISCUSSION

Only by educating men about the rights of women can the rights of women be realized.

Violence can be self-inflicted when girls absorb and turn inward the hatred of women that they experience around them.

Confidence comes from a sense of personal value, but many girls from childhood absorb a low sense of self-worth and self esteem by the culture surrounding them.

Launching your learning

Write an article for a teenage magazine on the plight of women in the world today.

Introduction

At a time when Islam is sometimes faced with hostile media coverage, particularly where the status of women is concerned, it may be quite surprising to learn that the majority of converts to Islam in Europe are women.

Women were given rights 1,400 years ago in the Qur'an. Some people argue that many women in the Muslim world are denied their rights today.

The veil – an imposition?

Some critics of women's rights in Islam argue that the wearing of the veil, compulsory in some Muslim countries, is an unnecessary imposition. However to Muslims the veil represents honour, dignity, chastity, purity and integrity. The Qur'an teaches that the fact that women belong to the female sex has no bearing on their human status or independent personality and is no basis for justification of prejudice or injustice against them. Women are recognized by Islam as full and equal partners of men in the procreation of humankind. He is the father, she is the mother, and both are essential for life. Her role is no less vital than his:

> 'O mankind! Verily We have created you from a single (pair) of a male and a female, and made you into nations and tribes that you may know each other...'
>
> Qur'an, Surah 49: 13

Equality

Muslims believe that the rights and responsibilities of a woman are equal to those of a man but they are not necessarily identical with them. Equality and sameness are two different ideas – men and women are not identical but they are created equals.

People are not created identical but they are created equals. With this distinction in mind Muslims argue that there is no room to imagine that woman is inferior to man. There is no ground to assume that a woman is less important than a man just because her rights are not identically the same as his. Had a woman's status been identical with a man's, she would have been simply a duplicate of him, which she is not. The fact that Islam gives her equal rights – but not identical – shows that it takes her into due consideration, acknowledges her, and recognizes her independent personality.

CITIZENSHIP CHALLENGE

'Equality and sameness are two quite different things.' Discuss.

Rights

Islam grants women equal rights to contract, to business, to earn, to possess independently and her property is as valuable as that of a man. If a woman commits any offence, her penalty is no less or more than a man could expect in a similar case. If she is wronged or harmed, she gets due compensations equal to what a man in her position would get.

Privileges

Women also enjoy certain privileges. They are exempt from some religious duties, for example prayers and fasting, during their periods, and from all financial liabilities. Islam places great store on the role of the mother in family life and a mother enjoys recognition and honour in the sight of God (Qur'an, Surah 31: 14–15 and 46: 15).

As a wife a woman is entitled to demand of her prospective husband a suitable dowry that will be her own. She is entitled to complete provision and total maintenance by her husband and does not have to work or share with her husband the family expenses. She is free to retain, after marriage, whatever she possessed before it, and the husband has no right whatsoever to any of her belongings.

Freedoms

Almost fourteen centuries ago, the Prophet Muhammad (pbuh) declared that women, just as men, have a right and a duty to educate themselves. This declaration has been implemented by Muslims throughout history. Women are also entitled to freedom of expression as much as men. It is reported in the Qur'an and in Islamic history that women not only expressed their opinions freely and participated fully in public life, but also engaged in serious discussions with the Prophet himself.

However, their rights are different because their roles are different. Men must support the family:

> 'Men are the protectors of women because Allah has given the one more strength ... and because they support them from their means.'
>
> Qur'an, Surah 4: 33

Women have the right to choose who they marry, to divorce, to study, to own property, to conduct business and to take part in politics.

The Prophet Muhammad (pbuh) stressed the importance of women and the respect which should be shown to them when he said:

> 'Paradise lies at the feet of your mother.'
>
> Sunan An-Nasa'i

▲ Muslim women in Pakistan marching for justice

58 Rights: POLITICS AND RELIGION 1

The kingdom of heaven on earth

> 'And God saw everything that he had made, and behold, it was very good. And there was evening and there was morning, a sixth day.'
>
> Genesis 1: 31

Artists, musicians, mystics, poets and prophets throughout the ages have had visions of a world that is 'very good' – free from conflict, violence and ignorance – a world where everyone lives together in peace, justice and solidarity.

Making vision a reality

> 'You shall not kill.'
>
> Exodus 20: 13

This Commandment is sacred to Jews, Christians and Muslims alike. Tragically, followers of these traditions sometimes kill other human beings.

Religious people, if moved by their conscience, sometimes speak out against killing and injustice. Jews, Christians, Muslims, Hindus, Buddhists and Sikhs increasingly find themselves involved in issues about right and wrong, injustice and discrimination. Sometimes however, their involvement causes controversy.

Moral issues and politics

During the 2001 British General Election the Roman Catholic Church provoked a storm of protest when it called on voters to consider withholding support from candidates who supported a woman's right to have an abortion, as well as demanding that their views on the moral issues surrounding euthanasia and embryo research be known (see Unit 15).

Women's sexual health groups reacted furiously after the launch of a document entitled 'Vote for the Common Good', which said abortion should be top of the list of questions a potential voter should ask. **The Brook Clinic** (see Addresses/websites) which provides free sexual advice for young people said it was a 'sad day' if people were being told how to vote.

Jesus and politics

In first-century Palestine the people were ruled over by the cruel and powerful Roman Empire. During Jesus' life many of his followers hoped – given the tremendous following he was attracting – that he would lead a movement to overthrow the Romans, and create a just and fair society. However, the New Testament portrays Jesus as a peaceful teacher who spoke of an inner, not outer, world.

In the Temptation Story Jesus was shown 'the kingdoms of the world' (Matthew 4: 8) and tempted by the Devil to 'turn stones into bread' (Matthew 4: 3). Jesus replied:

> 'It is written, Man shall not live by bread alone ... You shall not tempt the lord your God.'
>
> Matthew 4: 4, 7

Later when he made a very public entrance into Jerusalem (Mark 11: 1–10) – he arrived peacefully on a donkey not on a warlike white stallion.

2000 years on little has changed and millions are being oppressed by those in power. The world is no better today than when the Roman armies looted, raped and slowly and agonizingly put to death in public anyone who challenged their authority – 'freedom fighters' and 'terrorists' (see Units 54–5).

Liberation theology

Liberation theologians argue that Christians have a moral **responsibility** to take positive action to fight slavery, social injustice and the misuse of power by governments and multinationals.

Liberation theologians argue that Jesus' vision of a Kingdom of Heaven is possible in *this* life. The movement is very strong amongst priests in Latin America, Asia and Africa who are prepared to break laws which enslave and exploit innocent people. They are inspired by the life and words of Jesus who proclaimed:

> 'The Spirit of the Lord … has sent me to proclaim freedom for the prisoners and … to release the oppressed.'
>
> Luke 4: 18

Martin Luther King

Martin Luther King (1929–68) was born in Atlanta, Georgia, in the heart of the American south. From an early age he was aware that black people were not treated as equal citizens in America. Four million Africans had been torn from their homes and shipped to America to work as slaves (see Unit 35). Even though slavery had been abolished in 1869, most blacks still lived in poverty in the richest nation on earth. They earned half of white people's wages; many could not vote; they lived in ghettos and they were segregated (separated) in public places.

Martin Luther King was a Christian and a Baptist minister. He believed that the only way to achieve equality was by non-violent and peaceful forms of protest.

Not all blacks agreed with him. The Black Power movement, led by Malcolm X, believed that equality would only be achieved by force, because whites refused to listen.

In parts of America black people could only sit at the back of buses and even the old had to give up their seat if a white person asked them. Martin Luther King organized a 'bus boycott' and black people refused to use the buses until they were desegregated. This movement became known as the Civil Rights Movement and in 1960 Martin Luther King became its leader. In 1956 the US government passed a law making it illegal to segregate people on buses. Martin Luther King campaigned endlessly and organized various forms of peaceful protest. Often the police reacted violently.

Throughout his life Martin Luther King was confronted by racist violence. His home was bombed, he was stabbed and his family received death threats. But he kept to his Christian belief that violence and hatred could only be conquered by love and forgiveness. In 1964 he was awarded the Nobel Peace Prize, and, finally in 1965, equal voting rights were given to black people. In 1968 he was shot dead by a white man.

Launching your learning

In a famous sermon Dr King said:

> 'I have a dream that my four little children will one day live in a nation where they will not be judged by the colour of their skin, but by the sort of persons they are. I have a dream that one day … all God's children, black, white, Jews and Gentiles, Protestants and Catholics, will be able to join hands and sing in the words of the black people's old song, Free at last, free at last, thank God Almighty, we are free at last!'

1 Create a flow chart (with words and pictures) of Dr Martin Luther King's life.

2 Write a speech entitled 'My dream of the kingdom of Heaven on earth'.

Jerusalem

> 'I will rejoice in Jerusalem: and delight in my people; no more shall the sound of weeping be heard in it, or the cry of distress.'
>
> Isaiah 65

Jerusalem is the world's most holy city to Jews and Christians. To Muslims, Jerusalem is the third most holy city after Mecca and Medina. The most holy place in Judaism is in the Old City of Jerusalem in an area known as the Temple Mount. This area is known by Muslims as Haram al-Sharif, where the Archangel Gabriel took Muhammad to heaven, and within it are two sacred sites, the Dome of the Rock and the al-Aqsa mosque. Jerusalem also contains the Church of the Holy Sepulchre, believed by Christians to be Jesus' crucifixion and burial site.

Intifada!

As well as being of religious significance, the Temple of the Mount/Haram al-Sharif are of enormous political importance.

The current 'Intifada' – translated as 'uprising' – by the Palestinians began in 2000 when the Israeli Prime politician, Ariel Sharon, with a group of heavily armed body guards led Israeli politicians into this sacred area. This part of Jerusalem only fell under Israeli control in 1967. The United Nations has consistently demanded Israeli withdrawal. Most Israelis however believe that Jerusalem should be the undivided capital of Israel; this is unacceptable to the Palestinians.

Settlements

The Israeli government, ignoring United Nations' demands, has built settlements on Palestinian land, forcibly removing Palestinian families from their homes with bulldozers and tanks. There are currently five million Palestinians living outside Palestine as refugees. When these refugees attempted to return to their homes, Israel closed its borders and denied them entry. Jewish settlers on the other hand enjoy the full privileges and protection of the Israeli state as they claim Palestinian land for their own.

▲ Hamas, an Islamic resistance movement in Palestinian territory, has 'taken up the sword' in response to Israeli oppression

Power and prayer

Israel controls all the ports and roads in and out of Palestine and sometimes collectively punishes Palestinians by closing them. Every shipment of food and medicine must pass under Israeli supervision. Palestinians are regularly stopped and questioned by the army and police as they go about their daily lives and Palestinians require an 'occupation signed permit' to travel – even when they need to travel to pray.

Resistance!

This situation fuels much of the anger, instability and hostility in the region. America is viewed as favouring and supporting Israel. They have given over three billion dollars every year in military and economic aid to Israel. The continuing expansion of Jewish settlements in occupied lands and the status of the Dome of the Rock at the Temple Mount in Jerusalem are major flash points.

In recent years many anti-Western terrorists have come from Palestinian and Lebanese families directly harmed by the actions of the American-backed Israeli government. American calls for the rule of law and respect for human life ring hollow as her agents support governments that violate international law. After the attacks on America in 2001, Osama bin Laden, leader of the terrorist network *al-Qaida*, demanded that Israel and its American backers work for justice in Palestine and the Middle East.

Islamic resistance movements include Hezbollah and Hamas (in Arabic, an acronym for '*Harakat Al-Muqawama Al-Islamia*', meaning 'courage'). Many people who 'take up the sword' do so because they believe there is no other way to express their protest effectively. They also do so, in part, because of the concept of Jihad (see Unit 66). Other Palestinians and their supporters, who believe in the Islamic ordering of society, engage in peaceful confrontation, dialogue and in practical ways of restructuring society rather than in violence.

Afghanistan

The Soviet invasion of Afghanistan in 1979 provoked a violent armed response – a Jihad (see Unit 66). Various groups defined themselves as Islamic resistance movements (see Unit 60) and were supported, for political reasons, by the US who called them 'freedom fighters'.

After twenty years of war, one of these groups, the hard line Islamists known as the Taliban took control. The Taliban showed no respect for other 'infidel religions', and, in 2001, provoked international outrage when they destroyed a huge statue of the Buddha in Bamiyan in Afghanistan. This statue was a sacred place for Buddhists who, for hundreds of years, had paid homage there to the Emperor-turned-Buddhist-pacifist, Ashoka (circa 268 BCE). In the same year the Taliban ordered that all Hindus in Afghanistan should wear yellow badges so that they 'could be distinguished from Muslims' – triggering uneasy memories of Jews forced to wear yellow stars in Nazi Germany (see Unit 34).

FOR DISCUSSION

If you feel that nobody is listening to you and you suffer injustice and discrimination have you a right to take part in violent confrontation to correct what you believe are fundamental errors in the organization of human society?

Launching your learning

A Write a review of the above Discussion and try and relate it to some of the issues in the three units on politics and religion.

B Why is Jerusalem such an important city?

C What is the 'Intifada' and why are Islamic resistance movements protesting?

D In what ways did the Taliban put back human rights by centuries?

60 Rights: POLITICS AND RELIGION 3

The rise of Islam

The Prophet Muhammad fled the city of Mecca in 622 CE. By 630, only eight years later, he was back in Mecca as ruler. Although the Muslims began as a small group in Arabia, within a century they had created an Empire stretching from Spain to India; leading the world in medicine, science, mathematics, geography and literacy.

Invasion

When the French General Napoleon captured Egypt in 1798 he shattered any illusions held by the Muslim world of this unchallengeable superiority. Addressing his soldiers on the eve of this historic invasion he said:

> 'You are going to undertake a conquest, the effects of which upon commerce and civilization will be incalculable.'

The Western Christian world began to have a more dramatic and direct impact than ever before on the Muslim world. Ever since Napoleon's invasion the Muslim world has had to come to terms with the impact of Western influences on ideas about democracy, nationalism, modernization and religious revival.

Secularism and reformism

The Muslim world has responded in different ways. Some governments and institutions embraced Western ways and separated religion and politics; known as **secularism**. Other Islamic countries used Western ways in governments and institutions and also continued to apply Islamic values, known as **reformism**. Others stressed a total return to Islamic ways in both the public and private spheres of life, known as **Islamism**.

Islamism – a definition

Islamism considers that secular forms of governments and institutions are foreign to a true Muslim society. Islamists feel justified in working to overthrow secularist and reformist Muslim regimes that claim to be Muslim but which do not follow Islamic values.

Islamism is fuelled by social, religious and economic stresses in many Muslim countries: lack of democracy, corrupt political leaders, millions of Palestinian refugees, extreme wealth for a minority and extreme poverty for many, and poor human rights records. Perhaps the greatest stress of all comes from the Israeli-Palestinian conflict (see Unit 59). Another stress is the presence of American troops in Saudi Arabia, where the two most sacred places in Islam, Mecca and Medina, are located. Many Muslims see this as a **desecration of holy ground**.

Despite media stereotypes (see Unit 94), Islamism is not medieval but responds to the stresses and strains of the twenty-first century. Islamism is a huge change from traditional Islam. Whereas traditional Islamic law (**Sharia**) (see Unit 48) is a personal law, Islamists interpret it as applying wherever a Muslim happens to be. In Sudan, for example, where traditionally a Christian was perfectly entitled to drink alcohol because he was a Christian and Islamic law applied only to Muslims, the Islamist regime has banned alcohol for *all*, Sudanese, Christian and Muslim alike.

Divided loyalties

In 2001 some young British Muslims were reported to have gone to Afghanistan to fight against America and its allies. These British citizens see their religious priorities – including Jihad against America and its allies – as overriding their loyalties of being a British citizen.

Globalization (see Unit 62)

Globalization is seen as a threat by some Muslims who wish to uphold their traditional values. Globalization is seen as originating from the US. Its agents are multinational corporations, satellite TV companies, Hollywood and the stock markets. From an Islamist point of view America is the secular and **decadent** imperialist power of the twenty-first century, even supporting oppressive regimes in Gulf States like Saudi Arabia and Kuwait because of their massive oil reserves. Young people in countries like Saudi Arabia – frustrated with the failure of economics, politics or nationalism to give them the better lives they seek – have turned to Islam as a revolutionary solution. In the 1980s many looked to leaders like Iran's Ayatollah Khomeini (1900–89) who provided the vocabulary for hatred of America as **'the Great Satan'** and in the twenty-first century to men like the Saudi dissident Osama bin Laden (b. 1956), as a revolutionary solution.

Critics argue that 'Islamism' distorts Islamic religion and civilization by turning it into an **ideology** (a set of ideas typical to a political group) an '-ism', like other '-isms' such as communism, fascism and nationalism.

Fundamentalism

One of the most controversial religious terms is 'fundamentalism'. In its original meaning a *fundamentalist* means someone who believes in the fundamentals of religion, that is, the Holy Scriptures. In the Muslim world *fundamentalism* is confusing because by definition every Muslim believes in the fundamentals of Islam. The vast majority of Muslim fundamentalists strictly follow the teachings of Muhammad, promote regular attendance at mosques and promote the reading of the Qur'an. Many promote the concept of **theocratic government** in which Sharia (Islamic law) becomes the law of the state. But within the Muslim world are many different ideas about how, and to what extent, to apply Islamic ideas to the modern world.

After the terror attacks on America in 2001, the media wrongly used the term *Muslim fundamentalism* to refer to the beliefs of the suspected terrorists who happened to be Muslim. Most Middle Eastern terrorists are probably fundamentalist Muslims, but they share little with their fellow fundamentalists. They represent an extremist wing of fundamentalism composed of people who believe that the Islamic state must be imposed using violent action if necessary. They sometimes use terror tactics as a response to a perceived threat – namely the fear that the secular western world will erode or even destroy Islam.

Launching your learning

A Find out the meaning of the following words and phrases:

Secularism, reformism, Islamism, desecration of holy ground, Sharia, decadent, ideology, 'the Great Satan', fundamentalism, theocratic government.

B Use some of these words and phrases in answering the following questions:

1 Why was Napoleon's invasion historic?

2 How has the Muslim world responded since Napoleon's invasion?

3 What stresses exist in the Muslim world?

4 Why it is misguided to call Middle Eastern terrorists 'fundamentalists'?

C Find out more about the following: Saudi Arabia; the Israeli-Palestinian conflict; Sudan; Iran; Ayatollah Khomeini; Osama bin Laden.

CITIZENSHIP CHALLENGE

Discuss the possible consequences of a person's religious loyalties overriding their loyalties as citizens.

CITIZENSHIP CHALLENGE

The poor are getting poorer

A Look at the photographs of wealth and poverty in Bangladesh. Try and write a caption for them.

B What does it say about the state of the world today that:

- Europe spends £9 billion a year on ice-cream when it would cost only £7 billion to provide clean water and sanitation for all the world

- in the UK each person consumes enough water to shower all day (150 litres of water) if they want to.

  In Africa people are surviving on a daily ration less than the equivalent of a 60-second shower

- for the cost of two fighter aircraft (£25,000,000), 300,000 hand pumps could be installed in villages in Africa

- nearly a billion people entered the twenty-first century unable to read a book or sign their names

- the developing world now spends $13 on debt repayment for every $1 it receives in grants.

KEY IDEA

Ending world hunger alone will not end world poverty. People are hungry not because of lack of availability of food, but because they are too poor to afford the food.

The digital divide

In Africa only nine out of 100 people have a radio and one in 500 a TV. 90 per cent of foreign news published in the world's newspapers comes from just four Western agencies.

Parable of the divide

The following is an updated version of the 'Parable of the rich man and Lazarus' (Luke 16: 19–31).

> There was a rich nation whose people used to dress in whatever clothes they wanted and buy whatever cars they wanted, which emitted untold amounts of carbon dioxide. These people ate beef at fast-food restaurants whenever they wanted; they created a whole new industry around beef-eating even when it was grown by tearing down rain forests where the poor lived in another country far away, even though it was explained to them how they and especially their children depended on these very rain forests so far away for their health.

> Now at the rich country's border there lay many poor countries to the south; these countries were called 'Third World'. They were covered in sores of poverty, unemployment, lack of food and medical care, and the debts they owed the rich nation. Much of their land and soil and forests had been stripped bare by the nation's companies, who paid to support the dictators and their military guards.

> The sores of the 'Third World' included 500 million persons starving; one billion persons living in absolute poverty; 500 million persons with no access to basic healthcare; half a billion persons with no work and an income of less than $150 per year; nearly a billion illiterate persons; two billion people with no dependable water supply; the wiping out of forests and the erosion of soil. These sores and more were present daily for the rich nations to behold, but they turned their backs and pretended that such suffering was not 'newsworthy'. They built a culture of denial and left the dogs to lick the sores of the poor.

> And the poor nations died and were carried by the angels to the bosom of Abraham. The rich nation died and was buried.

> In the torment of Hades the rich nation looked up and saw Abraham a long way off, with the 'Third World' beginning to rise from the dead straight out of Abraham's bosom. So it cried out, 'Father Abraham, pity us and send the "Third World" to dip the tip of its finger in water and cool our tongue, for we are in agony in these flames.'

> 'My child,' Abraham replied, 'remember that during your life good things came your way, just as bad things came the way of "Third World". Now the "Third World" is being resurrected here while you are in agony. But that is not all: between us and you a great gulf has been fixed to stop anyone, if they wanted to, crossing from our side to yours, and to stop any crossing from your side to ours.'

> The rich nation replied, 'Father, I beg you then to send "Third World" to the other nations in our common alignment – Japan, the European Union, Canada, Australia, New Zealand – to give them warning so that they do not come to this place of torment too.'

> 'They have Moses and the prophets of East and West,' said Abraham, 'let them listen to them.'

> 'Ah, no, Father Abraham,' said the rich nation, 'but if someone comes to them from the dead, they will repent.'

> Then Abraham said to the rich nation, 'If they will not listen either to Moses or to the prophets or to Jesus, they will not be convinced even if someone should rise from the dead.'

From *Creation Spirituality* by Matthew Fox

Launching your learning

After reading the Parable of the divide, briefly explain the moral of this parable. (Use information in Units 43–5 and 61–4.)

'Everyone has the right to a standard of living adequate for their health and well being, including housing.'

United Nations Declaration of Human Rights

Absolute poverty – a definition

Absolute poverty is a condition of life so characterized by malnutrition, illiteracy, disease, high infant mortality and low life expectancy as to be beneath any reasonable definition of human decency. 35,000 people every day starve to death. Absolute poverty kills a small child every 2.4 seconds.

The powerless ones

Absolute poverty is a trap that imprisons one-fifth of the world's population. 90 per cent of those affected are small farmers or landless labourers. They are the powerless ones – exploited by landlords, businessmen, Western companies and corrupt politicians – who have little or no access to education, technical aid, the media, clean toilets or safe water, hospitals or transport.

Needs

Food

Food helps us grow and develop. We need the right amount of food and the right kinds of food.

Water

We need clean, safe drinking water. 80 per cent of all sickness and disease is caused by inadequate water and sanitation causing an estimated 50 million deaths each year.

Children are hardest hit and many die before they reach five years old.

Housing

Housing provides us with protection and security. Today, more and more people are forced into cities in search of work where there is not enough decent housing.

Health

One day we will all need some form of healthcare. Healthcare 'ensures a state of complete physical, mental and social well-being and not merely the absence of disease or illness' (World Health Organization). 70 per cent of the citizens of the world do not have access to organized healthcare.

Education

We take education for granted in Britain but in the poorest countries of the world only four adults in ten can read and write and less than one in four children go to secondary school.

Work

Today world unemployment stands at around 500 million.

Globalization – a definition

Multinational corporations affect nearly everyone's lives today. Hugely powerful businesses with factories all over the world own and control the economies of small and even large countries. Globalization is the process by which Western goods and business practices are marketed around the world, often swamping local economies and destroying traditional ways of life for many (see Units 63 and 64).

Media spins

'THERE ARE TOO MANY PEOPLE.' **Overpopulation** – the bogey word. But which countries are overpopulated? Those consuming the most? America with six per cent of the world's population consumes over 30 per cent of the world's resources.

'THERE IS NOT ENOUGH FOOD.' There is! The world is producing enough food to feed every man, woman and child. Enough grain is produced to provide every person with more than 3,000 calories a day. And that is without counting beans, fruit and vegetables. But that is not all! Often enough food is available even in those countries where many people go hungry. The poorest people, with little power, live on the worst land, while the best and most productive land is used for cultivating crops for export – sold to earn money to pay off debts and to buy much needed imports.

'NOTHING GROWS WITH ALL THOSE DROUGHTS.' In Africa or India the terrible droughts and floods are not the unexpected disasters we always imagine. In the Sahel region of Africa drought is practically part of the environment cycle, and in Asia everyone knows that floods will occur regularly. The problem is that as the poor get poorer, their ability to cope with such disasters is reduced and they become more vulnerable to these environmental 'shocks'.

'ALL THAT TEA AND SUGAR WE BUY, DOES THAT NOT HELP?' Yes, we buy food and other crops from developing countries. They sell them to help pay off their debts and to earn money to develop their economies. But the prices paid for their exports are generally decreasing, while at the same time the imports they need to buy from the developed world are getting more expensive. Tanzania receives less and less for its exports of coffee and cotton, but at the same time it has to pay more and more for imports, such as tractors and machinery. This vicious circle is repeated across the developing world.

And the biggest untruth of all – 'IT HAS GOT NOTHING TO DO WITH US'.

FOR DISCUSSION

A It has been estimated that more people have died as a consequence of hunger in the past six years than have been killed in all the wars, revolutions and murders in the past 150 years. What are basic needs? Do we take them for granted?

B Sometimes, between adverts, pop videos and 'reality TV', we glimpse a hungry, homeless and frightened child – somewhere. Why is so much TV time given over to fantasy when real life stories about living and dying in the real world, with real people, in real situations, are far more real? (See Unit 85)

Launching your learning

Imagine that you have been asked to make a 30 minute documentary for television on world poverty. Using the ideas and statistics in the four units on world poverty in this book write down a plan, a sequence and the methods you would use (including soundtrack and interviews) to get your message across.

▲ The struggle for existence

63 Rights: *WORLD POVERTY 3*

Mayday, Mayday, Mayday, Mayday, Mayday, Mayday, Mayday!

'I must try and show you this. There is a child, I think maybe it's four-months old. The doctor says, "No, it's two-years old". It squats on baked mud, a tattered dusty piece of cotton hangs from one shoulder onto its distended stomach. Its face is huge. A two-year-old face on a four-month body. The eyes are moons of dust and flies caked by tears so big they don't dry until they reach the navel. The child stares. Between its legs flows a constant stream of diarrhoea. The immediate earth around its legs is damp with it. I am watching a child die. In total silence and surrounded by its family it eventually begins to shit out its own stomach. He dies soon. He just dies. Big deal. A jumble of bones and dry skin, wet eyes, flies and shit. In that place where humans have abandoned, humanity thrives. A handful of grain each. I am tired with grief and despair and a consuming rage for humanity. The shame, the shame, the shame.'

Bob Geldof

Mass demonstrations against the injustices of capitalism, take place every year on 1 May. These have become headline news. But what are these Mayday protests about?

- Multinational corporations are unbelievably powerful, controlling trillions of pounds of the world's wealth. They look for cheap labour so that they can make huge profits. They are so powerful they are not answerable to anyone.

- Multinational corporations are owned and controlled by a few incredibly rich people who have governments in their back pockets. What goes is what they say goes!

- The International Monetary Fund – IMF – and the World Bank are the two most powerful institutions in the world. Their main concern is 'economic growth' not economic justice.

- A handful of millionaires now own as much wealth as the world's poorest 2.5 billion people. The combined wealth of the world's 200 richest people hit $1 trillion in 2002; the combined incomes of 582 million people living in the 43 least developed countries is $146 billion.

▲ 'The shame, the shame, the shame'

- Half the world – nearly three billion people – live on less than two dollars a day.

- Twenty per cent of the population in the developed nations consume 86 per cent of the world's goods.

- Even non-emergency food aid, which seems a noble cause, is destructive, as it under-sells local farmers and can affect the entire economy of a poor nation. If the poorer nations are not given the sufficient means to produce their own food and if they are not allowed to use the tools of production for themselves, then poverty and dependency will continue.

TALKING POINTS

'The people always pay.'

Professor Noam Chomsky

'We are interconnected. God said that He created us as a family. We are sisters and brothers and there are no outsiders. Until the world recognizes that we have to share, as families share, we will constantly be surprised that there are huge pockets of resentment, of anger, and that a few seem to benefit from globalization, and the rest have to pay a very, very heavy price.'

Former Archbishop Desmond Tutu, Nobel Peace Prize winner

Sapped!

SAP means 'structural adjustment policies'. Competition between companies involved in manufacturing in developing countries is often ruthless. It is described as 'a race to the bottom'.

World poverty is caused by the way that global markets and trading practices are structured. Economic policies imposed on the poor by the most powerful money institutions, the IMF and World Bank, have a devastating effect. **Structural adjustment policies** mean that nations lent money are done so on condition that they cut social spending to remain attractive to foreign investors, and become mainly commodity exporters. For poorer nations this leads to a spiralling race to the bottom as each nation must compete against others to provide reduced wages and cheaper resources to corporations and richer nations.

Countries must export more in order to raise enough money to pay off their debts in a timely manner. Because there are so many nations being forced into the global marketplace before they are economically and socially stable it is like a big **price war**.

The resources then become even cheaper from the poorer regions, which favours Westerns consumers. Investors concerned only about profits can then pull out very easily if things get tough. In worst cases **capital flight** can lead to economic collapses like in the Asian global financial crisis of the late 1990s.

Launching your learning

A Explain the following words and phrases. Try and use them in answering the questions below.
The World Bank, structural adjustment policies, price war, capital flight.

B What is the difference between 'economic growth' and 'economic justice'?

C Why is it important that countries are able to produce their own food?

D Explain why poor countries are forced to divert available resources away from domestic needs like hospitals and schools.

51 of the largest 'economies' in the world belong to corporations. Not nations. These include General Motors, Ford, Exxon, Shell, IBM, Sony, and Nestlé. Their billionaire owners are now as powerful as presidents and prime ministers. This situation raises many moral issues.

FOR DISCUSSION

How would you feel if your school was sold for a fat profit to make way for another supermarket and you had to travel miles to a new school and make new friends?

The death of democracy

Until the 1980s, one of the roles of governments was to control the supply of money and the movement of goods and capital into and out of their countries.

Not anymore. Today no government, including the American government, can control the flow of capital. A huge shift has taken place. Power is no longer in the hands of politicians, but in the hands of business leaders.

This erosion of **democracy** – of ordinary people's ability to control their own destinies and that of their country – results in voter apathy and a low turnout of voters at elections.

Takeovers

Corporations are stepping into areas that governments are abandoning. All over the world, corporations, not governments, are making decisions that will shape our future.

In Britain, many new NHS hospitals are run by private businesses and in education businesses are building and running schools for profit. While the schools and hospitals may be efficiently run, the problem is that the businesses that own the buildings can close them down and sell them for profit without regard for the needs of the local community.

Consumer power

The question now is, 'What are the responsibilities of these global corporations?' If the corporations care more about profits than about health, pollution or human rights, what can ordinary people do? While **voter apathy** is on the increase, more people are realizing that **consumer activism** can have a real effect on the policies of the multinationals.

It has been observed that the most effective political decisions are now those made in the supermarket or at shareholders' meetings. When genetically modified (GM) foods were introduced in the 1990s, the British government supported their introduction even though they were clearly unwanted by the British people. It was the supermarkets, not the government, who responded to consumer demand and removed GM products from their shelves overnight.

Corporate power

Global corporations can now play one government off against another to make sure they get the best terms for their businesses. They can say to governments: 'If you want our investment and the jobs it will bring, you will have to agree to our conditions – no taxes, no regulations, no environmental restrictions, no healthcare for our employees, low wages and no trade unions in our factories to protect the workers' rights'.

All over the world, illiterate peasant women are recruited from villages and taken to work in compounds guarded by high walls and security guards. They earn less than £2 a day to make trainers and football shirts for the high street shops in your town.

Manipulation

Global corporations now sponsor university departments and many people think this threatens the independence of the research and teaching in these departments. For instance, if GM companies sponsor food science research, they are going to withdraw their funding if the research finds that their products are harmful to consumers or to the environment.

Protest!

Many people question the values and behaviour of these companies. Around the world, environmentalists and political activists are opposed to the **globalization of capitalism**. They oppose the ever-growing power of the global corporations and financial institutions by street protest and education.

Consumer groups try to persuade their governments to pass legislation to protect their children and the environment from these companies. However, the problem with **consumer campaigns** is that they are single-issue protests and do not represent a real opposition to corporate globalization.

The Internet

Many people think that new forms of democratic opposition should be explored, and the Internet is increasingly being used for political debate and activism. In the future, the Internet may well replace parliaments and politicians and empower people to practice a genuine form of democracy, not just put a cross on a piece of paper every four or five years.

CITIZENSHIP CHALLENGE

In the 2001 general election in Britain only 59 per cent of those eligible to vote, voted, and six out of ten 18–25 year olds did not bother. This was the lowest turn out since the end of World War I (1914–18) when women did not have the vote and millions more were disillusioned with politicians.

A Explain what the dangers are of the erosion of democracy. Is there any point in voting when corporations are more powerful than individual nations? Will you vote at the next general election? Why are more people having less faith in politicians?

B Do you think that environmentalists and political activists opposed to the globalization of capitalism can make a difference?

C What is 'consumer power'? Next time you go shopping think about what you are buying. Who made it? How much were they paid? Who is making the profits? Become a global citizen. Find out about brand names and why some of the clothes you buy keep the poor poor. More people are finding out about corporate responsibilities, accountability and human rights issues through the Internet. Huge May Day demonstrations against capitalism have been organized on the Internet. Find out more by logging on to the search engine Google and typing in words like: no logo; world poverty; mayday; anti-globalization.

66 War and peace: 1

Every day on the news and in newspapers there are reports of wars. Although human beings are capable of the most remarkable achievements it seems that we still cannot live together in peace.

Human cost

- Estimates of the numbers of people killed in a war can never be precise. During World War I (1914–18) some nine million men were slaughtered and over 21 million wounded. World War II (1939–45) was responsible for the death of 18,360,000 soldiers and some 39 million civilians. In the 1960s during the Vietnam War, two million people died; in Cambodia during the Khmer Rouge regime an estimated three million people died and in 1994 at least half a million people were slaughtered in the Rwandan **genocide**.

- Since 1945 there have been hundreds of wars and the average death toll from war is put at over 2,500 people every day – over 100 people every hour.

- At the beginning of the twentieth century, nine out of ten victims of war were soldiers; at the beginning of the twenty-first century nine out of ten victims are civilians.

- Millions have been maimed for life or tortured. As well as shattered bodies there are shattered minds. In 1971 between 200,000 and 400,000 women were raped in Bangladesh during a nine-month conflict.

Militarism – a definition

The use of military force is the opposite of freedom because it is a violent attempt to force one's will on another. The military is the arm of the state and is sworn to obey its commands. It is like a machine with many human cogs to operate the technologically sophisticated instruments of killing.

Economic cost

- Every cruise missile fired costs £700,000. During the first night of bombing over Afghanistan in 2001 the Americans fired over 200. The world spends nearly £2 million a minute on the military.

- Military dictators in the developed countries spend twenty times more on their military programmes than on helping the poor. Arms dealers make fortunes out of modern warfare (see Unit 71).

The poverty draft

Basic training for the military reveals how people are stripped of their individuality and independent thinking skills and natural feelings, and are turned into efficient killing machines programmed to take orders without question. Only in this way can humans be conditioned to kill other humans so easily. In many nations, military service is compulsory while in the US the unemployment problem causes the poor to join the armed forces for the economic security offered. This is sometimes known as the 'poverty draft'.

My Lai massacre

During the Vietnam War, on 16 March 1968, in just four hours, 120 American soldiers from 'Charlie Company' massacred nearly 500 Vietnamese civilians in the village of My Lai. No shot was fired at the Americans but they burnt down every house, raped women and girls and then killed them. They stabbed some women in the vagina and disembowelled others.

▲ The US sprayed 18 million gallons of deadly herbicides over South Vietnam between 1961 and 1971, resulting in thousands of defective births

One soldier who killed 25 women and children, described what happened to him:

> 'After I killed the child, my whole mind just went. And once you start it's very easy to keep on. Once you start. The hardest – the part that's hard is to kill, but once you kill that becomes easier to kill the next person and the next one and the next one. Because I had no feelings or emotions or no nothing. No direction. I just killed. It can happen to anyone.'

Indeed the Vietnam conflict was described by many servicemen as 'hell on earth', where terror, fear and confusion created men operating without emotion, rationality or conscience.

The causes of war

Wars are mainly fought for power and to gain control over resources and trade. The US President Woodrow Wilson recognized that this was the case during World War I:

'Is there any man, is there any woman, let me say any child here that does not know that the seed of war in the modern world is industrial and commercial rivalry?'

This is particularly true in the Middle East today, where some of the most bloody wars have taken place over recent years. For example, the Iran-Iraq war, between 1980 and 1988, claimed one million lives. The causes can be found by looking at energy resources. The huge oil resources of the Arab world meant that these countries, with their cheap oil, could have dominated the world oil industry and all the thousands of products that derive from oil, like medicines, plastics, synthetic fibres and so on, as well as enriching other industries such as steel, copper and aluminium. However, this potential wealth challenged the superiority of the Western economy. So, over the years, America and its allies deliberately destabilized these regions in order to control the world's resources. The US has many arms trade related interests in the Middle East. By having pro-US monarchies at the helm and promoting policies that often ignore democracy and human rights, arms deals are worth billions of dollars (see Unit 71).

CITIZENSHIP CHALLENGE

A Keep your eyes on the television news and newspapers this week. Find out where in the world wars are going on. Try and find out what is happening and the reasons why people are fighting. Keep a record of your findings and report back to each other in class after one week.

B In your opinion is violence and war the most effective way of solving disputes? What alternatives are there?

C What effects can military training have on individuals?

'The first casualty of war is the truth'

At the beginning of the Gulf War in 1991 a Kuwaiti princess appeared on TV to tell the world how, when Iraqi troops had taken over a hospital in Kuwait, they had disconnected the life-support machines for premature babies. This was a lie.

Governments have enormous **censorship** (see Unit 86) powers over what we see and hear. This is especially true during times of war and conflict. The language they use in the media is aimed to impress on the listener and watcher that we are the 'good guys', protecting 'national security' or 'freedom of speech' and this may involve 'surgical bombing', 'covert operations' or 'collateral damage'. But what do these phrases really mean?

During the 'surgical strikes' and 'precision bombing' of Iraq in 1991 and Afghanistan in 2001 thousands of innocent civilians were slaughtered, yet British and American politicians dismissed this as 'an unfortunate consequence of war'.

War crimes

The concept of war crimes is a recent one. Until World War II, general opinion was that war was a nasty affair but after it was over everyone could carry on as normal. This changed after Nazi atrocities – against Jews, gypsies, homosexuals, the disabled and other minority groups – came to light. Nazi war leaders were brought to trial at Nuremberg and sentenced to death for their **crimes against humanity**. Several Japanese commanders were also hanged for the atrocities they inflicted.

However, the people who judge war criminals are those who belong to the winning side and the Allied troops were not always the 'wholesome heroes' often depicted by Hollywood films like *Pearl Harbor*. In 2001 a colour film of World War II in the Far East was discovered, shot by an unknown combat cameraman. It showed chilling scenes and eye-witness accounts of American soldiers looting and shooting Japanese wounded as they lay helpless on the ground and of British-led troops collecting Japanese ears and heads.

War crimes were in the news again in the 1990s when hellish images of brutality, 'ethnic cleansing' and concentration camps in Bosnia Herzegovina provoked a swell of public calls to punish the guilty. An international tribunal was established in The Hague to deal with Balkan war criminals. The **International Criminal Court** hears cases of **crimes against humanity**, genocide, torture, rape and other forms of sexual abuse that occur during wartime – including enforced prostitution and sexual slavery.

Biological and chemical weapons

▲ Bio-terrorism alert in Washington

Bio-terrorism – the use of biological agents – occurred in Tokyo in 1996 when a religious cult released the nerve gas Sarin in a subway killing thirteen people, and in 2001 when anthrax was discovered in Florida and Washington.

The **Chemical Weapons Convention**, signed by 163 countries, outlaws the development, production, stockpiling and use of chemical weapons. It also calls for the elimination of these weapons and production facilities by 2007.

Twenty countries are believed to have the means to produce chemical weapons – including Britain, the US, Israel, India, Russia, China, Iraq and Libya. In 1988 Iraq gassed the Kurdish town of Halabja with nerve and mustard gas, killing 4,000 and injuring 30,000 people. It also used chemical arms during its 1980–88 war with Iran.

Biological and chemical weapons are seen in the developing world as the 'poor man's atom bomb', although the effects can be just as deadly over a longer period of time and more sinister. Just a tiny amount of lethal substance may spread rapidly and a country's population may be wiped out within months or even weeks. The attraction for the weapon's users is that when the disease eventually dies out a country's valuable infrastructure is left intact with its population disabled or wiped out.

Jihad – a definition

The attacks on the World Trade Centre by suicidal hijackers in America on 11 September 2001 were described as 'Jihad' by some people, but acts of terror can never be equated with the true meaning of Jihad.

Jihad is an Arabic word meaning 'struggle' or 'striving' to serve Allah – often translated in the West as 'Holy War', which Muslims agree is a fair translation.

Greater Jihad is the way in which Muslims make a personal effort to follow Allah's commands and struggle to fight evil on a personal level within themselves.

Lesser Jihad is to defend Islam and come to the aid of any fellow Muslim attacked for practising Islam.

Muslims may fight in self-defence but are forbidden from starting the fighting. The aim of fighting must be to create a society where people are free to live their lives without beliefs or politics being imposed on them. There must be no hatred or revenge in the fighting. As soon as peace is offered the fighting must stop and any differences between people must be resolved.

FOR DISCUSSION

A   In Matthew 24: 6–7, Jesus is quoted as saying: 'And you will hear of wars and rumours of wars.' Will we ever see a world free of war? What are the causes of war?

B   'The first casualty of war is the truth.' What does this statement mean?

C   'Holy wars' pose many moral issues: Who really knows what is right? Is it right to kill to protect one's religion or set of beliefs? How can anyone know that 'God is on their side'?

Launching your learning

Explain the meaning of the following words and phrases:
Censorship, surgical strikes, precision bombing, crimes against humanity, Chemical Weapons Convention, bio-terrorism, Greater Jihad, Lesser Jihad.

67 War and peace: 3

Conscientious objectors

Many humanists and Quakers (see Addresses/websites) are pacifists. They believe that if killing is wrong then war must be wrong because war is basically a matter of killing. Pacifists refuse to fight or serve in the armed forces. Many were imprisoned during the two World Wars of the twentieth century and many today are Prisoners of Conscience (see Unit 54). During the wars, pacifists were often accused of cowardice. However, they were prepared to go into battle zones in the ambulance services and care for the wounded and the dying – jobs that demand as much courage and skill as that of any soldier.

Mahatma Gandhi

The British Empire extended to India where Mahatma Gandhi led the struggle for Indian independence by promoting **ahimsa** – meaning 'non-injury' – as a means of non-violent struggle. Gandhi (1869–1948) defined ahimsa as 'the avoidance of harm to any living creature in thought, word or deed'. His millions of followers resisted the British by non-cooperation with laws they considered unjust. Although beaten, the Indian protestors repeatedly got to their feet and offered their broken skulls and limbs for further abuse. Their show of courage caused many of their attackers to throw down their weapons and refuse to beat those who, for the sake of their beliefs, were not afraid of maiming or even death.

Gandhi believed that non-violence, **satyagraha** (literally 'truth-force'), gives the 'masses a weapon – enabling a child, a woman, or a decrepit old man – to resist the mightiest government successfully'. He taught that if humanity continues to use the philosophy of 'an eye for an eye' to solve disputes then we will all 'soon be blind'.

It is sometimes thought that Gandhi taught absolute pacifism, the view that violence is never justified, but in fact he maintained that it is better to resist with physical force than to be a coward. If, for example, my family is threatened with armed robbers and I say to them out of fear of my own life: 'I forgive you for what you are about to do', and then walk away, leaving my family to rape and butchery, then this is a display, not of non-violence, but of cowardice. Gandhi taught that a person in such a situation should resort to the use of **necessary force** rather than justify his cowardice through the philosophy of non-violence. Non-violent direct action is:

- **Humane** – it avoids killing or hurting other human beings
- **Universal** – it cuts across barriers of sex, age, race and class
- **A civilian method** – everyone can become involved
- **Voluntary** – people are not forced into a military type machine
- **Radical** – it can change society for the better
- **Creative** – it works positively without destructive means
- **Dignifying** – people stand up for themselves and refusing to let go of their argument however much they are provoked
- **Respectful** – of the **sanctity of life**.

His holiness, The Dalai Lama

▲ 'Violence begets violence. Violence means only one thing: suffering' The Dalai Lama

The Dalai Lama (b. 1935), the spiritual leader of Tibetan Buddhism, has become very popular in recent years as a teacher of universal tolerance and forgiveness.

> 'According to my own little experience, the more I meditate on compassion and think about the infinite number of **sentient beings** who are suffering, the more I have an immense feeling of inner strength.'
>
> His Holiness, The Dalai Lama

Compassion

The Dalai Lama has called *compassion* the universal religion. He believes that for us to be happy, it is important to have a spiritual dimension to our lives: religious beliefs are one level of spirituality and we are free to believe or not, but there is another level of spirituality, called *basic spirituality*, which is actually more important because it is universal.

Basic spirituality

Basic spirituality is the cultivation of the basic human qualities of goodness, kindness and caring. Whether we are believers or non-believers, this kind of spirituality is essential, as we are all members of the human family and we all need these basic values.

Kindness and compassion are basic good qualities of human beings, and by their practice it is possible to become good human beings, moral people, without any religion. But the important thing, whether we are believers or not, is the practice of these basic spiritual values, for it is through this practice that we can become happier people. This substitution of positive values for negative ones is part of a process of training the mind that is the essence of the spiritual life.

FOR DISCUSSION

A 'Hitler would not have taken any notice of non-violent direct action.' Discuss.

B What did Gandhi mean by using necessary force rather than justifying cowardice through the philosophy of non-violence?

C What is ahimsa and who are *sentient beings*?

D What is happiness? Is it wrong to harm other people to obtain your own 'happiness'? Is it possible to be happy knowing that you have hurt another?

CITIZENSHIP CHALLENGE

Discuss whether violence is always:

1 indiscriminate

2 difficult to limit

3 unjust

4 destructive

5 uprooting

6 a vicious circle.

68 War and peace: THE JUST WAR

Introduction

In 1999 Tony Blair, the Prime Minister of Britain and a self-confessed Christian, called British involvement in the Balkans War a 'just war'. For some people the idea of Christians going to war and killing other human beings seems to contradict Jesus' teachings in the Gospels: 'Blessed are the peacemakers'.

So how has it come about that through the centuries Christians have become involved in war? And what exactly is a 'just war'?

Christian pacifists

Early Christians took Jesus' teachings on non-violence very seriously and were **pacifists**. For nearly two centuries they refused to serve in Roman armies although by the end of the second century CE some Christians did military service. The church taught that clerics, priests, monks and nuns could not fight. However, when the stability of the Roman Empire was threatened by invasions of barbarians from the north, Christians began to argue that there might be times when they could be justified in waging war, but only if certain conditions were met. This position came to be called the 'just war'.

The Doctrine of the just war

A just war is a war that *must* be fought but only if certain *conditions* are met. These conditions are designed to prevent war happening and to limit its effects if it does take place. The ideas were developed by Thomas Aquinas (c.1225–74) and Francisco de Vitoria (1483–1546) and are still used by Christians today. The conditions of a just war are:

1   *The war must be declared by a legal recognized authority*, for example, a government. During most of the time the just war theory has operated, 'declaration by a legitimate authority' has meant declaration by a king or sovereign head of state or a government.

2   *The cause of the war must be just.* The war must be fought with the intention to establish good or to correct evil. Its purpose must be to promote peace. The war must be carried out with the intention that good shall result rather than evil. A war cannot be just if it is waged with a wrong intention, such as the desire to secure vengeance or to satisfy lust for domination.

3   *The war must be the last resort.* A state should only go to war AFTER all diplomatic negotiations have been tried and have failed. War must only be declared as a last resort. No war is justified if there is ANY chance of resolving the conflict by non-violent means, such as discussion, negotiation, the employment of economic sanctions or other means short of military action.

4   *The war must be waged on the basis of the **Principle of Proportionality**.* The relationship between ends and means must be proportionate; that is, you must use only enough force to achieve your goals, not more. There cannot be excessive destruction. The good to be accomplished must outweigh the otherwise evil acts that will be exercised in bringing about the good end.

5   *The war must have a reasonable chance of success.* Unless there is a reasonable chance that the objective for waging war can be achieved it is immoral to incur the damage and destruction that will result.

6 *Only sufficient force must be used.* Civilians must not be involved. Warfare must be waged with as much moderation as possible and so indiscriminate bombing, torture, rape, looting and massacres are prohibited. Care must be taken to see that prisoners of war and people not involved in military activities are not killed. This condition refers not only to the actual war itself but also to the terms of settlement at the end of the war – terms that must include justice rather than vengeance.

destroyed this once beautiful city. The emergency services were destroyed along with the homes and lives of 135,000 civilians for virtually no military purpose. In terms of the just war doctrine the action was *not* justified because for a war to be a just war *all* of the conditions must be met.

Again, the use of atomic weapons in 1945 on Japan was not an act of moderation, nor was any justice shown to the hundreds of thousands of innocent civilians killed and maimed.

CASE STUDY – WORLD WAR II

Was the war against the cruel dictatorship of Hitler's Nazi regime during World War II (1939–45) a just war?

- It was fought between Germany and her allies and countries, such as Britain, who were all legal authorities.

- Germany was attacked for invading and suppressing other countries.

- The intention was to correct the evil Germany was doing.

- The Allies felt that they had a reasonable chance of success and they did win.

- All forms of negotiation with Hitler and the Third Reich had failed.

- Most of the fighting was limited to the armies concerned and to harbours and munitions sites.

Launching your learning

A Explain the conditions of a 'just war', in your own words.

B Which conditions of a 'just war' were fulfilled during World War II and which were not?

C Apply the six conditions to a war that is being waged today and try and work out whether this war can be called 'just'.

▲ 'There cannot be excessive destruction'

This looks as though all the conditions of a just war were met. However, actions such as the Allied bombing of the German city of **Dresden**, or the dropping of atomic bombs on the Japanese cities of Hiroshima and Nagasaki (see Unit 69), broke the final condition.

The bombing of Dresden in 1945 in Germany by over 2,000 bombers lasted continually for two days and completely

69 War and peace: NUCLEAR WAR

'Destroyer of worlds'

In 1945 the scientist Robert Oppenheimer (1904–67), the creator of the atomic bomb, after watching the first test of his creation, quoted from the Hindu Scriptures the *Bhagavad Gita*.

In 1998 The Indian Prime Minister Vajpayee, leader of the BJP, the 'Hindu fundamentalist' party, after watching the first test of India's nuclear bomb, likewise quoted from the *Bhagavad Gita*:

> 'Now I have become death, the destroyer of worlds.'

More countries than ever before possess weapons of mass destruction – nuclear, chemical and biological weapons. Over the last 50 years the nuclear weapon states have wasted a great deal of money building up nuclear arsenals whilst leaving the urgent problems of poverty and pollution under-resourced.

Hiroshima

The first atom bomb, weighing two kilograms and little larger than a cricket ball was dropped on the Japanese city of Hiroshima by American and British forces. Lord Philip Noel-Baker, a Nobel Peace Prize winner, wrote:

> 'Hiroshima, 6 August 1945, 8.15 am, a perfect summer morning … above something falls … there is a sudden searing flash of blinding light, hotter and brighter than a thousand suns. Those who are looking at it have their eyes burned in their sockets. They will never look on men or things again … there are no ashes, even on the pavement – nothing but black shadows on the stones. Then comes the blast. For two kilometres in all directions, every building, every structure is levelled to the ground … Then the fireball touches the earth … Swept by tornado winds they rush together in a single firestorm.

> Tens of thousands more, trapped by walls of flame that leap higher than the highest tower in the city, swiftly, or in longer agony, are burned to death. And everything goes black. The mushroom cloud rises to the very vault of heaven.'

The two atomic bombs dropped on Hiroshima and Nagasaki killed over a third of a million people in a hell we cannot imagine and left their scar on generations to follow. But many historians argue that the war in the East was coming to an end before the bombs were dropped. Even if the use of nuclear weapons did end the war quickly, did it make the devastation of Hiroshima and Nagasaki morally justifiable?

Secrecy

So great are the vested interests in nuclear weapons that military affairs are classed 'top secret'. Even when people are opposed to nuclear weapons, politicians go ahead with their deployment. Governments argue that they need to 'defend' themselves against 'the enemy'. But who is the 'enemy'?

Mushrooming

Many people opposed to the existence of nuclear weapons argue that the real enemy is world poverty – made worse by the misallocation of billions of pounds on weapons of destruction. In truth, nuclear weapons have become a sort of 'status symbol' showing the world how 'modern and powerful' their owners are.

India and Pakistan recently joined the 'nuclear club'. The following countries also own nuclear weapons or are trying to develop them: Egypt, France, Israel, Iran, Iraq, Argentina, North Korea, South Korea, Taiwan, China, Russia, Brazil, Britain, Syria, the US and South Africa. This increase is known as **proliferation**.

Trident

Today's nuclear arsenals contain the combined potential fire power of over one million Hiroshimas. The nuclear load carried by a single Trident submarine – of which Britain has several – is equivalent to eight times the total fire power used during the whole of World War II and has the explosive capacity to destroy all the major cities of the northern hemisphere.

On the brink

A nuclear war could begin in many ways, including: the deliberate decision to launch a nuclear strike; some form of nuclear terrorism; a systems malfunction or escalation from conventional war.

In 1995 Russian President Boris Yeltsin was told that a nuclear missile was speeding towards the heart of Russia. Russian nuclear forces, already on a hair-trigger alert, were put on even higher alert ready to launch at his command. The fate of the planet hung in the balance as hundreds of millions of people were going about their daily lives. Russian policy called for a 'launch on warning' – 'use them or loose them'. Yeltsin waited. And within those fateful moments the Russians were able to declare a false alarm. An ultimate nightmare had barely been avoided.

MAD

During the 'cold war' America and the former Soviet Union engaged in a policy called 'deterrence'. This is based on the idea of **'mutually assured destruction'** (**MAD**) – you will not destroy us because if you do we will destroy you.

The futility of this state of affairs prompted a public outcry about nuclear weapons. However, those who support the **Deterrence Theory** argue that this 'no win' situation has meant that a major world war has been avoided.

Indeed, since the awesome display of destructive power at Hiroshima and Nagasaki, no such conflict using nuclear weapons has taken place.

For reasonable followers of the world's faiths, the idea of using nuclear weapons is evil because it means that the environment will be shattered and plant and animal life destroyed. However, concerns are rising that extreme Christian, Hindu and Muslim fundamentalist leaders may be willing to use them in some sort of 'holy war'.

TALKING POINTS

'On the assumption that a third world war must escalate to nuclear destruction, I can tell you that the fourth world war will be fought with bows and arrows.'

Albert Einstein

'We have guided missiles and misguided men.'

Martin Luther King

'Those that survive a nuclear war would envy the dead.'

Nikita Krushchev   ex Russian President

'Nuclear weapons have changed everything except our ways of thinking.'

Albert Einstein

CITIZENSHIP CHALLENGE

Using the information in this unit, prepare a short presentation on different aspects of nuclear war, particularly on the question: 'Can the use of nuclear weapons ever be justified?' (See Unit 68).

70 War and peace: SON OF STAR WARS

In 2001 the US defence secretary Donald Rumsfeld insisted that going ahead with a missile defence system was a 'moral issue'. In this Unit we will look at the issues involved in what has become known as '**Son of Star Wars**'.

Treaties

- **The Nuclear Non-Proliferation Treaty**, agreed by 187 countries aims to prevent the spread of nuclear weapons and weapons technology and to further the goal of achieving nuclear disarmament. Or, to put it more bluntly, this treaty was to prevent new members from joining the 'nuclear club'.

- **The Comprehensive Test Ban Treaty** was designed to prevent testing of nuclear weapons and so reduce the chance of an arms race.

- **The Strategic Arms Reduction Treaties, START I and START II**, were designed to reduce Russian and American weapons.

- **The Anti-Ballistic Missile (ABM) Treaty (1972)** prohibits the use of defensive systems that might give an advantage to one side in a nuclear war. In 2001 US President George Bush announced a withdrawal of support for the ABM treaty, saying it was an 'outdated Cold War relic'. Why did Bush do this?

'Son of Star Wars'

Missile tests by Iran and North Korea in late 1998 and sensational charges of Chinese nuclear espionage during 1999 provoked America to go ahead with its controversial anti-missile shield, designed to shoot down incoming missiles.

In the 1980s, America wanted to deploy **Star Wars**, an ambitious space-based arsenal of military satellites, capable of detecting and destroying enemy missiles. Today's proposed 'Son of Star Wars' has the same intention but relies on missiles fired from the ground or ships. The process has been described as shooting a bullet with a bullet.

Supporters say the system is needed to protect the US against 'rogue states' with nuclear weapons such as Iran, Iraq and North Korea, and guard against any accidental launch of missiles by countries like Russia.

Critics argue

- For all its sophistication and for all the billions of dollars it would cost, the system would not have protected the thousands of people brutally murdered by the suicidal bombers with penknives and knowledge of jet handling who crashed into New York and the Pentagon in 2001.

- It may actually fuel an arms race and breaks the Anti-Ballistic Missile Treaty.

- $60 billion has been spent on missile defence projects since 1983 yet produced precious little beyond a string of technical failures. Problems include: the enemy's element of speed and surprise and the ability to create relatively cheap decoys that can confuse and overwhelm even the most sophisticated defensive system.

- If the US creates a defence system this will allow them to pursue their own globalization and national interests even more aggressively. Other nations will have heightened fears for their own security and so buy more arms. Ironically, this could be the reason that the US could eventually feel threatened.

■ Risk of war means potentially high profits for arms manufacturers. The go-ahead for Son of Star Wars has been spurred on by intensive pressure from a network of major weapons contractors, like Boeing and Lockheed, as they would profit from the public funding.

▲ Son of Star Wars could not have prevented the devastation caused by the hijacking of civilian airliners in New York In 2001

Non-violent direct action

Son of Star Wars relies on early-warning radars in America, Alaska, Greenland and Fylingdales in North Yorkshire, Britain. Protests against the system have grown and two peace activists at Fylingdales were given three month jail sentences after being found guilty of 'criminal damage' in 2001. The Ministry of Defence say the total damage they caused was £900. The sentences are unusually harsh for criminal damage of this order.

Criminality

Peace protestors argue that the 'legal system backs up the criminality of the nuclear weapon states'. In 2001, Church of Scotland Minister, Reverend Norman Shanks was among many church ministers arrested at a protest. He said:

'There is clear justification, both within the traditions of the church and on the basis of scripture, for people – whether ministers or lay people who have Christian convictions – to stand up and speak out for what they believe, even if that involves civil disobedience.'

These protestors belong to **Ploughshares** (see Addresses/websites), a campaign involving humanists, pacifists and religious followers who work to disarm the UK nuclear weapons system in a non-violent, open and peaceful manner. Its supporters act to uphold international humanitarian law and to expose the illegality of nuclear weapons.

TALKING POINT

'If you look at world history, ever since men began waging war, you will see that there's a permanent race between sword and shield. The sword always wins. The more improvements that are made to the shield, the more improvements are made to the sword. These missile defence systems will spur sword makers to intensify their efforts.'

French politician Jacques Chirac

CITIZENSHIP CHALLENGE

Dialogue
Find a partner and imagine that one of you supports Son of Star Wars and the other does not. Using the information in this unit write down the conversation that takes place between you.

Press release
Write down a short press release of no more than 40 words on 'the sword and the shield'.

71 War and peace: THE ARMS TRADE

Ethical?

Although politicians in Britain have talked about 'an ethical foreign policy' the fact remains that the trade in weapons is far from being ethical. War is big business.

The world spends more on arms than it spends on anything else. The buying and selling of weapons is one of the major causes of world poverty. The people who sell arms rely on a world where war is commonplace. War, or threat of war, means money for them.

Peace does not benefit weapons manufacturers. Peace would not make any sense at all, for example, to the Carlyle Group, which makes its money from military conflicts. Carlyle is run by men with impeccable credentials. Managing directors and chairmen include a former US defense secretary, a former US secretary and George Bush Senior's campaign managers.

TALKING POINT

The cross of iron
'Every gun that is made, every warship launched, every rocket fired signifies in the final sense, a theft from those who hunger and are not fed, those who are cold and are not clothed. This world in arms is not spending money alone. It is spending the sweat of its labourers, the genius of its scientists, the hopes of its children. This is not a way of life at all in any true sense. Under the clouds of war, it is humanity hanging on a cross of iron.'

Dwight D. Eisenhower – President of the United States (1953–60)

Human rights

Respect for human rights is overlooked as arms are sold – often secretly – to known human rights violators, military dictatorships or corrupt governments. The new arms are often used to prevent any form of democracy in those countries. The worst offenders who sell these arms are the US and Britain.

Politics

Arms sales go alongside political interests. For example, Britain and the US sell weapons to Turkey. These have been used against the Kurds in what some have described as the worst human rights violations and ethnic cleansing since World War II. Britain and the US turn a blind eye to these atrocities because the 'political handshake' allows them to set up bases in key Turkish locations in order that they can spy on the Middle East.

Real costs

■ Six times more public money goes into weapons research than into research on health protection.

■ Dictators in the developing world, often supported by the West, spend 66 per cent more on the military than on education.

■ There is one soldier per 240 people in the poor world and only one doctor per 2,000 people.

■ If redirected, the money consumed by the military could eliminate poverty in the developing world. For instance, one Patriot missile costs $1 million. The price of 23 of these could keep two million Mozambicans in seeds, clothes, pots and storage facilities for one year. A B52 bomber uses 3,600 gallons of fuel per hour of flight – enough fuel for an air ambulance to carry out ten hours of 'mercy flights'.

Propaganda *(see Units 91 and 96)*

Amazing, breath-taking air shows leave us in awe at modern technology – almost making us forget the purpose of such aircraft. Recruitment adverts show us the 'brotherhood of man' using 'emotional manipulation', making us forget that the military is about killing people. Major defence contractors own CBS and NBC, two of the largest US television networks. A Lockheed advertisement actually claimed that 'peace means less jobs'. The advertisements and propaganda are about minimizing casualties to make us believe that in future wars no one will be killed.

Five steps towards a better future

1 **Campaign**
Nearly all arms-producing countries sell weapons to nations with terrible human rights records. **CAAT (Campaign Against the Arms Trade)** (see Addresses/websites) works towards abolishing the arms trade and puts pressure on the British Government to stop selling arms to such countries.

2 **Educate**
Children need to be taught that war is obscene. They should be encouraged to resolve disputes peacefully. They should be taught that differences in culture and nationality should not lead to prejudice and conflict.

3 **Expose**
The arms trade thrives on secrecy. Organizations like CAAT and some British MPs are demanding that the Government publish details of all arms dealings.

4 **Work**
Many people work in the arms industry. Some Trade Unions have put pressure on companies to redirect their resources away from arms manufacturing towards socially worthwhile projects.

5 **Think**
We have wrongly got used to the idea that war is inevitable. It is crucial that we learn how to discuss and debate things instead of reacting violently.

CITIZENSHIP CHALLENGE

A Using the information in this Unit, design a poster based on Eisenhower's 'Cross of Iron'.

B World military expenditure was $800 billion in 2000. If you were a leader of a peaceful world how would you redirect this money and what would you spend it on?

C Give reasons why rich countries like America or Britain turn a blind eye to human rights abuses.

D Discuss the viscious cycle below and the statement 'peace means less jobs'.

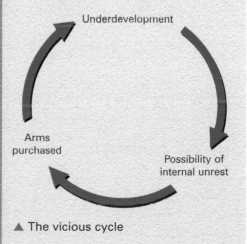

▲ The vicious cycle

We have long lived under the illusion that human beings are the masters of the planet who can do what they want. The reality is very different. There are real limits within which we must operate if we are to survive.

▲ It would take 5.4 Earths to provide for the world's population if everyone lived like the average American

Human impact on the environment

When our ancestors were hunter-gatherers, our impact on the environment was limited. But soon after the invention of agriculture, around 7000 BCE, and the resulting rise in human population, the first signs of environmental destruction due to human activities appeared.

Out of balance

It was only 300 years or so ago that the Industrial Revolution brought the first signs of a massive imbalance between humankind and nature. Attitudes in the Western world towards the environment were such that people seldom questioned the way they treated the natural world – exploiting and abusing it at will. Little thought was given to industrial pollution and the terrible consequences of upsetting the fragile balance of the world's ecosystems. To the ambitious industrialists, the earth's resources appeared to be infinite.

The Green Movement

During the 1960s and 1970s, studies on the destructive effects of human activities, together with fears that natural resources are running out, made more and more people worried about the future. The Green Movement was born. Organizations like Greenpeace and *Friends of the Earth* (see Addresses/websites) attracted tens of thousands of people the world over in the struggle to change people's attitudes about our planet.

Bad news!

- **Pollution** – the waste from cars, factories and homes causes problems like acid rain, poisoned rivers and oceans and an increase in disease from poor air, water and soil. Chemicals and pesticides destroy parts of the insect chain – killing off part of the food chain. Their over-use threatens to destroy the rest of that chain, including human beings who are at the top of some food chains. Chemicals and pesticides run off into seas, streams, rivers and water tables causing immeasurable damage.

- **Energy wastage** – It would take 5.4 Earths to sustain the world's population if everyone lived like the average American. Natural resources are running out: by 2020 the consumption of energy in the world will increase by more than 50 per cent. Today there are 500 million cars in the world and by 2020 there will be an estimated one billion cars.

- **Deforestation** – There are less than twenty per cent of the world's forests left. The world's forests are the lungs of the planet, without them the world would be unable to breathe.

- **Desertification** – In Roman times, North Africa was used for the growing of grain. Today vast areas are desert. Intensive farming and poor land management have turned large parts of the world into infertile desert.

- **The ozone layer** – The ozone layer around the Earth protects life from the harmful ultraviolet rays of the sun. Pollution has destroyed parts of the ozone layer making it thinner than it has ever been causing an increase in cancers.

- **Water shortage** – Two people in three across the world will face water shortages by 2025. Millions of 'water refugees' will be forced from their homes to seek clean water supplies elsewhere. Water shortages threaten to reduce the global food supply by more than ten per cent.

- **Species extinction** – Over-fishing, over-farming, deforestation and desertification have upset the delicate natural balance of life on earth. The disappearance of certain species of plants, maybe holding the key to some of our incurable diseases, is an irreversible process.

- **Global warming** – This could alter 35 per cent of the Earth's existing habitat by the end of this century. Plants and animals will have to migrate permanently to find new habitats and some will not be able to move fast enough. Global warming results in an increase in droughts and the spread of deserts.

- **Overpopulation** – Rapid population growth and relatively high fertility levels in the world's 48 least developed countries, and rising life expectancy everywhere, will push the world's population from 6.1 billion in 2001 to about 9.3 billion by 2050. These increases will put great pressure on food and water resources in many parts of the developing world.

CITIZENSHIP CHALLENGE

In pairs discuss the following:

A   Does it matter if a species dies out? Would it matter if human beings died out? Would it matter less if humans died out but other forms of life survived? Give reasons for your answers.

B   Discuss whether it is morally wrong not to recycle cans, bottles, paper and vegetable waste.

C   Is it right to build a dam that will supply water to thousands of people, but will destroy the habitat of many plants and animals?

D   Find an example of an environmental problem in this week's news. What are the causes? How could the problem be solved?

WEBSITE

Visit *www.lead.org/leadnet/footprint* to measure your 'ecological footprint'.

73 The environment: 2

Jewish and Christian scripture

Most of the world's religions have stories about the creation of the world. In Christianity and Judaism, the stories of the creation are found in the first two chapters of the book of Genesis in the Tenakh. Genesis means 'beginning' and the Book of Genesis describes the relationship between the Earth, God and humanity. God created the world *ex nihilo* (from nothing):

> 'In the beginning God created the heavens and the earth.'
>
> Genesis 1: 1

After creating the earth, the sky, the seas and plants, God made birds and fish on the fifth day and animals and humans on the sixth day.

> 'So God created man in his own image, in the image of God he created him; male and female he created them.'
>
> Genesis 1: 27

In the Tenakh, the Jews were told to take care of Creation and rest the land once every 50 years so that it would produce more in the future (Leviticus 25: 8–11). They were also ordered not to destroy trees when they were attacking a city:

> 'When you lay siege to a city … do not destroy its trees by putting an axe to them, because you can eat their fruit. Do not cut them down.'
>
> Deuteronomy 20: 19

In the New Testament, Jesus often referred to the beauty of nature in his teachings:

> 'Consider how the lilies grow. They do not labour or spin. Yet I tell you, not even Solomon in all his splendour was dressed like one of these.'
>
> Luke 12: 27–8

Supremacy

> 'Then God said, "Let us make man in our image, in our likeness, and let them rule over the fish of the sea and the birds of the air, over the livestock, over all the earth, and over all the creatures that move along the ground" … God blessed them and said to them, "Be fruitful and increase in number; fill the earth and subdue it. Rule over the fish of the sea and the birds of the air and over every living creature that moves on the ground".'
>
> Genesis 1: 26 and 28

Some people have suggested that the historical roots of the environmental crisis we face today are to be found in the Judaic-Christian tradition. They point to the way that successive generations of Christians have interpreted the Creation Story in the Book of Genesis as God giving humankind absolute dominion and supremacy over the natural world. In the Western world, Christianity has been the dominant religion and the idea that humanity 'rules over' nature has influenced the way people have treated the natural world.

Stewardship – a definition

Over recent years, however, many Christians, on seeing the devastating effects of 'progress' have reinterpreted Biblical teaching. Occasionally, apocalyptic visions of humanity acting as its own executioner, by creating a world inhospitable to life, have given impetus and urgency to the idea of **stewardship**. Stewardship is the idea that human beings are the custodians and trustees of creation. Our role is to act as 'stewards' to the natural world – to look after the planet and maintain it for future generations.

As such we cannot escape the duty to act responsibly towards the created world – a sacred gift:

> 'Then the Lord God placed the man in the garden of Eden to cultivate it and guard it.'

> Genesis 2: 15

CITIZENSHIP CHALLENGE

A Is it quite simply human **greed** that has led to the devastating effects of pollution, deforestation and the mindless plundering of the earth's natural resources?

B As stewards, have we human beings a right to exploit nature solely for our own gain?

C We are stewards of creation, which means that we are responsible for all living things. But what do you understand by *stewardship*? Do you think it means 'power over' or could it mean 'to take care of'? How will your definition affect the way you treat the natural world?

The Christian Churches

It is only in the last twenty years or so, as awareness about the environmental crisis has grown, that Christian churches have began to speak out about the damage that has been done. This concern is in the following statement by the Roman Catholic Church in 1988:

> 'The earth and all life on it is a gift from God given us to share and develop, not to dominate and exploit. Our actions have consequences for the rights of others and for the resources of the Earth.

We have the responsibility to create a balanced policy between consumption and conservation. We must consider the welfare of future generations in our planning for and utilization of the Earth's resources.'

Worship and thanks

At the heart of modern Christian views on the environment is the belief that the mystery, beauty and order of the natural world is evidence that the planet has been created. Life, therefore, has meaning and purpose and is not the product of blind chance. In the mysterious cycles and patterns of the seasons, in the enormous variety of life and in the intricate balance of the ecosystem, Christians see the work of a Creator God. They give thanks in their weekly worship and during **Harvest Festival** for the miraculous way in which the earth provides for us.

Chico Mendez

Some Christians have dedicated their lives to protecting the environment, for example, Chico Mendez (see Addresses/websites) – founder of the Alliance of the People of the Forest. Mendez was a Brazilian rubber tapper. He showed the world that it is possible to generate income from the forest without destroying it. He won admiration around the world as the leader of non-violent protest against deforestation by the cattle barons and plantation owners. He was brutally murdered in 1988 at home in front of his family by paid assassins.

TALKING POINT

'It would not occur to you to cut off your leg because your leg is part of you. Well, so are the trees in the Amazon basin; they are our external lungs. We are just beginning to wake up to that. We are gradually discovering that we are the world.'

Joanna Macy, writer

The sanctity of life

All religions teach that life is a gift. Once a life has been given, no human being has any right to destroy it. This principle does not only apply to human life, but to all biological life as well, and, indeed to the life of our planet, which in itself is a living organism. The message of the great teachers of all the world religions is that the universe and everything in it is divine.

Nature is alive

This message about the sanctity of life has been around for all of human history. From the time of our remotest ancestors until the seventeenth century, it was taken for granted that the world of nature was alive. But in the last three centuries, growing numbers of educated people have come to think of nature as lifeless. This has been the central teaching of science – the mechanistic theory of nature – teaching that nature should be mastered, controlled, until we have power over 'things' (that is, nature).

'Progress'?

However, this message of control, which tells us that we need to master things to make 'progress', has led us to the brink of self-destruction. It has meant that humankind, in the pursuit of progress and material wealth, has ceased to respect life on earth. Throughout history all cultures, except our own modern one, have taught reverence for life. 'Reverence' means 'great respect and admiration mixed with love'.

Connections

The view that nature is lifeless and so can be treated as an object is slowly beginning to change. Modern physics forces us to see the universe not as a collection of lifeless physical objects, but rather as a complicated web of relations between the various parts of a unified whole.

In other words all things are connected. In ordinary life we are not usually aware of this unity and we divide the world into separate objects and events. It is of course useful that our minds do this, but it is an illusion. In reality the universe is one.

Mystics and physicists

The principle of unity is apparent to the physicist who explores reality at the atomic level and it becomes even more apparent as she/he goes down into the realm of subatomic particles. In fact this awareness of the unity of all things, where all things are seen as interdependent and inseparable parts of the cosmic whole is a similar view to that held by mystics.

Hindu view

'The human role is not separate from nature. All objects in the universe, beings and non-beings, are pervaded by the same spiritual power. The human race, though at the top of the evolutionary pyramid at present, is not seen as something apart from Earth and its many forms. People did not spring fully-formed to dominate lesser life, but evolved out of these forms and is integrally linked with them.'

Hindu statement, *The Assisi Declarations* of 1986

Sikh view

Many Sikhs come from farming backgrounds where they have close association with nature. They support initiatives for the protection, preservation and care of the environment. Sikhs believe that there are 8,400,000 life forms and the soul may transmigrate to any of these. The human form is rare and carries with it a responsibility to the world. Harmony with other parts of nature is essential. In Japji Sahib, which is recited by Sikhs every morning, this relationship with nature is very deep:

'Air is the Guru, water the father
Earth the great Mother,
Day and night are male and female nurses,
In whose lap the whole world plays.'

Japji Sahib: Guru Granth Sahib

Muslim view

'The central concept of Islam is tawhid or Oneness of God. Allah is Oneness; and His Oneness is also reflected in the oneness of mankind and the oneness of man and nature. His trustees are responsible for maintaining the oneness of His creation, the integrity of the Earth, its flora and fauna, its wildlife and natural environment. Oneness cannot be had by discord, by setting one need against another or letting one end predominate over another; it is maintained by balance and harmony. Muslims say that Islam is the middle path and we will be answerable for how we have walked this path, how we have maintained balance and harmony in the whole of creation around us. So oneness, trusteeship and accountability, that is tawhid, khalifa and akhirah, the three central concepts of Islam, are also the pillars of the environmental ethics of Islam. They constitute the basic values taught by the Qur'an. It is these values which led Muhammad, the Prophet of Islam, to say:

"Whoever plants a tree and diligently looks after it until it matures and bears fruit is rewarded".'

Muslim Statement, *The Assisi Declaration*

ANCIENT ENGLISH VIEW

A member of the Leominster Morris who annually perform the Wassail (Anglo Saxon derivation 'wass hael', meaning 'be whole', 'good health') every Twelfth Night, which ensures, at the darkest time of the year, the return of the sun and the fertility of the apple crops.

Launching your learning

Write down your thoughts and views about the following phrases:

1 Nature is alive.

2 Progress has led us to the brink of self-destruction.

3 All things are connected.

Genetically engineered foods (**GE foods**), also known as genetically modified foods **GM Foods**, or genetically modified organisms (**GMOs**), have made a big splash in the news recently. Astonishing progress is being made. But do genetically modified foods pose a huge health risk? What are the environmental consequences of GM Foods?

Gene – Genie?

A particular gene in a fish, responsible for protecting that fish from cold temperatures, is selected. This gene is then transferred into a tomato or strawberry. The tomato or strawberry will now be able to produce a protein that increases its cold resistance.

Scorpion poison genes have been added to cabbages to kill caterpillars.

Genetically engineered foods – a definition

The term 'GM foods' is most commonly used to refer to crop plants created for human or animal consumption using the latest molecular biology techniques. These plants have been modified to bring out desired characteristics, improve resistance to herbicides and improve nutritional content.

The enhancement of desired characteristics has traditionally been done by breeding, but this takes time. Genetic engineering, on the other hand, can create plants with the exact desired characteristic very quickly and with great accuracy. Genetically modified foods also include fruits and vegetables containing vaccines to make them bigger and to increase their shelf life.

Agribusiness

The demand for 'good quality' food puts enormous pressures on the modern farmer. Small farms, facing bankruptcy, are increasingly selling up to huge companies which use the latest biotechnologies. Modern farming has become a huge industry – sometimes called **agribusiness**. Agribusiness aims to boost crop yields by protecting plants from pests and developing plants with more resistance to herbicides. Today an estimated 35 million acres of land around the world have been planted with commercial GM crops.

Food for the future?

Supporters of genetically modified foods argue that GM crops will ensure an adequate food supply for the booming world's population (see Unit 72) in a number of ways:

- **Pest resistance** – Much modern food is produced using chemical pesticides. Consumers do not want to eat food that has been treated with pesticides because of the potential health and environmental hazards. Growing GM crops can help reduce the amount of chemical pesticides used.

- **Cold tolerance** – Unexpected frost can kill off sensitive seedlings. Anti-freeze genes from fish enables plants to survive cold temperatures that would otherwise destroy seedlings.

- **Drought tolerance** – As the world population continues to explode and more land is needed for food, GM crops can be engineered to grow in formerly barren and inhospitable places.

- **Nutrition** – Many of the world's poor rely on a single crop such as rice for their diet.

Rice, however, does not contain adequate amounts of all necessary nutrients to prevent malnutrition, but if rice could be genetically engineered to contain additional vitamins and minerals, malnutrition could be prevented.

Frankenstein foods?

- **Increasing poverty** – While these arguments might seem convincing, critics of GM crops argue that people are going hungry not because there is a shortage of food produced, but simply because *they are too poor to buy it*. Far from feeding the poor, genetic engineering is going to result in many more people starving as their cash crops are replaced by genetically engineered substitutes.

- **Threat to farming methods and the food supply** – If agribusiness controls the supply of seeds, traditional agriculture, which saves part of the crop for sowing the next year, will be threatened.

- **Harm to other organisms** – Recent studies in America showed that genetically modified corn caused high mortality rates in monarch butterfly caterpillars. It was thought that pollen from the corn was blown by the wind onto plants in neighbouring fields eaten by the caterpillars.

- **Reduced effectiveness of pesticides** – Just as some mosquitoes developed resistance to the now banned pesticide DDT, other insects could become resistant to GM crops engineered to produce their own pesticides.

- **Human health** – Introducing a gene into a plant may create new allergies and other long-term health problems. In 2001 the British Medical Association called for a five-year moratorium on genetically engineered crops, because of concerns that they might increase human resistance to antibiotics.

- **Superweeds** – Some crop plants, engineered to survive herbicides (weed-killers) could cross-breed, resulting in the transfer of the weedkiller-resistant genes from the crops into weeds. These 'superweeds' could spread and dominate the ecosystem. This could have devastating environmental consequences. Genetically modified plants might breed with wild species and so spread their genes far and wide.

Summing up

Genetically modified foods have the potential to solve many of the world's malnutrition problems and help to protect the environment by increasing food yield and reduce reliance on chemical pesticides and herbicides. Yet there are many challenges ahead, especially in the areas of testing, regulation and international policy. Some people feel that genetic engineering is the inevitable way forward and we cannot afford to ignore a technology that has such enormous potential benefits. Others think that we must proceed with caution to avoid causing harm as a result of our enthusiasm for this powerful technology, while others argue that we cannot afford to dice with the natural world, 'play God', as we do not know the long-term environmental and health consequences.

CITIZENSHIP CHALLENGE

Dialogue

In pairs, imagine that one of you is a scientist who supports GM foods and the other is an environmentalist who rejects GM foods. Make up a conversation you might have about the potential risks against the potential benefits of GM foods. Write out your dialogue and then perform it.

▲ Changes in the climate are already having catastrophic effects. Unless something is done climate changes caused by human pollution could get much worse

Global warming – a definition

There is mounting evidence that the world is getting warmer. The fifteen warmest years in the last century have occurred since 1980. Ice is melting on every continent. The snow/ice pack in the Rockies, the Andes, the Alps and the Himalayas is shrinking. The volume of the ice cap covering the Arctic Ocean has shrunk by more than 40 per cent over the last 35 years. Global warming is primarily a result of the industrialization and motorization levels in the rich countries of the world.

Since pre-industrial times, atmospheric concentrations of 'greenhouse gases' (GHGs) – carbon dioxide, methane and nitrous oxide – have grown by 31 per cent, 151 per cent and 17 per cent respectively. This is largely because of fossil fuel use, land use change and agriculture.

GHGs, which trap the sun's rays, create a **hothouse effect**, resulting in an increase in the Earth's temperature. In 1995, the *Intergovernmental Panel on Climate Change (IPCC)* estimated that temperatures are set to rise by as much as 4°C by 2090. But recent IPCC estimates project that temperatures will rise by as much as 5.8°C by 2100. This will be accompanied by a rise in sea level and changes in weather patterns and will have a worldwide catastrophic impact on agriculture and water resources.

According to a group of UN-sponsored scientists, developing countries are twice as vulnerable to climate change than industrialized countries. Small island states are three times more vulnerable. According to Christian Aid (see Addresses/websites), industrialized nations already owe 600 billion dollars to the developing nations for the damage caused by climate changes.

Car chaos

The world's 700 million motor vehicles pump more than 500 hundred million tonnes of carbon dioxide into the atmosphere every year. Car engine pollutants are a major cause of global warming. It's a strange world where biological diversity is declining at a dangerous rate, while the artificial diversity of the machine – the car – is exploding. One car is produced every second, or one new car for every two babies born. We are repopulating our dying world with creatures of our own invention. In cities around the world 'rush hour' lasts all day.

Britain under threat

Between 1987 and 2001 Britain experienced three winter storms of a strength that would normally be expected once every 200 years. In February 2001 a Government report by the *Expert Group on Climate Change and Health* warned that climate changes over the next 50 years will cause death and destruction on a major scale in Britain unless preventive action is taken now. Rising sea levels caused by the melting of the Arctic ice-cap and severe storms are likely to cause catastrophic flooding, devastating tens of thousands of homes. Hotter summers in Britain are expected to result in 30,000 extra cases of skin cancers, unless pollution is cut, and 10,000 extra cases of food poisoning. Even outbreaks of malaria could occur.

Kyoto

In 1997, in Japan, the **Kyoto Conference on Climate Change** took place. There, developed countries agreed to specific targets for cutting their emissions of greenhouse gases. The US proposed to just stabilize emissions and not cut them at all, while the European Union called for a fifteen per cent cut.

Profits before principles

In March 2001, US President George Bush, a former Texan oil businessman, shocked the world when he said that he opposed the agreement by nations to cut pollution and fight global warming (see Unit 52). The US is the most powerful and influential country in the world and, incidentally, the worst polluter. The US has four per cent of the world's population, yet **emits** (sends out) 21 per cent of the world's carbon dioxide; and CO_2 is just one of many greenhouse gases. Bush was elected with the backing and the contribution of millions of dollars by the oil industry who stand most to lose if the Kyoto Protocol goes ahead.

Big business on the defensive

There were many political factors involved during the Kyoto Conference. The oil industry launched a huge campaign in the media to discredit the conference. They argued that cutting emissions will hurt the global (or US's) economy and affect people's jobs. They complained that the Kyoto Protocol does not commit developing nations to the same levels of reductions in global warming pollutants. However, it is not the developing nations who have caused the pollution for the past 150 or so years. It would be unfair to ask them to cut back at the **same** levels for the mistakes of the currently industrialized nations. One of the reasons President Bush gave against the Kyoto agreement was that India and China would not be subject to Kyoto measures. He did not mention the fact that India and China's emissions are far less than the US's.

Launching your learning

A Explain in your own words why the world is getting warmer.

B What problems might people in Britain face if global warming continues?

C What is the Kyoto Agreement? Why did the US oppose it?

World poverty and the environment

At first glance, world poverty and environmental issues may seem like separate issues. However, they are very closely related.

The more developing countries stay in debt the more they will be under pressure to milk the earth's resources.

When poor countries face natural disasters, such as hurricanes, floods and fires, the cost of rebuilding becomes even more of an issue when they are already burdened with debt.

▲ Gorillas could be extinct in the next ten years

▲ Humans have destroyed over 30% of the Natural World since 1970

GRASP

Industrialization is often to blame for losses in **biodiversity**.

In 2001 the **Great Apes Survival Project (GRASP)** was launched by **UNEP**, the **United Nations Environmental Programme** (see Addresses/websites). Some experts predict that gorillas, orang-utans and chimpanzees could be extinct in Africa and South East Asia within ten years. One species of chimpanzee shares more than 98 per cent of its DNA with humans. During recent years, thousands of orang-utans have been killed or driven from their homes by illegal loggers, and thousands of chimpanzees have been killed for food. Gorillas play a crucial role in forest ecosystems by dispersing seeds and pruning trees.

Biodiversity

In 2001 a report by the *Worldwide Fund for Nature* maintained that humans have destroyed more than 30 per cent of the natural world since 1970. The fourth most populous country in the world, Indonesia, houses ten per cent of the earth's remaining tropical forests.

Not only are forests depleting year by year, but species that depend on the forests are also disappearing, and these species are needed to ensure a stable **ecosystem**.

The 'Person of the Forest', or Orang-utan, is one such species at risk due to excessive logging and poaching. Other species at risk in Indonesia include the Sumatran tiger, Sumatran and Javan rhino and the Asian elephant.

Who cares?

Why is biodiversity important? Does it really matter if there are not so many species?

Yes it does matter and it affects us all. Biodiversity actually boosts ecosystem productivity where each species, no matter how small, all have an important role to play. This enables the ecosystem to recover from a variety of disasters. This is obviously useful for humans as a larger number of species of plants means more variety of crops and a larger number of species of animals ensure that the ecosystem is naturally sustained.

Extinction

It is feared that human activity is causing the **extinction** of various animal species, marine life, forests and the ecosystems that forests support.

Climate changes and biodiversity

The *World Resources Institute* reports that there is a link between biodiversity and climate change. Rapid global warming can affect ecosystems' chances to adapt naturally.

Coral reefs

One type of ecosystem that perhaps is neglected more than any other is the richest in biodiversity – the coral reefs. Reefs are useful to the environment and to people in a number of ways. However, all around the world, much of the world's marine biodiversity faces threats from human activities as well as natural. It is feared that very soon, many reefs could die off.

The 1999 Biosafety Protocol

The 1999 Biodiversity Protocol meeting in Colombia broke down because the US and five other countries felt that their business interests were threatened.

Launching your learning

A Find out the meaning of the following words:
Biodiversity, ecosystem, extinction

B After looking at the units on world poverty and the environment, try and explain how they are related.

C If humans have destroyed more than 30 per cent of the natural world in the last 30 years what, in your opinion, can be done by (a) individuals; (b) governments; and (c) the international community to prevent us destroying the world forever?

TALKING POINT

'"All beings tremble before danger, all fear death", said the Buddha. In Buddhism there is the idea of interdependence, the experience that everything depends on everything else. All that lives, all that exists is connected.'

Testing the Global Ethic

The work into **conservation** by charities and environmental activists is often undermined by those who have other interests, particularly money and power.

Tigers

The population of tigers in the last century has declined by 95 per cent. Many **conservationists** fear that they will be extinct by 2010. Tiger bone is in high demand for Chinese medicine; and other medicines containing tiger parts have been making their way to North America. It is not just tigers either. Rare leopards, deer and other animals are also being illegally traded.

AIDS research

Scientists now believe that they have found the origins of AIDS. The source comes from a type of chimpanzee that is immune to the virus. Unfortunately the forests in which they live are being opened up by logging companies resulting in a destruction of the chimpanzee's habitat.

Big business

Another source of problems that can affect an environment and the species that live in it stems from greedy or careless management of industrial waste by governments and large corporations.

Toxic spills

A damn on a gold mine owned by *Aurul SA* burst in 2001, spilling waste water, highly contaminated with cyanides and heavy metals.

From the river in Romania, it made its way into Hungary. According to the **World Wide Fund for Nature**, a rare species of otter that was only 400 strong before the spill, can no longer be seen. More than 100 tonnes of dead fish have been collected from the river's surface, but many more are believed to be lying on the river bottom. In addition to those species directly affected by the toxic spill, there is a secondary danger to all species which feed on anything living in the river. Farmers have reported dead or blinded livestock. The ecological damage has been huge. Scientists fear that it will take many years to restore the waters.

In Russia, nuclear radioactive waste, dumped into the sea, is threatening the Arctic region.

Noise pollution in the sea

The US Navy and NATO have been using and testing Low Frequency Active Sonar (LFAS) to detect enemy submarines. Many dolphins and whales who use their own sonar to navigate the oceans have been severely affected. The sound is so loud that it can kill and maim whales, dolphins and sea life. LFAS is known to be harmful to humans as well. The US Navy is moving ahead with plans to deploy a new extended-range submarine detection system that will introduce noise into the world's oceans, billions of times louder than that known to disturb whales.

Scientists fear that LFAS, together with a growing number of industrial sources of noise, from super tankers to the giant air guns used in oil exploration, could interfere with essential biological functions – mating, feeding, navigating, nursing and communicating – of already depleted or endangered species whose survival depends on their ability to hear and be heard (see Addresses/websites).

CITIZENSHIP CHALLENGE

A For more information on animal and nature conservation in general:

- www.environmental defense.org
  www.enn.com
  www.fragilecologies.com

- The World Wide Fund for Nature (www.panda.org/) presents information about all aspects of nature.

- The web directory (www.webdirectory.com/) is a search engine for environmental issues. They have thousands of links.

- The Africam (www.africam.mweb.co.za/) in Zambia and South Africa has video cameras placed near a couple of waterholes and updates its pictures every 30 or so seconds.

- The Environment News Service (http://ens.lycos.com/index.html) provides some good news.

B Study the photographs in this unit. What do they tell you about the environment and the future? Create a caption for each photograph above. Have you, as global citizens, any power to save the planet from total destruction?

79 The environment: ANIMAL RIGHTS 1

Introduction – animals and us

We humans *use* animals for a variety of purposes: for food; as pets; as work tools; as a means of entertainment in zoos and circuses; as sport; as laboratory tools for medical research or the testing of products and for clothing, decoration and shoes. Most people accept that animals are used to make our lives better (or at least prefer not to think about it).

Others, however, argue that because they are living creatures, animals have **rights** and it is wrong to exploit and use them for human ends. They are concerned about the way animals are used or abused in scientific research or testing; about the way people hunt and kill animals just for sport or for the fur; about eating other living creatures; about endangered species and about what happens to the animals we eat before they arrive in the supermarkets.

It is not surprising that the issue of animal rights causes so much strong feeling.

Attitudes to animals

Attitudes today

The growth in the number of vegetarians in the UK is a good indication of the growing interest in animal rights and personal health. In 1945 there were an estimated 100,000 vegetarians while today this figure is thought to be over four million. Cosmetic stores like *The Body Shop* – the first store to claim that none of their products were ever tested on animals – have become increasingly popular, while many other firms and supermarkets have followed suit and now sell animal friendly products, such as free range meat.

Public protest

Animal rights organizations, such as **Animal Aid, Compassion in World Farming** (see Addresses/websites) and the **RSPCA**, have become increasingly popular. In 1995 a woman was killed in the UK during a protest blockade to stop calves being transported to Europe in terrible conditions. The famous French actress and long-time animal rights activist Bridget Bardot attended her funeral in Coventry Cathedral. Some more extreme protests between December 2000 and February 2001 included ten nail bomb attacks against businesses by animal rights activists and two car bomb attacks against individuals connected with hunting. In February 2001 a prominent animal rights activist was sentenced to six months in jail after admitting sending threatening letters to employees of the animal research company, *Huntingdon Life Sciences Laboratory*.

Animals and religion

Awareness of animal rights is nothing new. Most of the world's major religions preach **compassion** for animals and teach that their lives are precious and should be respected. Compassion is quite a bit thinner on the ground in the Western tradition however:

- Rene Descartes (1596–1650) a philosopher whose thought greatly influenced Western thinking, argued that animals are little more than robots lacking minds and souls.

- Thomas Aquinas (1225–74) taught that animals are 'enslaved for the uses of others'.

- Those individuals who put compassion for animals into practice – like St Francis of Assisi (1182–1226) – were often considered eccentric.

■ With moves to abolish the human slave trade, people began to think about another form of slavery – that of animals. Abraham Lincoln (1809–65), former President of the US, for example, pronounced that it was only a matter of time before animals had legal rights.

Disconnected

On the face of it, average modern city-dwellers do not seem to have much of a relationship with animals at all. If they do, it is probably with a domesticated cat, dog or fish. But if you start looking at the products they buy, what they are made of and how they are made, you may find that people are much more connected with the animal world than their ancestors ever were. However, it is a very different connection. It is often a distant and a dead connection. What do you think? Are we more in contact with animals today – or less so?

Vegetarianism

Some people feel so strongly about animal rights that they refuse to eat meat products. A **vegetarian** is a person who lives on the products of the vegetable kingdom, with or without the use of eggs and dairy products, but excluding entirely the consumption of any part of the body of an animal as food – this includes chicken and fish. A person who eats only a little meat/fish or chicken, or mostly eats vegetarian food is not a vegetarian. A person who does not eat red meat but eats chicken or fish is not a vegetarian. (Whatever he or she might try to tell you!)

The concept of **ahimsa** (non-violence and respect for life) prevents a Hindu from causing harm to any creature and therefore many Hindus are vegetarian. Cows, for example, are so highly revered that the killing of them is banned. Cows that no longer produce milk are retired, not slaughtered. Special sanctuaries called **goshallas** have been created for them.

Vegans

A **vegan** is a person who lives on the products of the plant kingdom to the exclusion of all products from the animal kingdom. A vegan consumes no animal by-products, for example, eggs, cheese or dairy products. Vegans avoid both animal derivatives and animal-tested products in their lifestyle. This means the avoidance of meat, milk, eggs, butter and so on, as well as leather, wool, cosmetics, soaps and shampoos derived from animal ingredients or tested on animals.

Launching your learning

A What do the following terms mean? **Compassion, animal rights, ahimsa, goshallas, vegetarian, vegan.**

B Give the views of three individuals from the past who have expressed an opinion on animals.

C Why do you think *The Body Shop* is proud of the fact that it does not test its products on animals?

D Why do you think people are so concerned about how animals are treated?

TALKING POINTS

'The question is not, can they reason? Nor, can they talk? But can they suffer?'

English philosopher Jeremy Bentham (1748–1832)

'One is almost inclined to say that men are the devils on earth and animals, the tortured souls.'

German philosopher Arthur Schopenhauer (1788–1860)

▲ Fifty millions animals worldwide die in laboratories

Do we abuse them?

Before you read this section, take a look at the box 'Animals are us'. Think about what it says as you consider the rights and wrongs of conducting experiments on animals.

Animal experimentation

The benefits

For many years animals have been used for medical research. New drugs are often tested on animals, such as mice, rats or cats, to see if they are suitable for use by humans. Medical advances which have depended on animal research include anaesthetics, open-heart surgery, whooping cough and polio vaccines, multiple sclerosis, kidney transplants, high blood pressure drugs, AIDS research, psychiatric drugs, life support systems for premature babies and gene therapy.

Thousands of lives are saved each year through medicines and surgical techniques first tested on animals. Most people agree that the benefits to humans in terms of reduced suffering and cures for disease outweigh the suffering inflicted on the animals. They do not like to think about what happens in the research laboratories, but accept that it is necessary and for the good of humankind in general.

Opposition

A growing number of people, however, cannot accept that experimentation on animals is justified. They point out that every year more than two and a half million animals suffer and die in British laboratories in the cause of human health. At least 50 million do so worldwide. They also argue that the information the experiments provides may not be that valuable. The **British Union for the Abolition of Vivisection** (BUAV) (see Addresses/websites) argues that experiments are unreliable because they tell us about animals, not people.

Since the 1970s, animal rights activists have argued that animals have rights and should not be used for experiments regardless of the possible benefits to human health. They argue that simply because chimpanzees, rats, dogs, cats and farm animals are not members of our species, that does not give us the right to abuse them and kill them for our own ends.

Although they may not be able to do higher mathematics, chimpanzees have the same rich emotional and social life as humans and, as they basically have the same nervous system and lower brain (where emotions come from), they are capable of feeling pain and distress in exactly the same way as us.

Speciesism – a definition

Animal rights activists accuse scientists of **speciesism**: a prejudice towards the interests of members of one's species and against those from other species. Sometimes their opposition leads to direct action.

Vital research?

Much of the research involving animals is to test drugs and research into possible cures. Many animals, however, are used in countries around the world to test cosmetics and toiletries. The companies producing them need to know that they will not have harmful effects on humans. Some of these companies' products may seem vital to us, but do we really need to torture animals simply to bring a new kind of make-up or deodorant to the supermarket shelves?

ANIMALS ARE US

Human beings have much in common with other animals:

- **Genetic structure** – Humans share 98 per cent of their genetic structure with chimpanzees.

- **Pain** – Humans share the capacity to suffer and feel pain with all vertebrates including fish.

- **Caring** – Humans share the capacity for caring about other mammals, as do elephants, whales and dolphins. Elephants will administer first aid to wounded companions, applying clay to stop the flow of blood.

- **Communication** – Humans communicate with one another, as do other animals.

- **Social** – Humans are social animals and live with or live near each other, as do most animals.

The 1986 Animals Act

In 1986 the government passed the **Animals Act** to control animal experiments. It incorporates the 'Three R s' principle for animal research:

- **Reduction** – Cutting the number of animal experiments, for example, by swapping information between countries.

- **Refinement** – Extracting the maximum amount of information from the minimum number of experiments.

- **Replacement** – There are many possible replacements for higher animals in experiments, including the so-called 'lower organisms', for example, the horseshoe crab.

TALKING POINTS

Here are two comments by university professors. Read them before discussing the questions below with your classmates:

'If possessing a higher intelligence does not entitle one human to use another for his own ends how can it entitle humans to exploit non-humans for the same purpose?'

Pete Singer – Philosopher and Professor of Bioethics

'You can't go to a doctor without having a treatment that has been tested on animals – you can't pick and choose.'

Colin Blakemore – Professor of Physiology

A If experimenting with animals saves human lives, does that make it acceptable?

B Is there a difference between experiments that test possible life-saving drugs and those tests carried out for cosmetics and toiletries?

Fox hunting

Fox hunting is an issue which arouses great emotion in people. The issue of fox hunting has caused considerable friction between those wishing to keep it as a country sport, and those who declare it a blood sport and want to see it banned.

What hunt supporters say

Hunt supporters see foxes as a menace. They point to the way that foxes kill livestock, such as chickens or lambs, often killing more than they need for food. They believe that foxes need to be controlled and that hunting is as effective a way of doing this as any other. They argue that hunting dogs kill foxes far quicker than by other controlled means and so this is the least cruel method. Hunting, whether with rod, line, net, gun or dog should not, they argue, be made a criminal offence where the species hunted is not endangered or protected and the method of hunting is conducted in accordance with recognized codes of practice which minimize animal suffering.

Hunt supporters also say that hunting is part of the country way of life that has existed for centuries and the activity plays a significant role in the control, conservation and management of the species and its habitat. It is a basic freedom of country people to take part in any sport they like and the government should not try to stop them – especially as they see the government as led mostly by 'townies' who do not understand the country way of life. If hunting is banned, should shooting follow – and even angling?

What hunt opponents say

Anti-hunt campaigners on the other hand, consider that hunting foxes is nothing more than a cruel blood sport enjoyed by just a small number of country folk. Hunt opponents also argue that foxes are not the menace they are made out to be and other ways of controlling them would be less cruel. Being chased for miles by packs of hounds and then killed by them is barbaric and obscene. A number of people feel so strongly about fox hunting that they become **hunt saboteurs** and attempt to disrupt hunts. Sometimes this leads to violence between hunt supporters and the saboteurs.

CITIZENSHIP CHALLENGE

One of the aspects of citizenship which you cover in school is concerned with 'learning more about fairness, respect for democracy and diversity'. The hunting debate provides a good opportunity for exploring these issues.

Use the websites listed here to find out what you can about the arguments for and against hunting. Consider them as impartially and objectively as you can (that is, use reason not emotion to decide how you feel) and then prepare a letter to your local MP setting out either your support or your opposition to the banning of hunting.

Pro hunting website:
www.countrysidealliance.org

Anti hunting websites:
www.league.uk.com (League Against Cruel Sports)

▲ Sport or barbarity?

Hunting and the Law

In 2002, British Members of Parliament voted for a ban on fox hunting. However, a ban cannot become law until it is passed by the House of Lords, where there is much opposition to a ban.

Genesis and animals

The Book of Genesis in the Tenakh is the story of how God created the natural world. God tells Adam and Eve that man should rule over the earth and all the creatures in it (Genesis 1: 26) and humanity has been given seed-bearing plants and fruit to eat (Genesis 1: 29). There is no mention of people eating animals and the arrangement for humans to have a vegetarian diet comes after the arrangement for people to rule over the earth.

Noah's Ark

Later on in Genesis (chapters 6–9), we find the story of God flooding the world and Noah's Ark. After the flood has subsided, God tells Noah and his family that they can now eat 'everything that moves' (Genesis 9: 3). This seems like God is giving them permission to eat meat. So within a few pages of the first book of the Tenakh, there seems to be two different and contradictory commands.

Today, modern Christians and Jews are just as likely to be meat eaters as anyone else.

Christian view

The basis of traditional Christian thought about animals has come mainly from Thomas Aquinas who argued that animals and plants were a lesser life-form than humans. For many people this view remains the basic Christian teaching to this day – you may have heard people saying that animals have no 'soul'.

Over time, however, Christian writers have had different views on animal rights.

- Humphrey Primatt, an English vicar in the eighteenth century, wrote a book about animals and cruelty. He said all life was created by God and that any creature that can feel pain has the right to not have pain inflicted upon it – this includes animals. Primatt's work lead to the foundation of the **RSPCA** (Royal Society for the Prevention of Cruelty to Animals) in 1824.

- A famous Christian theologian from Germany, Albert Schweitzer (1875–1965) taught that *all* life is sacred – meaning animals too. In his book, *Civilization and Ethics*, he argues that people, animals and plants are created by God and to injure or kill any life-form on purpose is to act against God's creation.

- Another Christian theologian, Karl Barth (1886–1968), answered Schweitzer in a way that almost went back to the Aquinas argument. He said that since God became man in the human form of Jesus, humans are more important than other life-forms – in other words animals cannot be equal to humans.

'Dolly'

The blistering pace of technology makes cloning possibilities appear to be endless. Cloning was first brought to public attention in 1997 when scientists in Scotland produced a sheep called **Dolly**, cloned using DNA from another sheep. Since then scientists have produced **Geep** – half goat and half sheep, and have cloned monkeys.

Humonkeys

What about combining humans and monkeys to make a 'half and half breed'? This is not impossible in today's sophisticated laboratories.

KEY QUESTIONS

1 How many genes would *humonkeys* have to have to gain human rights?

2 Would *humonkeys* be recognized as morally responsible individuals if they are able to talk?

3 Would theologians decide that *humonkeys* are able to receive salvation like human beings?

Return of the mammoth?

Scientists are now working on ways of bringing extinct species, using cloning techniques, back to life.

In October 1999 a team of scientists successfully airlifted a twenty-five ton male woolly mammoth from its grave in Siberia where it had been frozen for 20,000 years. It was complete except for its head. Since mammoths have been extinct for over 10,000 years, some scientists proposed that attempts be made to breed a living mammoth from DNA or cell nucleus retrieved from the body.

A modern elephant ovum would be used because it is the closest living relative to the mammoth. If successful, this would produce an elephant with some mammoth features.

KEY QUESTIONS

Remarkable stories like these raise some important issues:

1 Should human beings interfere with the evolutionary process?

2 If evolution proceeds through natural selection and the survival of the fittest, did mammoths become extinct for some reason? Was their extinction necessary in order to keep a balanced ecology?

'Bessie'

Throughout the world many species of animals and birds are threatened with extinction. Could cloning help to prevent this from happening?

Are not humans, as 'stewards of creation', responsible for the survival of other life forms by any means necessary?

As many of the remaining threatened species do not readily mate in captivity, scientists argue that cloning is their only hope. In October 2000 American scientists impregnated a cow with a cell cloned from an Asian gaur – a rare wild ox. They removed the DNA from a cow's ovum, fused it with DNA taken from a skin cell of a gaur, and produced a gaur calf called **Bessie**.

The techniques of transferring the nucleus of one species into another are still in their early stages and mistakes and errors do occur. For instance it took 277 attempts to produce Dolly and many lambs were produced with abnormalities.

Human health

Recent crises in farming like BSE and foot and mouth have made many people question the ways in which we produce meat. **The Church of Scotland**, after carefully studying the ethical implications of cloning, has called for a ban on animal cloning as a means of meat and milk production.

Tetra

In 2000 there were more than 80,000 new animals with mutant genes born in British laboratories. Genes from humans are already working in microbes, fish, mice, rabbits, cows, sheep and pigs. In 2000 scientists in America announced that they had cloned a monkey called **Tetra**. They hope that cloning will produce identical laboratory animals for animal research and testing. Much of the research on animals aims to improve human health. Experience gained in cloning animals may improve our understanding of genetics and disease, and could have a number of positive results for humans:

- **'Humanized pigs'** could provide heart, liver or kidney transplants for humans in the future. Cloned pigs could produce organs that will not be rejected by humans. This would save many lives because thousands of people die each year waiting for available human organs. However there are enormous health risks (see Unit 25).

- **Transgenic animals**, which carry genes from human and other species, are used for research into treatments for genetically transmitted diseases such as sickle-cell anaemia.

- **Biological proteins** are essential for treating diseases, including diabetes, Parkinson's Disease and cystic fibrosis. However, these proteins are difficult to make. Animals can be genetically altered in order to produce proteins in their milk. These materials can be separated from the milk and used in medicine.

The proteins would be extracted and used for artificial tendons, ligaments or tissue repair. A sheep's genes can also be altered so that it produces protein molecules in its milk – 50 sheep could produce enough clotting factor to treat all the haemophiliacs in the UK.

Pets

Although the issues of human and animal cloning will be hotly disputed for many years to come, there is already a market for clones, though not human ones, yet. The cloning of pets is already being carried out in the US. Rich people are prepared to have the DNA taken out of either an existing pet or one that has just died and have it cloned to produce a new pet.

Launching your learning

A What do you understand by **transgenic**?

B What do you understand by **geeps**?

C What do you understand by **humonkeys**?

D What are **Bessie**, **Dolly** and **Tetra**?

FOR DISCUSSION

A Transgenic pigs may only have a tiny amount of human genes in them, but a richer mix could be made. At what point do these pigs stop being pigs? How many genes do these animals have to have to gain human rights?

B Even if engineering animals provides us with benefits, do animals not have rights too?

C Do you think that cloning and engineering animals is 'playing God' and may ultimately destroy the natural order forever?

83 The environment: ANIMAL RIGHTS 5

Jain view

About 2,500 years ago in India lived Vardhamana. His followers are called Jains. They believe that Vardhamana was 'The Great Hero' or 'Mahavira'. The key to Mahavira's teaching are:

> 'There is nothing so small and subtle as the soul, nor any element so vast in space. Similarly, there is no quality of the soul more subtle than non-violence and no virtue of spirit greater than reverence for life (ahimsa).'

Ahimsa, he said means: 'Do not injure, abuse, oppress, insult, torment, torture or kill any living beings.' The Jain tradition teaches: 'Ahimsa para dharmah' (Non-violence is the supreme religion). All souls are equal, irrespective of species and all have the power for spiritual growth.

Jains go even further than their Hindu or Buddhist neighbours, who might be equally concerned not to injure any living creatures. Jain monks can be seen in India with their mouths covered to prevent harming any living beings in the air. They also carry a brush, gently sweeping any insects that might be on their path.

Maharira once said:

> 'One who neglects or disregards the existence of earth, air, fire, water and vegetation, disregards his own existence, which is entwined with them.'

Muslim view

The Qur'an teaches that Allah created a balanced natural world and made humans its **custodians**:

> 'Allah has made you custodians and inheritors of the earth.'

Qur'an, Surah 6: 165

The Qur'an also teaches that Allah is compassionate and merciful to animals:

> 'There is not an animal that lives on the earth, nor a being that flies, that is not part of a community like you.'

Qur'an, Surah 6: 38

This teaching of respect and care for all creatures means that in everyday life Muslims have certain established principles.

- It is forbidden to be cruel to animals – domestic and farm animals should be treated well and work animals should never be made to carry excessive loads.

- Hunting for sport or pleasure is forbidden. Hunting for food must be done without deliberate cruelty. Killing animals for human vanity, such as the fur or ivory trade, is forbidden.

- Animal experiments and vivisection for cosmetic or luxury goods purposes are also forbidden, as is factory farming.

Halal

Any animals killed for research purposes should be killed by **halal** methods – the animal's throat is slit with the sharpest possible knife while a prayer to Allah is said. This is believed to be the quickest and most painless way to slaughter an animal. Many non-Muslims think that halal slaughter is cruel. However, when the method of halal slaughter was first written down 1,300 years ago, it improved the existing way in which animals were killed and was as humane as possible at the time. Also, the methods of slaughter in modern factory slaughterhouses are often brutal and cruel with production lines of animals all watching each other go to their death.

Some people argue too that under the rules of a halal slaughter a BSE type of crisis would be unlikely.

IslamVeg is an organization run by Muslims in the US who believe that the best way to follow the teachings of the Qur'an is to be vegetarian. They argue that nowhere in the Qur'an does it say that people have to eat meat and the methods of modern meat production, combined with the treatment of animals in factory farming in all countries, means that Muslims sometimes cannot be certain that meat is really halal.

CITIZENSHIP CHALLENGE

1 A French philosopher called Voltaire (1694–1778) once said:

'I disagree with what you say, but I will defend to the death your right to say it.'

Do you think that it is acceptable to extend this right so society allows a small number of animal rights protestors to decide whether laboratories carry out animal experiments?

2 'You cannot have rights without duties.' Consider this statement with reference to animal rights.

Launching your learning

A Explain religious attitudes to animals and the responsibilities human beings have towards the animal kingdom.

B Analyze how these religious attitudes and teachings might be applied to current practices and arguments about animal rights.

C 'Although a particular animal experiment causes distress to animals, if it can save human lives it is acceptable.' What do you think? Give reasons for your answer.

Summing up

We can easily forget what an important part animals play in our lives. They are used by people all over the world and even if we live in a city environment and are seldom in contact with them their role in our lives is significant. Over recent years an increasing number of people have been asking the question: 'Have animals, like humans, got rights?' If they have, then what are our responsibilities towards them and how should we treat them? If we think that animals are on Earth only to be used by humans, and they do not have rights, do we still have responsibilities towards the way we treat them? Issues surrounding animal rights also raise questions about how we see ourselves because the way we treat animals reflects something about the way we view ourselves and the planet we share with them.

▲ 'There is not a bird that flies that is not part of a community like you.' The Qur'an

84 The media: MEDIA MOGULS

'Everyone has the right to freedom of opinion and expression; this right includes freedom to hold opinions without interference and to seek, receive and impart information and ideas through any media and regardless of frontiers.'

Article 19 of the Universal Declaration of Human Rights

▲ Fantasy across frontiers

The media age

Never before in history have people been so dominated by the **mass media** – television, magazines, newspapers, books, video, radio, advertisements, the Internet, the cinema – spewing out images and words. Billions of hours of our collective attention are directed towards sources of information, communication and entertainment.

From birth to old age, from *Tweenies* to *Last of the Summer Wine*, from *Beano* to *People's Friend*, everyone is exposed to some form of the media. Its influence on our thoughts, attitudes and behaviour is not to be underestimated.

We can watch history as it happens. The world did not watch the Fall of Rome, the Crusades or the Great Fire of London, but when the twin towers of the World Trade Centre in New York collapsed in September 2001 after being struck by two planes, the cameras were there (see Unit 70).

Who owns the media?

Never before has there been such a concentration of power in the hands of so few people. It has been estimated that less than 500 billionaires own more than half of the world's wealth. Many of these people have either made their fortunes in the media industry or used their wealth to control a part of it. They have learnt how to create a market. They have attracted consumers who have bought into their ideas about beauty, femininity, masculinity, success, happiness, love and sex and about how to make friends and influence people.

The hard sell

The media sell a product to a market. The product is *us*, audiences. The market is other businesses – advertisers. A successful media company is one that attracts many people to its outlets. It would be surprising if the sellers, the media owners, tried to make the audience, you and me, buy something that was not created by them. The choice of media content is created by and reflected in, the interests of the sellers.

KEY IDEAS

While media technology offers more choice, especially through digital technology, the media itself, in terms of who owns it, is shrinking.

A handful of corporations control the world's information. The global media industry is fast becoming more powerful than many governments.

Monopoly

In 2001 one of the biggest business mergers in history took place when *America Online* (AOL) and *Time Warner* become one. A vast empire of broadcasting, music, films and publishing joined forces with one of the world's largest Internet providers, all fed to consumers through *Time Warner's* cable network. This multinational corporation has the power to choose what they *want* to show. The problem such business mergers pose is that they result in one corporation forming a **monopoly** – complete unshared control. The unique advantage of having power over the media is that challenging opinions and opposing views can be prevented from getting a hearing.

News corporations

Newspapers are a powerful instrument all over the world. Newspapers are often owned by individuals who, quite naturally, have their own views and their own particular **bias**, particularly about politics. The *Sun*, for example, is owned by Rupert Murdoch whose *News Corporation* owns over 100 newspapers and eight publishing houses worldwide, as well as numerous television networks including *Sky, BSKYB, Phoenix TV* and *Fox TV*. Murdoch is very powerful and is unlikely to encourage people to question a system that has made him so powerful. In 1999 two reporters working for *Fox TV* were sacked for reporting about the use of growth hormones in milk. The General Manager of *Fox* told them: 'We paid $3 billion for these television stations, we'll decide what the news is. The news is what we tell you it is'.

Phoenix TV recently began broadcasting to China. The Chinese Government stands accused of violating Human Rights. Murdoch, however, to make sure that he becomes even richer and more **powerful**, has made an agreement with the Chinese government: if *Phoenix TV* refuses to report items like the illegal and cruel Chinese military occupation of Tibet (see Addresses/websites), then it is free to broadcast and advertise in China.

TALKING POINT

'It has often been said that journalism's role is to afflict the comfortable and comfort the afflicted. Sadly, too many media owners – many of whom have great power – see the role of the media differently: they believe the role of the media is to comfort the comfortable and ignore the afflicted.'

Frank Vogl, Journalist

FOR DISCUSSION

The media has created **a global consumer** – someone continually being persuaded or influenced to buy what the media, usually owned by multinational corporations, produce. The owners of these corporations become very rich. They cannot become so mega rich without exploiting others. You cannot **exploit** women and men without **deceiving** them. Deception by the media is **subtle**. It works on the conscious and the unconscious levels. It gives you the impression that you are free to choose while it robs you of all the means of free choice.

85 The media: *TUNING IN*

Today, watching TV often means fighting, violence and foul language – and that is just deciding who gets to hold the remote control.

Television

It has been estimated that the average person in Britain will spend about eight years of their life watching television. Television viewing is now the main leisure activity in most families. On an average day in Britain 38 million people watch TV for at least three hours. Before the age of fourteen the average child will have seen about 18,000 'deaths', usually murders, on their TV screen. Many people are increasingly concerned about the massive influence television has, particularly on the young. They argue that although TV has some very positive aspects – for example, it informs, educates and can reduce loneliness – it also has many dangerous aspects.

Couch potatoes

When we spend hours in front of 'the box' a whole range of leisure pursuits, social meetings and information sources are cut off from us. Television viewing is **passive** – people *switch off* from friends and neighbours. As more and more people stay in as 'couch potatoes', community living becomes a thing of the past. Health can even be affected, for example obesity.

TV addicts

Research suggests that children who are television **addicts** have weaker imagination and concentration levels than those who do not watch much TV. As a technology, television works by electronic scanning, shutting down the functioning of those parts of the brain that help us to think clearly and independently.

The good life?

Day after day TV exposes viewers to a false portrayal of people, concentrating on the violent and the sensational. The values and goals striven for are often superficial. Wealth, power, glamour, physical beauty or physical strength are seen as being desirable or necessary for a **good life**. Television has its own set of values. It tells us what happiness is, what success is, what we should buy and how we should behave.

The watershed

The choice of material for children's television is governed by guidelines. On the BBC and ITV there is a 9 pm **watershed**. After this time certain programmes are thought to be unsuitable for children. These include programmes that show violence, bad behaviour by **role models**, racial stereotypes, drug-taking, smoking, the use of knives, or criminal techniques, cruelty to children or animals, explicit sex and swearing. The guidelines do not ban all violence, but they stress that the consequences of violent behaviour should be shown and that news producers should consider the ages of the audience in the early evening.

Screen violence

Recent surveys in Britain reported that two-thirds of nine to eleven-year-olds have watched eighteen-rated videos, such as *Pulp Fiction* and *Silence of the Lambs*, and that 71 per cent of people believe there is a link between screen violence and violent crime. Warner Home Videos chose not to release *Natural Born Killers* on video following the massacre of children at Dunblane in 1996. Similarly, Warner Cinemas in 2000 decided not to show the film *Kids*, depicting child sex scenes.

The news media *(see Unit 86)*

When we see the 'News' on TV, or read the 'News' in a newspaper, or listen to the 'News' on Radio 1, we think what we are hearing is the **truth**. However, the people who decide what news items are to be covered shape the news for us by selecting and editing items.

Some tabloid 'newspapers' are known to create stories where none exist. For some, like the *Sun* or the *Star*, headline news can mean Martine McCutcheon's latest hairstyle rather than the death of a homeless woman in Manchester. And the *Sun* puts a different interpretation on events than, say, the *Independent*. What the *Independent* calls a 'demonstration' the *Sun* might call a 'riot'. Exaggerating stories to make them more 'newsworthy' is known as **sensationalism**.

Some newspapers will set out to damage a person's reputation if their interests are threatened. For example, when the MP Clare Short put forward a Bill in Parliament trying to ban sexist images on 'page three', (see Unit 39) the *Sun*, ran a series of nasty personal articles on her.

Bias

Newspaper reports of the 2001 May Day demonstration (see Unit 63) in London highlight the way that truth is manipulated. Compare the language used by the *Sun*:

> 'Anarchist mobs … shaven headed yobs … thugs … rampage … mayhem … rioters'

with the language used by the *Guardian*:

> 'anti-capitalist demonstrators … activists … protestors'.

Bias is just as obvious in the use of photographs and their captions see below.

Launching your learning

Find out the meaning of the following words and phrases:
Passive, the good life, watershed, role models, objectionable, truth, sensationalism, bias.

▲ 'The thin blue line holds back anticapitalist protesters' *The Guardian*

▶ 'Nuts in May' *The Sun*

86 The media: *THIS IS THE NEWS!*

▲ News is often unbalanced in its coverage of *all* the facts

The issues

Although many countries have signed the Universal Declaration of Human Rights (see Unit 52), freedom of opinion, expression and information is still not universally given.

Even in the developed and freer nations, news and information is subject to **partiality** and **unbalanced** coverage or just plain **omissions** of the major issues.

Although we have more TV channels than ever before they do little to bring us the **fair, objective**, tough reporting that is truly needed to bring global peace and stability.

Most people get their view of the world from the mainstream media. It is, therefore, important that mainstream media be objective and present accurate representations of what goes on around the world.

Rwanda

In 1999 the United Nations Secretary-General Koffi Annan criticized international news reporting in many developed nations for declining coverage of world events. One example was the genocide in Rwanda in Africa in the 1990s.

In 1994 at least half a million people were massacred in a **genocide**, perhaps as many as three quarters of the Tutsi population. At the same time, tens of thousands of Hutu were slaughtered because they opposed the killing campaign and the forces directing it.

During the horrific genocide in Rwanda, the media played a major part in creating an atmosphere for the terrible human suffering that occurred. A report by **Human Rights Watch** (see Addresses/websites) found that the killing campaign was planned for a long time and the international community was aware of what was going on, yet ignored it, even when they were present during the systematic killings.

KEY IDEAS

Poor and misrepresented press coverage of the developing world by the developed countries such as the UK can lead to stereotyping (see Unit 34).

Accurate media representation of world issues is crucial. Whenever media reports are censored or biased then people's basic rights are undermined.

Censored!

- A government which censors the information available to its people in a state of national emergency is a government which seeks to keep the people in a state of ignorance.

- As long as people have sought after power they have tried to control communication channels and information.

- The more mass media that exists, and the more powerful the development of information technology, the more we can be controlled.

- With mass media, the simplest method of control is by straight censorship, that is by banning certain types of information.

- In many countries people are thrown into prison because of what they have written, or what they have said. And where the state can manipulate the media without opposition, what is printed or broadcast bears little resemblance to the truth (see Unit 85).

CITIZENSHIP CHALLENGE

A Look at the photograph in this unit. What does it tell you about the media?

B Some commentators have argued that if the crimes against humanity in Rwanda had taken place in Europe they would have made headline news for weeks. Why do you think they feel this way? Can you think of reasons why events in Rwanda were barely mentioned in the tabloid newspapers or on the mainstream news?

C Look at what is current in the news. Often news reports are just presented as facts. However, it is sometimes hard to verify the reports and they end up being accepted as *facts*, rather than just one *perspective* – an opinion. Can you distinguish between 'facts' and 'opinions'?

D The multinational companies have control in the production and maintenance of electronic components, computers and telecommunications technology. As national economies rely more and more on these technologies, the power of these companies increases. What problems could this cause?

E Compare and contrast 'objective and fair' news reporting with 'partiality and unbalanced' news reporting. Give examples.

87 The media: COMMERCIAL BREAK

Modern life is one long commercial break

The images and language of advertising are all around us, increasingly 'in your face'. A person living in a British city is bombarded, every single day, by over 1,600 advertising images.

Advertising tries to sell us not just clothes and records but a whole lifestyle. We are told that if we buy the 'right' trainers and the 'right' mobile phone and listen to the 'right' music then we will be successful and popular with our friends. Later on we will have to have the 'right' job, the 'right' car and the 'right' house, and when we are old we will no doubt need the 'right' pension and the 'right' old people's home.

Positive images

Advertising *can* be used for good. For example drink driving campaigns or shock images, such as *Barnardo's* 2000 campaign, which showed pictures of a baby dependent on heroin, drew attention to the plight of some children. The advert on this page aims to encourage positive attitudes.

Selling audiences

When TV sells advertising space it is selling audiences. It offers advertisers a known audience to which to advertise. The fee is fixed according to what kind of audience it is. If a programme is mainly watched by people in their twenties to forties it will cost more to advertise in its commercial breaks than, say, in a programme aimed at younger or older people with less spending power. Advertisers over recent years, playing on people's fears and insecurities, have targeted 'low yield' groups in the afternoon, for example the elderly who are persuaded to part with their savings in return for some kind of healthcare plan.

Subtle

Many adverts rely on simple visual clues, like the *Silk Cut* cigarette adverts which use photographs of pieces of cut silk and no words at all. Advertising is more of a code than a language. Words are used in compressed and witty ways, for example, one advert uses three letters: NRG. It is left up to the **consumer** to **decode** the advert. The more time it takes to decode the longer we are in the grip of the advertiser's power.

SLAVES TO FASHION

Adverts tempt people to follow the latest fashion. Some football clubs change their strips frequently so that old strips worn by supporters are outdated and they have to buy new ones to 'keep up'. The fashion industry is involved in **child labour**: Michael Jordan earned US $20 million a year for endorsing Nike shoes – more than **Nike's** entire 30,000-strong Indonesian workforce earned making them.

Targeting the kids

Children's spending in Britain and the US has roughly doubled every ten years for the past three decades. $2 billion is spent annually to target young consumers. Marketing strategies measure humans in terms of their lifelong consuming value (£70,000 per person is the going estimate) and advertising is everywhere. It is estimated the average child sees between 20,000–40,000 commercials every year.

At six months of age, babies are forming mental images of corporate logos and mascots. A child wakes up in London or New York in her *Disney* character pyjamas, rolls out of her *Barney* sheets, her toothbrush and toothpaste are covered in cute licensed characters. Gathering up her *Pokemon* cards and strapping on her *Rugrats* backpack, she heads off to school.

But in America advertising does not stop at the school gates. The school is the biggest ad space of all! *Channel One's* news broadcasts are provided free to schools who must promise that the students will watch its commercials; computers fill students' screens with ads; soft drink and fast-food companies take over cafeterias; hallways, posters and book covers all become billboards.

Consumerism

The lifestyle sold to us by the media is only one possible lifestyle among many. It is a **consumer** lifestyle for a **materialist** society. Sometimes the power of the media makes it seem as if there is no alternative to **capitalism** and materialism. However, in other times and places people have developed many different lifestyles and ways of organizing society. Some of these societies were religious societies, such as Tibet, where Buddhist monasteries and teachings were a central part of the culture, until the Chinese invaded; while societies such as Tanzania in the 1960s and 1970s, tried to create a **socialist** way of life with equality of opportunity for all.

Christmas

People's lifestyles in Britain were much less commercially orientated in the past. The annual festival of consumerism that we know as **Christmas** is very different today from what it was 40 years ago. For a few days all businesses would close down to mark the religious occasion with a token exchange of gifts. Today many people ignore the deeper religious meaning behind the festival and think of Christmas in terms of shopping. The pressure of commercialism marks Christmas out as a peak time of year for suicides, separations and debt.

FOR DISCUSSION

A Many advertisements today try and persuade us to buy things we do not need, with money we do not have, in order to impress people we do not know.

B Adverts try to manipulate audiences. If you buy a certain brand of hair gel, the advert implies that you will be attractive to the opposite sex.

C Adverts make us discontented with what we have got. If we were contented we would be happy and would not want more. But maybe? If I buy their product, I will be rich, powerful, sexy, loved, a player in their glamorous world.

D Images encouraging young people to act and behave in ways that are beyond their years, for example 'Boy Mags' for ten-year-old girls with pin-ups of fifteen-year-old boys, or adverts for fizzy alcoholic drinks clearly aimed at the young, should be banned.

88 The media: CELEBRITIES

Chris Evans, Posh Spice, Zoe Ball, 'Nasty Nick', Vinnie Jones – are all TV personalities. But what exactly is 'personality' and why does the media portray these people in the way it does?

Personality – a definition

The dictionary gives a number of definitions:

- personal existence or identity; the condition of being a person
- the distinctive qualities of a person
- a famous person; a celebrity.

The word 'personality' comes from the Latin *persona* and the Greek word *prosopon*, which originally meant the mask worn by actors in the ancient Greek theatre. The *persona* was the actor's mask, a character in a play. In English the word *persona* still has the meaning of a *mask*, an aspect of the personality shown to others, of an assumed role.

▲ Famous for being famous?

Unmasked

This is really quite important if we think about it. The word we use for our identity for 'who we are' comes from a word meaning a *mask*. If we are no more than what we want others to think we are, then we can reinvent ourselves every six months, like the pop star Madonna. We can cut and dye our hair, change our clothes and makeup, listen to different music, buy a new mobile phone and even change our friends. But does this make us any different underneath? Is there a real character, an 'essential me', behind the mask of personality, or is 'what you see, what you get'?

Famous for being famous

A celebrity is a well-known person, someone who is *celebrated*. In your grandparents' time, a celebrity was a person popular perhaps because of their achievements as a scientist, an author, an actor, a musician or a sportsperson, but nowadays many celebrities are famous just for being famous.

Soap and spice

Why is it that we become so identified with the lives of footballers, rock singers, TV 'celebrities' and film stars? Is it just because they are rich and we are not? Or do we admire them because they are admired?

One clue can be found by looking at soap operas. It has been observed that the poorer the country, the richer the characters in its soap operas. For instance, in Brazil, where desperate poverty is widespread, soap operas about the super-rich are very popular. In India, the man who drives the rickshaw will spend his work-breaks reading and talking about cricket players and Bollywood film stars. Their fabulous wealth makes them not only admired but almost worshipped. Celebrities have become gods, stars in the heavens, and for many have replaced the gods of their religion.

Stars in their eyes

The cult of celebrity is based on dreams. The media has developed a culture of **individualism**. It glorifies the individual hero, the star. We dream of being like those whom we admire, we dream of being rich and famous, supposedly 'successful' and surrounded by everything we could want in life. But deep down we know it is a dream, and no more likely to come true than winning the lottery. Yet it is this dream that is sold to us by the mass media that surrounds us in our daily lives. Many religious thinkers believe that we are living in a dream and that the great religious teachers – Moses, Jesus, Krishna, Buddha, Muhammad (pbuh) and Guru Nanak – came to show us how to wake up.

The real self

Many religions teach that there is a permanent identity, a soul or 'real self' behind the personality, behind the mask. The personality is more like a suit of clothes that we can put on and take off.

Sometimes we say that so-and-so is nice but 'has no personality'. If someone 'has personality' we mean that they have a lively character or socially attractive qualities. But does this mean they are a nice person? After all, we can 'smile as we kill', and someone can have a wonderful personality but a very bad character; they may be very attractive and popular, but also lie, steal and betray their friends. In the end, do we want our friends to be admired and envied, or to be loving, trustworthy and 'there for us' in times of need?

TALKING POINT

'Celebrity is not always a useless thing I suggest. In fact it's the only way anyone can get people to listen to us. It is a currency of a kind and if I can spend it on behalf of *Jubilee*, I will.'

Bono, lead singer of *U2* and campaigner for *Jubilee Plus* (see Addresses/websites)

CITIZENSHIP CHALLENGE

A With a friend, pick out any two famous personalities and try and work out, if you can, their real character behind the mask of personality, or is 'what you see, what you get'?

B Over the next week talk to an older person, maybe a grandparent, and ask them to write down the names of ten people who they looked up to when they were young. You should also write a list. Compare them. What have all these people done?

C Why does Bono believe that 'celebrity is not always a useless thing'?

Reality TV

The twenty-first century is seeing a new type of TV programme – '**reality TV**'. These shows are popular despite being unscripted and unrehearsed. It is this 'live' quality that makes them exciting to large numbers. 'Reality-based' TV uses ordinary people instead of professional actors.

Television ethics

Reality TV – watching ordinary people in extraordinary situations – has sparked an international debate on **television ethics**. It raises issues about privacy and the sorts of messages the media gives us about human nature.

Big Brother

Big Brother locked volunteer contestants in a house wired with live recording equipment linked directly to an Internet site and broadcast at regular intervals on national TV. Everything they did and said was visible. They had to remain there for ten weeks if they wanted to claim the 'cash prize'. Contestants were nominated out of the house throughout the ten week period by the group members and the watching public. It was sold to viewers as a **social experiment** – to see what the participants would do when left to their own devices.

When contestants were released they became instant celebrities. They had fan clubs, were in the papers, and were recognized on the street.

Bums on seats

Some people say shows like this are just boring. Why do people want to watch a bunch of strangers sitting around a house all day?

TV, they say, used to be like the movies – an escape from reality, a unique story, specially crafted, either funny or exciting, or intelligent, or emotional ... or something! TV producers admit the plot lines on these shows are mostly unremarkable. Yet they are very popular.

Television is a competitive business and producers are concerned about **ratings** – 'bums on seats' – how many people they can get to watch their programme. They are concerned that people will not switch on unless they are given more of everything – particularly more sex, more drama and greater opportunities to show people being unpleasant to one another. Viewers, like heroin addicts, need a greater dose each time than that which got them off before.

Millions were happy in 2000 to watch *Big Brother's* contestants hide each other's cigarettes but that was because they had never seen anything like it before. Now producers think that the only way of keeping their interest alive is to increase their dose of sex and drama. And the sequel to the series was seen to involve noticeably more sexual suggestion, and 'accidental' nudity and partial nudity. Looks and 'sex appeal' had a direct link with contestant popularity.

Survivor!

One contestant on the Swedish show *Operation: Robinson* did not survive. He killed himself a month after he got 'voted off' the island.

Survivor, shown on ITV in the summer of 2001, was set on a harsh snake infested island where the castaways had to trek two miles for water, light fires and kill rats for food.

Unlike *Big Brother*, which allowed things to happen and was character driven, the responses of those on *Survivor* were dictated and policed by the show's producers who created an extreme and unusual artificial environment.

Unlike *Big Brother*, in which nothing much really happened for long periods, *Survivor* was such an endless whirl of activity that viewers did not really get to know the characters.

'Trust no one'

Survivor advertised itself with the words: '*Trust no one*'. Critics argued that it gave a negative view of human nature – survival depends on shoving aside anyone in our way; or on deceiving and using people. It gives the message that stripped of civilization people quickly turn, quite naturally, into competitive, selfish and cruel primitives.

TALKING POINT

'"Don't trust any one" is the show's depressing slogan, and it's easy to see why they had to keep the castaways busy. The more they let them hang about, the more they would have found them forging bonds that led to cooperation, because that's what happens when people are thrown together. The desperate pretence that self-interest is the ultimate "truth" of our beings would be shown up for what it is, a fiction that only functions as long as it is rigidly policed.'

Charlotte Raven – TV critic

Voyeurism and exhibitionism

In ordinary life, watching the private details of a stranger's life is called spying, or voyeurism, and is frowned upon, if not illegal. But 'reality TV' concentrates on, and celebrates, **voyeurism**. Supporters say most people have fantasies of peering through their neighbours' walls.

Reality TV allows them to indulge those fantasies in a relatively safe, controlled way. On the flip side, the people being peered at are volunteers. They *want* to be watched – a characteristic some would call **exhibitionism**. In this case exhibitionism and voyeurism combine to create wildly popular television.

CITIZENSHIP CHALLENGE

A   Why does Charlotte Raven think that self-interest is not the ultimate 'truth' of our beings?

B   Before 'reality TV' only the beautiful, the wealthy or the well-connected could be famous. Reality TV picks average people off the street and makes them famous. Do you think the success of 'reality TV' has something to do with how it provides the average person with the experience of 'celebrity'? (See Unit 88.)

▲ Who could *you* trust?

90 The media: MAKING THE CUT

▲ Offensive, obscene, objectionable?

Eminem's hit single *Stan* – a song featuring a crazed fan, suicide and murder – leapt straight to the top of the UK charts in December 2000. But Eminem is as controversial as he is successful. His songs have attracted strong criticism from people appalled at their violent content directed at women and gay people and want his songs banned. This is not the first time that popular culture has sparked a moral panic. Everything from novels to horror comics have been accused of 'undermining moral values'.

In the 1950s it was Elvis' dancing that upset the authorities – TV appearances were filmed from the waist up so his pelvic thrusts could not be seen. In the 1960s the Rolling Stones' *Let's Spend the Night Together* was banned by the BBC or given restricted play.

In the 1970s the Sex Pistols' *God Save The Queen (it's a fascist regime)* – caused a stir and some DJs refused to play it.

Censorship – a definition

Censorship is carried out by a **censor**, an official who examines the media with the power to remove anything thought to be offensive, obscene or objectionable.

Hate sites

On the Internet it is easy for anyone to produce a website and mix fact and fiction to attract surfers. Many neo-Nazis and racists have set up sites that incite hatred and feed ignorance. The anti-racist organization **Searchlight** fights racism (see Addresses/websites).

Pornography

Pornography is a huge multi-billion pound industry. It is estimated that in the US alone the 'porn' industry is worth more than the music and film industries combined. You do not have to look far to find the evidence – thousands of 'sex sites' appear on the Internet and top shelves of newsagents are saturated with pornographic images and photographs.

There are forms of technically legal **child pornography**, where women have their pubic hair shaved and are posed to look like little girls. There is also sexual violence, with women being humiliated, whipped and beaten. Illegal pornography also circulates – sold from under the counter and on the Internet – featuring women bound and gagged, raped and tortured, and sometimes murdered, in the sinister and shocking world of '**snuff pornography**'.

Paedophiles

Hard core material is being found on Usenet Newsgroups where individuals exchange views.

Some of these groups are international paedophile rings producing and exchanging child pornography. Children using chat rooms have been lured into meetings with paedophiles and then raped in front of cameras.

In 2001, after a huge international police operation, seven British men were found guilty in the 'Wonderland Case' after police seized 750,000 images of child pornography and 1,800 hours of video footage depicting child pornography, some of which involved children of less than two years of age.

British and European police are committing more resources to tackle Internet crime. Behind the pornographic images are real children who have been severely damaged and traumatized by their experiences.

The prevention of child sex abuse online is now amongst their highest priorities. Charities like **Barnardo's**, **Childline**, and the **Children's Society** work to heighten public awareness about the Internet and children's safety. They lobby governments and the Internet industry to encourage them to do more to protect children. They also helped to introduce new legislation authorizing maximum sentences of ten years, rather than three years, for offences relating to possession of child pornography.

CITIZENSHIP CHALLENGE

A Can songs really provoke violent behaviour? If the authorities ban Eminem today what is to stop them banning anything else they do not like tomorrow? After all, *Romeo and Juliet* starts with young men joking about 'thrusting maids to the wall'. Should Shakespeare's play be performed, let alone be taught in classrooms?

B If just a few people are offended by sexually explicit films, violent lyrics, or 'video nasties' should they be banned? Do you think these films or lyrics influence or change the way that we see ourselves and the way that we relate to other people?

C Are there certain images that you find offensive or obscene or objectionable yet somebody else does not?

D Can we always trust that censors are working for the public interest?

E Look at the United Nations Declaration on Human Rights (see Unit 32). Are there any basic human rights being broken by censors who ban songs with violent lyrics?

91 The media: BIG BROTHER IS WATCHING

'No one shall be subjected to arbitrary interference with his privacy.'

Article 12 of the United Nations Declaration on Human Rights

Information technology – a definition

Information technology is the means by which information is transmitted using technology.

KEY ISSUES

The right to privacy
George Orwell in his novel *Nineteen Eighty Four* (written in 1949) foresaw state control, **invasion of privacy** and even 'thought control' through the mass media. The situation today, though less extreme, is disturbing.

Privacy can be invaded through sophisticated technology like the computerization of personal files. The key issue here is how far should states go to protect public interest without invading the individual's privacy? For example, the authorities can justify using sophisticated surveillance techniques to listen to telephone conversations or watching emails of suspected terrorists, criminals or paedophiles, in the interests of law and order. But should they have the power to invade *anyone's* privacy? Could it be argued that secret methods of surveillance threaten a cornerstone of British law: a person is 'innocent until proved guilty' (see Unit 54)?

Propaganda – a definition

- Propaganda is a persuasive technique. It is used by those with power to persuade and influence others' opinions by spreading certain beliefs, ideas or news.

- Society is controlled for the benefit of the powerful through propaganda. If a country wants to declare war on another country, there will be loud propaganda about 'human rights abuses'. Thus the public are kept ignorant of the fact that many violent events – planned, financed, armed and guided by their own nation's intelligence services – even happened.

- Propaganda does not work through argument or debate, but through the **manipulation** of symbols and basic human emotions.

- When most people think about propaganda, they think of the enormous political campaigns waged by Hitler and Stalin in the 1930s. Today, however, we are immersed in propaganda of varying sorts. Propaganda can be as blatant as a swastika or as subtle as a joke.

TALKING POINT

'We live in a dirty and dangerous world. There are some things the general public does not need to know about and shouldn't. I believe democracy flourishes when the government can take legitimate steps to keep its secrets and when the press can decide whether to print what it knows.'

Washington Post owner Katharine Graham

Sound bites

We are confronted with hundreds of messages each day. Many people respond to this pressure by processing messages more quickly and, when possible, by taking mental short-cuts. Propagandists love short-cuts (as politicians love **sound bites**), particularly those which short-circuit reasoned thinking. They encourage this by agitating emotions and by exploiting insecurities. History shows that propaganda is more often than not successful.

Launching your learning

A Find out the meaning of the following words and phrases:
Information technology, invasion of privacy, manipulation, techniques of persuasion, sound bites.

B The following extracts in *italics* are taken from the **Catechism of the Roman Catholic Church**. They sum up the concerns of the world religions towards the mass media today. Look at the units on the media in this book. Write down examples of where and how:

▲ The internet hub: www.bigbrother?

- the media gives rise '*to a passivity among users, making them less than vigilant consumers of what is said or shown*' (see Units 85, 87, 89)

- journalists do not '*serve the truth, and offend against justice in disseminating information*' (see Units 85–6)

- totalitarian states '*falsify the truth, exercise political control of opinion through the media*' and '*secure their tyranny by strangling and repressing everything they consider thought crimes*' (see Unit 86).

FOR DISCUSSION

'At the end of the day, how many people can you spy on, how many bank accounts can you freeze, how many conversations can you eavesdrop on, how many e-mails can you intercept, how many letters can you open, how many phones can you tap? The sheer scale of the surveillance will become a logistical, ethical and civil rights nightmare. It will drive everybody clean crazy. And freedom – that precious, precious thing – will be the first casualty. It's already hurt and haemorrhaging dangerously.'

Arundhati Roy – Indian writer

CITIZENSHIP CHALLENGE

Look at the computer graphic opposite showing the complicated structure of the Internet. Write down your thoughts about the image. How has improved technology expanded the potential of our private lives, but also opened up increased possibilities of '*Big Brother Watching You*'?

Celebration

In 2001, Channel 4 in Great Britain broadcast for the first time a series of nightly reports by satellite directly from the **Kumbha Mela**, the great religious festival held once every twelve years in India. All sorts of colourful, strange and delightful monks, yogis and eccentrics appeared in our living rooms while the reporters struggled to convey the powerful feelings of love and worship felt by the millions of people attending the festival.

The overall effect of the broadcasts made some people realize that people could still cheerfully come together to celebrate a spiritual power beyond their personalities and possessions, and that many of these people,

though desperately poor by Western standards, were rich in ways which materialists could never understand.

The Mahabharata

The two great epic stories of the Hindu religion, the *Mahabharata* and the *Ramayana*, were recently serialized and broadcast on Indian television in weekly episodes. The whole country virtually came to a standstill for an hour each week as hundreds of millions of people tuned in to watch the heroes and gods whose stories they knew so well.

In some villages, with only one television, the whole village came to watch. Although the advertisers whose products were touted in the commercial breaks may have done well and the actors who played some of the leading parts in the *Ramayana* went into politics on the back of their popularity, the main effect of the televising of the stories of the gods was a revival of interest in Hinduism.

Some would argue that this is a positive and uplifting use for television: the dramatization and broadcasting of the great works of art and mythology, which have shaped the lives of millions, rather than soap operas about the petty squabbles and intrigues of publicans and shopkeepers.

Seven years in Tibet

In the 1990s, a number of Hollywood film stars became interested in Tibetan Buddhism.

They began to publicize the fate of Tibet since its invasion by the Chinese in 1951 and their brutal suppression of a Tibetan uprising in 1959. The Dalai Lama (see Unit 67), the spiritual and political leader of the country, was forced to escape to India, where he remains in exile to this day.

▲ Live, by satellite: yogi power!

At the time, the United Nations documented how the Chinese had killed a million Tibetans and completely destroyed virtually all their monasteries and religious buildings. Monks were shot or crucified (see Unit 51), many nuns were raped and tortured, landowners were beaten and often killed.

All this was well known to those who cared to look. However, for 30 years little was said or done about it and the continuing oppression and suffering of the Tibetan people was almost completely ignored.

The reason was not hard to find. It was to do with politics and business. For example, in the 1970s, the President of the US, Richard Nixon, made a trade agreement with China. Everyone involved kept quiet about the horrors that the Tibetan people had suffered because China and America wanted to trade with each other.

However, once Hollywood took an interest, the Dalai Lama became a media star. A number of his books were published to great acclaim and two epic films were made about his life: *Seven Years in Tibet*, starring Brad Pitt and *Kundun*. Both became box office hits.

God online

Vast amounts of information are now available from the Internet on just about any subject and many religious groups have websites publicizing their beliefs.

The problem is that without any form of control – **regulation** – over who can and cannot have websites, it is not always easy to know who we are dealing with when we browse a website. A site may be very professionally produced, but this does not tell us whether it is owned by sincere and genuine people or by the criminally insane. In the world of book publication, editors check books for factual errors before publication. However, on the Internet it is easy for anyone to produce a website and mix fact and fiction to attract surfers. Sanity-challenged people with an interest in money and power can easily 'cook up' secret teachings from a lost world and invite us to become initiated into the secrets of their cult – for a price! And of course, we can pay by credit card over the web.

'The God slot'

Religious programmes on British television include: *The Daily Service*, *Everyman*, which looks at moral issues, *The Heaven and Earth Show*, a light-hearted Sunday morning look at every kind of religion and spirituality, *Prayer for the Day*, *Songs of Praise*, *Sunday Half Hour*, *Sunday Worship*, and *Thought for the Day*. *Something Understood* examines some of the larger questions of life by taking a spiritual theme and exploring it through music, prose and poetry, bringing together the thoughts, ideas and works of the great thinkers, theologians, poets and composers. However, in comparison with the media's output of quiz shows and sport, little time is given to religion. Prime time viewing, when most audiences watch television, is taken up by soaps, when millions watch *Eastenders* or *Coronation Street*. Religious programmes are usually restricted to Sundays, but some commentators argue that in a multi-faith society other religions should get more coverage. In the US, however, TV evangelism, known as 'televangelism', can draw massive audiences as we shall see in the next Unit.

CITIZENSHIP CHALLENGE

Organize three class viewings of *Seven Years in Tibet* (129 minutes long). What did you learn about Tibetan Buddhism? When you have watched it, find out more about what is happening in Tibet today (see Free Tibet Campaign in Addresses/websites).

In the 1500s in Europe the Pope sent out monks and priests to sell 'indulgences' to raise money to rebuild St Peter's Cathedral and pay off some debts. Their message was simple: 'Give us money and your sins will be forgiven.' The media as it was then – the printing press – allowed what used to be a small-time operation to go into mass production. The Pope's representatives were told to enter a city with a showy procession and explain the new 'indulgences'.

Is the same thing happening with religion and the media today?

Televangelists – a definition

An 'evangelist' is someone who spreads a Christian message. A **televangelist** is someone who does it using TV and the mass media. At its best, evangelism may come out of genuine concern about the world and the fate of the people in it.

At its very worst, **televangelism** has bred corruption to the tune of a multi-million dollar industry, which has struck it rich filling stadiums, websites and TV screens, peddling prayer, hawking healings, and selling salvation and religious faith as though it were a set of encyclopaedias.

The gospel of greed

Many televangelists have a similar 'gimme gospel of greed' as those sixteenth-century priests – a $3 billion business which preys on the poor and the desperate; and they do it in the name of God! Many evangelists spread their message by pointing fingers – at other people's beliefs, politics or sexuality – telling them they are doomed to 'eternal damnation' unless they get it right like they did – saving the world by getting rid of differences that do not fit in with their view of the world.

The pro-wrestlers of religion

Showbusiness is as American as apple pie. And so is evangelical Christianity. It is natural then that the two have combined in the media world. There are an estimated 3,000 TV and radio evangelists in the US alone. Many televangelists have became millionaires. Critics consider televangelists to be like the 'pro-wrestlers of religion' – their 'crusades' resembling a carnival. The lure of magical demonstrations, exorcism, casting out demons and healing the sick have tremendous appeal to the masses. These evangelists also make huge sums of money from their 'Christian' spin-offs: self-help books, 'Christian' sex manuals, 'Christian' money guides, 'Christian' quiz shows, 'Christian' athletes, 'Christian' rock stars and 'Christian' T-shirts.

Spiritual superstars?

To the faithful millions in America who watch their channels, televangelists like Dr Gene Scott and Benny Hinn, are miracle men. In reality, they are just two more in a long list of religious con men, milking the most vulnerable members of society of millions of dollars. Their message is as simple as those sixteenth century priests: 'Give us your money and your soul will be saved'.

Dr Gene Scott, is a multi-millionaire. On his TV shows he barks: 'Get on the telephone' – his way of ordering faithful viewers to send cash to buy their salvation. And send they do, more than $1 million a month, according to some estimates. Through the years, the collections have helped support Scott's lavish lifestyle – chauffeured limousines, private jets, ranches, a mansion with round-the-clock bodyguard protection. In his sermons this 'Christian leader' is not afraid to get involved in politics: 'Nuke 'em in the name of Jesus!' he ranted during the Gulf War (see Unit 65 and 66).

Benny Hinn claims his powers come from God. His 'miracle crusades' are highly emotional, often bordering on mass hysteria.

Hinn claims his 'anointing' can cure all types of diseases. Swinging his coat during an 'anointing' his victims fall on the floor. He runs, screaming and yelling: 'The demon must bow to the master Jesus and be gone.'

Hinn has claimed that people only have to watch the show and touch their TV sets to be healed. He also claims that people can be cured just by attending his meetings, entering the building, or even as they drive into the parking lot – a ridiculous, but profitable idea!

Faith healers or fake healers?

- Many televangelists claim that they can heal the sick and exorcise demons. But rather than being guided by the 'power of their faith', many lure the desperate and the vulnerable for the sole reason of making money.

- The poor, uneducated, elderly and desperate are the faith healers' easiest and most common targets. The rich, if successfully conned, can be counted on to donate the larger sums needed to expand televangelists' empires. Parents of young children with terminal illnesses and accident victims are targets, too.

- All of these people suffer from stress and hopelessness. In desperation they may reach out to faith healers. The terminally ill are the most desperate and often have lost all hope.

- They are more likely to consider unorthodox recovery methods, providing ambitious faith healers with an opportunity to make loads of money. The financial benefits of faith healing do not go to the sick, maimed or infirm but to the televangelists' empires.

- To date there has been no scientific evidence that these crusades cure people with terminal disease. This sort of faith healing is rarely based on a sincere attempt to heal, but rather on a theatrical, pseudo-religious farce, designed to relieve the desperate of their money. The only thing getting healthy in these charades are the faith healers' bank accounts.

Launching your learning

What are televangelists? What are they selling? How do they sell it? Who buys it?

FOR DISCUSSION

1 'The whole point is that I'm trying to get you out of the wrong way of thinking that Jesus and his disciples were poor. The Bible says that he has left us an example that we should follow in his steps. That's the reason I drive a Rolls Royce. I'm following Jesus' Steps.'

Frederick K.C. Price, televangelist

2 The magazine **MAD** named televangelist Rev Jerry Falwell as the 'dumbest person of 2001' for blaming the 11 September terrorist attacks on gays, lesbians, pagans, abortionists and feminists.

Images

In the West when people think of Islam they often think about the images of Islamic societies that they have seen in the newspapers, on television or at the cinema: images of terrorists bombing New York; thieves having their hands cut off; scary bearded fanatical clerics screaming abuse at America and Britain; women oppressed and hidden behind the veil.

Movies from Hollywood with images of 'Islamic suicide bombers', like *Jihad in America*, *The Sword of Islam* and *The Final Battle*, reinforce the message that Islam threatens 'Western culture' and has to be dealt with through violence.

Islamic society is portrayed as oppressive and unjust. All this seems to come from another world, a Medieval world we have long left behind in the West, a world more like that of Robin Hood. Of course, the Islamic world was once Medieval, as was the Western world, and the Western world was as disease-ridden and cruel as the East. But the peoples of both East and West have since moved on to create modern societies.

The glories of Islam

The problem is that the image of the Islamic world in the West has not changed. Instead of emphasizing the achievements of the Islamic world in science, mathematics, medicine, architecture and art (see Unit 60), the Western media still portrays a warlike, barbarous world without democracy, justice or compassion. But in Medieval times, it was the Islamic world that was at the centre of civilization. Muslims invented chemistry, algebra, modern surgery, determined the world's circumference and Arabic was the international language of science and culture.

The Crusades

The Crusades were a series of wars, blessed by the Pope and undertaken by European leaders between 1095–1291. When Pope Urban II launched the First Crusade in 1095 he declared, 'God wills it!' making the Crusades a **'holy war'**.

Many crusaders were motivated by religious zeal to conquer the 'Muslim infidels'; but many too were motivated by the desire for land, plunder and the trading ambitions of the major Italian cities. They arrived in the Middle East like a horde of hooligans and started massacring Muslims, Jews and Christians alike, as they fought their way to Jerusalem.

It is the memories of the cruelties and atrocities committed by both sides in the Crusades that are drawn on by newspaper editors when they try to frighten us with stories of 'mad mullahs' or 'Saddam Insane'.

'Friends or enemies'?

When terrorists attacked America on 11 September 2001 Western governments immediately pointed the finger at the Saudi Arabian **dissident** Osama Bin Laden's *al-Qaida* network, based in Afghanistan.

The Taliban, who ruled over Afghanistan – a Muslim country of 26 million people – became headline news. What the media failed to concentrate on was how the brutal Taliban were financed and supported by the Americans in the 1980s as Afghanistan tried to defend itself against an invasion by the Russians, who at the time where the enemies of the West. Now the Taliban were 'enemies' and Afghanistan was bombed. The media also failed to concentrate on the fact that Saudi Arabia, a 'friend' of America – because of its huge oil reserves – is run by an equally cruel and corrupt group of very powerful men.

It seems Muslims are 'friends' if they agree with the West and 'enemies' if they challenge Western economic interests.

CITIZENSHIP CHALLENGE

Many Muslims found the author Salman Rushdie's novel, *The Satanic Verses*, published in 1988, **offensive** because it seemed to be repeating much medieval material about Islam. Some even called it '**blasphemy**'. In 1989 Ayatollah Khomeini of Iran issued a **fatwa** calling for Rushdie and his publishers to be killed. Have writers like Salman Rushdie the right to be free to write what they like, even if their work offends others?

Launching your learning

Find out the meaning of the following words and phrases:
The glories of Islam, the Crusades, holy war, offensive, blasphemy, fatwa, dissident.

95 The media: MUSIC ON MESSAGE

CITIZENSHIP CHALLENGE

A Desert Island Discs – You can only take ten songs with you. What would they be?

1 What, if anything, are they about?

2 Where are the artists from?

3 Are the songs about romance? Or reality? Or both?

B Why do the 'manufactured' bands on *Top of the Pops* not inspire teenagers to get things done? Does it matter if they do not?

Wannabes

The Western music industry is a multi-billion pound industry. Bands are sometimes 'manufactured' and produced. The media have the power to 'hype up' and sell bands. The more the media discuss and publicize them the bigger they stand to become and the more money record companies will make. An example of **media hype** is the uproar that accompanies an Eminem tour or album (see Unit 90).

Manufactured monkeys

In 2001 ITV's *Popstars* auditioned thousands of young 'wannabes' and picked five to form *Hear'say*. The band stand to receive about twelve per cent of retail sales and a further 25 per cent of income from the sale of merchandize and 'spin offs'.

Hear'say had the fastest selling single ever and their album sales reached 450,000 within its first week of release. 'Manufactured' bands are not new, for example *The Monkees* in the 1960s, *The Sex Pistols* in the 1970s (see Unit 90) and *The Spice Girls* in the 1990s.

Often music is specially written for the band. It does not necessarily relate to the artists' life or experience. In contrast, however, African music comes straight from a singer's soul.

Music on message

At a South African Freedom Day Concert in London in 2001 the Guest of Honour, Nelson Mandela (see Unit 54), held a pre-show meeting with all the bands. First, Mandela flattered the bands by telling them about the importance of music and then – not unnaturally – asked for a song. There was a second or two of panic.

REM said nothing, *The Corrs* looked flustered as they hastily conferred about whether to sing a verse and chorus of *Danny Boy*. And then, up stepped Baaba Maal, a singer from Senegal in West Africa, wearing a long brown robe singing a rousing song of praise and greetings. Afterwards Baaba Maal said about this moment of triumph:

> 'We're used to just singing like that in Africa, but the others weren't used to it. They should come to Africa.'

Music in Africa has never been separated from everyday life. Songs are usually message and moral songs – even the love songs tend to be message songs in the clothing of love-songs. Yossou N'Dour, another African superstar, who had an international hit, *Seven Seconds*, with Neneh Cherry, also wrote the album *Set*, which sparked a social movement.

▲ Baaba Maal on message

Yossou N'Dour's latest project is about the **digital divide** (See Unit 61). He aims to help Africans build Internet access and online communities so that Africa is not left behind in the post-industrialized world.

Roots and racism

The media often unintentionally **stereotypes** Africa as a land with insurmountable social and environmental problems. (See Unit 34.) This book maybe has done it. The truth is that there is another side to Africa (see Ziff, African Film Festival and VSO in Addresses/websites).

The song was a call for honesty and openness in public affairs and in business, and also in people's personal lives. *Set* in Wolof means 'clean' or 'pure'. Young kids in the ghettos of Dakar, in Senegal, and in other cities of the country were inspired to take it upon themselves to clean up their neighbourhoods, clearing away illegal garbage dumps, rehabilitating water supply facilities that the city government had let go to waste and painting murals on hundreds of city walls with messages and the faces of historical figures. 'Set – Setaal' ('Clean – Let's Be Clean') became a rallying cry for good behaviour in public, for getting things done without waiting for the government to do them, for taking responsibility for one's everyday environment, at the community level.

FOR DISCUSSION

After reading the units on the media, what do you understand by the term **'digital divide'** (see Unit 61)? What does it mean? Does any of it 'divide' your life or the lives of others, do you think?

96 The media: STAR TREK – THE ETHICS OF SPACE

To boldly go...

On 4 October 1957, the world watched in amazement as a tiny sphere called *Sputnik*, weighing no more than 84 kilograms, went spinning and beeping around the Earth. The space era had begun!

In 1961 the cosmonaut, Yuri Gagarin, became the first man to orbit the Earth, and in 1969 Neil Armstrong and 'Buzz' Aldrin became the first men to set foot on the Moon.

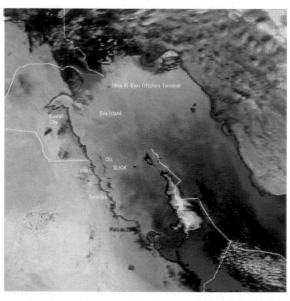

▲ Huge clouds of carbon monoxide from dry season fires in South America and Africa, and wintertime burning of fossil fuels can be seen from space spreading across the Southern and Northern Hemispheres

Is there anybody out there?

'In my Father's house are many mansions.'

Jesus in the Gospel according to St John

The search for signs of life in the solar system or in other galaxies – belonging to the realm of science fiction just a few decades ago – is now commonplace. In one Space Treaty, signed by nations involved in space exploration, astronauts are called 'envoys' (messengers) of the human race. Maybe by exploring space we might benefit from other planets or civilizations and what they might have to offer, for example minerals, ores, knowledge and wisdom? However, the likelihood is diminished by the astronomical distances involved.

Space colonies?

Our need for air, water and food and our physical fragility make space exploration a dangerous business. Manned space missions took a huge blow when, in front of the world's media, the 'Challenger' space shuttle exploded on take off, killing the astronauts. While some people believe that 'manned' space flights are necessary others argue that they use humans as little more than **robots** in the service of space technology.

'Manned' experiments are largely concerned with the human body's reaction to life in space, with the eventual aim to establish some kind of colony in space.

Benefits

- **Communication** – Space technology reduces times and distances and makes links between people, especially through the explosion of new information and communication technologies. These technologies create communication forums bringing together doctors and scientists regardless of the distance separating them.

- **Information** – Space technology provides us with huge amounts of information about the Earth and space.

- **Observation** – The world only learnt about the hole in the **ozone layer** (see Unit 72) because of satellite observations showing up the stratosphere above the South Pole.

name of 'national security'. However, it is *universal security* that the people of the world need, and not space overrun by paranoid nationalistic politicians and generals.

TALKING POINT

'Earth and Space are not ours. They are treasures, real and symbolic, which we owe to ourselves to safeguard for our descendants.'

UNESCO

Risks

- **'Big Brother' is watching!** – Technology is so precise that the position of individuals anywhere on Earth can be detected without their knowledge. Cameras in space can take pictures that, once enhanced, can identify individual faces in the street.

- **Pollution** – At present, several space vehicles with nuclear reactors are in orbit. Already some lethal radioactive debris has fallen to Earth. As humankind explores the universe ever more deeply, the need to develop systems of power becomes increasingly urgent. Many critics argue that **alternatives** to nuclear and oil energy should be used.

- **Globalization** – Space technology costs **trillions** of dollars. The astronomical costs of new information and communications technology prevent many poor countries from reaping the benefits. These technologies could lead to the **'globalization' of culture** and to a greater 'sameness' between cultures, languages and behaviour. This could bring about the disappearance of cultural diversity, a crucial part of our heritage.

- **War in space** – The huge advances made since the 1960s have often been driven by military goals cloaked under the

CITIZENSHIP CHALLENGE

A Find out:
   1 about alternative sources of energy.
   2 how much is a trillion? Ask a maths teacher.
   3 what the globalization of culture could mean.

B While *we* might benefit from other planets or civilizations and what they might have to offer, *what can we bring them?* Technology? Wisdom? Peace? Imagine you had been chosen to represent the young people of the world. You have to make a presentation about the world and its people to an 'alien'. You have only five minutes. Write down what you would say.

▲ Do we come in peace?

Addresses/websites

Life and death issues

Drug Abuse Resistance Education (DARE)
19 Forest Avenue
Mansfield
Nottinghamshire NG18 4BX
www.dare.uk.com

Terence Higgins Trust (HIV/AIDS)
52–54 Gray's Inn Road
London WC1X 8JU
www.tht.org.uk

Barnados
www.barnados.org.uk

Brook Centre (Sex and contraception advice)
www.brook.org.uk

CASCADE (Drugs information written by young people)
www.cascade.u-net.com

Childline
www.childline.org.uk

Church of England Children's Society
www.the-childrens-society.org.uk

DrugScope
www.drugscope.org.uk

EXIT (Voluntary Euthanasia Society)
www.euthanasia.org

Genetics Forum
www.geneticsforum.org.uk

Health Development Agency
www.had-online.org.uk

Help the Aged
www.helptheaged.org.uk

LIFE Organization (Anti-abortion)
www.lifeuk.org

National Abortion Campaign (Pro-abortion)
www.gn.apc.org

Parenting
www.bounty.com

Relate (Advice and counselling about relationships)
www.relate.org.uk

Royal Association for Disability and Rehabilitation (RADAR)
www.radar.org.uk

The Samaritans
www.samaritans.org.uk

Youth Work
www.youthwork.com/links

Social harmony

Commission for Racial Equality
Elliot House
10/12 Allington Street
London SW1 5EH
www.cre.gov.uk

Prison Phoenix Trust
PO Box 328
Oxford OX1 1PJ

Asian Dub Foundation Education (ADFED)
www.asiandubfoundation.com

Church Action on Poverty
www.church-poverty.org.uk

HateWatch (Racism and the Net)
www.hatewatch.org

Howard League for Penal Reform
www.howardleague.org

Institute for Race Relations
www.irr.org.uk

Lesbian and Gay Christian Movement
www.lgcm.org.uk

Prison Activist Resource Centre
www.prisonactivist.org

Prison Reform Trust
www.prisonreformtrust.org.uk

Race Relations/Civil Rights/ML King
www.racerelations.about.com

Searchlight (Combating racism)
www.searchlightmagazine.com

Shelter
www.shelter.org.uk

Women in Prison
www.womeninprison.org.uk

Rights

Amnesty International (British section)
99–119 Roseberry Avenue
London EC1R 4RE
www.amnesty.org.uk

Liberty (National Council for Civil Liberties)
21 Tabard Street
London SE1 4LA
www.liberty-human-rights.org.uk

Survival International
6 Charterhouse Buildings
London EC1M 7ET
www.survival-international.org

Al-Fatiha Foundation (Muslim gay and lesbian organization)
www.al-fatiha.net

Association for the Prevention of Torture
www.apt.ch

Asylum Aid
www.asylumaid.org.uk

Free Tibet Campaign
www.freetibet.org

Human Rights Watch
www.hrw.org

International Association for Religious Freedom
www.iarf-religiousfreedom.net

Jamaat-e-Islami (Human rights and Islam)
www.jamaat.org

Medical Foundation for the Care of Victims of Torture
www.torturecare.org.uk

Minority Rights Group
www.minorityrights.org

Nicaragua Solidarity Campaign
www.nicaraguasc.org

Physicians for Human Rights
www.phrusa.org

Refugee Council
www.refugeecouncil.org.uk

Sikh Human Rights Group UK
www.shrg.org

Stonewall (Gay rights)
www.stonewallsociety.com

UN High Commissioner for Human Rights
www.unhcr.ch

United Nations Children's Fund (UNICEF)
www.unicef.org.uk

United Nations Declarations of Human Rights
www.un.org/Overview/rights

Womankind Worldwide
www.womankind.org.uk

Women's Human Rights Resources Database
www.law-lib.utoronto.ca

Poverty

Christian Aid
35 Lower Marsh
Waterloo
London SE1 7RT
www.christian-aid.org.uk

Islamic Relief
19 Rea Street South
Birmingham B5 6LB
www.islamic-relief.org.uk

War on Want
Fenner Brockway House
37–39 Great Guildford Street
London SE1 0ES
www.waronwant.org

ActionAid
www.actionaid.org.uk

Catholic Agency for Overseas Development
www.cafod.org.uk

Child Poverty Action Group
www.cpag.org.uk

International Federation of Red Cross and Red Crescent Societies
www.ifrc.org

Jubilee
www.jubilee2000uk.org

MayDay (World poverty awareness)
www.mayday.org.uk

Muslim Aid
www.muslimaid.org

NetAid
www.netaid.org

Oxfam
www.oxfam.org

Reclaim the Streets
www.reclaimthestreets.net

Save the Children
www.savethechildren.org.uk

Tear Fund
www.tearfund.org

World Development Movement
www.wdm.org.uk

Peace

Campaign Against the Arms Trade
11 Goodwin Street
Finsbury Park
London N4 3HQ
www.caat.org.uk

Campaign for Nuclear Disarmament
162 Holloway Road
London N7 8DQ
www.cnduk.org

The Religious Society of Friends (Quakers)
Friends House
173 Euston Road
London NW1 2BJ
www.quaker.org.uk

Buddhist Peace Fellowship
www.bpf.org

Coalition to Stop the Use of Child Soldiers
www.child-soldiers.org

Pax Christi
www.paxchristi.org.uk

Peace Pledge Union
www.ppu.org.uk

Ploughshares Fund
www.ploughshares.org

Environment

Friends of the Earth
26–28 Underwood Street
London N1 7JQ
www.foe.co.uk

Greenpeace
Canonbury Villas
London N1 2PN
www.greenpeace.org

Animal Aid
www.animalaid.org.uk

British Union for the Abolition of Vivisection
www.buav.org

Compassion in World Farming
www.ciwf.co.uk

Countryside Alliance (Pro-hunting)
www.countryside-alliance.org

Environmental New Network
www.enn.com

Environmental News Service
www.ens.lycos.com

Leadership for Environment and Development
www.lead.org/leadnet/footprint

League Against Cruel Sports
www.league.uk.com

National Centre for Atmospheric Research
www.fragilecologies.com

Nottingham Hunt Saboteurs (Anti-hunting)
www.nhsa.enviroweb.org

RE Environment Project
www.reep.org

United Nations Environmental Programme
www.unep.org/grasp

Whales and Sonar Pollution
www.greennature.com

World Population
www.populationconcern.org.uk

WWF International
www.panda.org

Media

African Film Festival
www.zanzibar.org/ziff

BBC
www.bbc.co.uk

Channel Four
www.channel4.com

Everyman (Contemporary moral issues on the BBC)
www.bbc.co.uk/religion/tv_radio/everyman

McLibel
www.mcspotlight.org

Media Watch
www.mediawatch.com

Nation Records
www.fun-da-mental.com/media

New Internationalist Magazine
www.oneworld.org

No Logo
www.nologo.org

Space site
www.bbc.co.uk/science/space

U2 World Service Magazine
www.u2propaganda.com

War, propaganda and the media
www.globalissues.org/HumanRights/Media

Youth Watch
www.zmag.org/youthwatch

General

United Nations Association (UK)
3 Whitehall Court
London SW1A 2EL
www.una-uk.org

Voluntary Services Overseas (VSO)
317 Putney Bridge Road
London SW15 2PN
www.vso.org.uk

About.com
www.judaism.about.com
www.islam.about.com
www.christianity.about.com
www.buddhism.about.com
www.hinduism.about.com

British Humanist Association
www.humanism.org.uk

British Medical Association
www.bma.org.uk

British Orthodox Church
www.uk-christian.net

Buddhist Fundamentals
www.fundamentalbuddhism.org

Catholic Truth Society
www.cts-online.org.uk

Church of England
www.cofe.anglican.org

Consultants on Religious Tolerance
www.religioustolerance.org

Culham Institute
www.culham.ac.uk

Hindu Students Council
www.hindulinks.org

Sikhism
www.sikhs.org

UK Islamic Mission
www.ukim.org

World Health Organization
www.who.int

Subject index

Name index

Photo acknowledgements

Cover photographs by Format Photographs/Joanne O'Brien (protestors); Format Photographs/Ulrike Preuss (couple); Science Photo Library/James Stevenson (foetus).

The publishers and author would like to thank the following for permission to use photographs: AP Photo/Mark Lennihan on p. 156; AP Photo/Mohamed Zatari Stringer on p. 111; Associated Press/Javier Bauluz on p. 139; Associated Press/Kenneth Lambert on p. 134; John Birdsall Photography on p. 61; Erik Bjurstrom/Bruce Coleman on p. 169; Bronstein/Liaison/Gamma/Frank Spooner on p. 156; Coloursport/Matthew Impey on p. 90; C. Planet 24/Carlton Television on p. 181; DRIK on p. 124; Earth Satellite Corp/SPL on p. 194; Empics/Mike Egerton on p. 5; Environmental Images/I.S.F. on p. 165; Environmental Images/Ueli Hiltpold on p. 162; Format/Donna Binder on p. 34; Format/Karen Robinson on p. 159; Glasgow Museums and Art Galleries on p. 104; *The Guardian*/Martin Argles on p. 128; Rose Handy on p. 151; Images Sans Frontiers on p. 133; Angela Lubrano on p. 182; Murdo Macleod on p. 27; Magnum Photos on p. 94; Magnum Photos/Jean Gaumy on p. 190; Magnum Photos/Steve McCurry on p. 102; Magnum Photos/Nitin Rai on p. 86; National Youth Agency on pp. 84 and 176; Network/John Sturrock on p. 65; Page One on p. 178; Panos Pictures/Peter Barker on p. 25; Panos Pictures/James Bedding on p. 12; Panos Pictures/Jeremy Horner on p. 69; Panos Pictures/Simon Horton on p. 146; Panos Pictures/Roderick Johnson on p. 159; Panos Pictures/Mark McErg on p. 186; Panos Pictures/Eric Miller on p. 82; Panos Pictures/Caroline Penn on p. 8; Panos Pictures/Chris Stowers on p. 120; Scott Peterson/Gamma/Frank Spooner on p. 174; Photofusion/Robert Brook on p. 92; Photofusion/Gina Glover on p. 36; Popperfoto/Reuters on p. 53; Popperfoto/Reuters/Dan Chang on p. 173; Popperfoto/Reuters/Jim Hollander on p. 170; Popperfoto/Reuters/Jeff J Mitchell on p. 79; Popperfoto/Reuters/Sara K Schwittek on p. 143; Popperfoto/Reuters/Ian Waldie on p. 173; Press Association/Stefan Rousseau on p. 30; Redferns/Olivia Hemmingway on p. 75; Redferns/Simon King on p. 64; Redferns/Nicky J Sims on p. 193; Rex Features/SIPA on p. 113; Harjinder Singh Sagoo on p. 108; The Samaritans on p. 59; Science Photo Library/Makoto Iwafuji/Eurelios on p. 44; Science Photo Library/Dr Yorgos Nikas on p. 33; Science Photo Library/Alfred Pasteka on p. 47; Science Photo Library/Victor de Schwanberg on p. 48; Space Telescope Science Institute/Science Photo Library on p. 195; Frank Spooner/FDB-Thierry Falise on p. 109; Still Pictures/Hjalte Tin on p. 154; Still Pictures/UNEP/Hart mut Schwarzbach on p. 127; Sygma/Corbis on p. 117; Tibet Foundation, London on p. 137; TRIP/H. Rogers on p. 99; Victor Habbick Visions/Science Photo Library on p. 185; Visual News/Getty News Service on p. 112; Richard Wayman on p. 6.